THE FUTURE OF LIVED RELIGIOUS LEADERSHIP

AMSTERDAM STUDIES IN THEOLOGY AND RELIGION
(AmSTaR)

The *Amsterdam Studies in Theology and Religion* (AmSTaR) is a peer-reviewed publication of VU University Press in cooperation with the Faculty of Religion and Theology of the Vrije Universiteit Amsterdam. It publishes dissertations and scholarly monographs on a wide range of issues pertaining to theology and religion. The series is open to publications in English, German and Dutch.

Editorial Board

Prof. dr. J.W. van Saane
Prof. dr. J.T. Sunier
Prof. dr. E. van Staalduine-Sulman
Dr. P.G.A. Versteeg

Executive Editor

Prof. dr. C. van der Kooi

Volume 7

Vol. 1 – C. van der Kooi, E. van Staalduine-Sulman and A.W. Zwiep (eds.). *Evangelical Theology in Transition.* ISBN 978 90 8659 600 3.
Vol. 2 – Binsar Jonathan Pakpahan. *God Remembers: Towards a Theology of Remembrance as a Basis of Reconciliation in Communal Conflict.* ISBN 978 90 8659 603 4
Vol. 3 – Peter Ben Smit. *Tradition in Dialogue: A Historical Study of the Notion of Tradition in the International Bilateral Dialogues of the Anglican Communion.* ISBN 978 90 8659 604 1.
Vol. 4 – G.J. Buijs, J.T. Sunier and P.G.A. Versteeg (eds.). *Risky Liaisons? Democracy and Religion: Reflections and Case Studies.* ISBN 978 90 8659 605 8.
Vol. 5 – Hendrik M. Vroom. *Walking in a Widening World: Understanding Religious Diversity.* ISBN 978 90 8659 652 2.
Vol. 6 – Miranda Klaver, Stefan Paas and Eveline van Staalduine-Sulman (eds.). *Evangelicals and Sources of Authority.* ISBN 978 90 8659 735 2.
Vol. 7 – Rein Brouwer (ed.). *The Future of Lived Religious Leadership.* ISBN 978 90 8659 774 1.

The Future of
Lived Religious Leadership

Edited by

Rein Brouwer

VU University Press

This publication is made possible by the Van Coeverden Adriani Stichting, CLUE⁺, the Netherlands Organisaton for Scientific Research (NWO), and the Protestant Theological University.

VU University Press
De Boelelaan 1105
1081 HV Amsterdam
The Netherlands

info@vu-uitgeverij.nl
www.vuuniversitypress.com

© 2018 by the authors

Design jacket: Haags Blauw, The Hague (Bianca Wesseling)
Type setting: Arie Zwiep, Oudewater

ISBN 978 90 8659 774 1
NUR 700

All rights reserved. No part of this book may be reproduced, stored in a retrieval system, or transmitted, in any form or by any means, electronic, mechanical, photocopying, recording, or otherwise, without the prior written consent of the publisher.

Contents

List of Contributors vii

Introduction: The Future of Lived Religious Leadership 1
REIN BROUWER

1. Postcolonial Leadership between the Sovereign and the Beast 8
   JOHANN-ALBRECHT MEYLAHN

2. Discursive Leadership and the Other 26
   JOHN ELIASTAM

3. Leadership in a Deconstructed Church 48
   REIN BROUWER

4. Virtual Leadership? The e-Church as a South-African
   Case Study 65
   IAN NELL

5. Tweeting God: Redefining Future Christian Leadership through
   Twitter? 83
   JAN-ALBERT VAN DEN BERG

6. The Pastor as a Brand? The Use of Social Media by
   Pastorpreneurs for Personal Branding 99
   THEO ZIJDERVELD

7. Healthy Leadership: The Science of Clergy Work-Related
   Psychological Health 116
   LESLIE J. FRANCIS

8. Lay Leadership in the Church of England: A Study in an
   Urban Diocese 135
   DAVID W. LANKSHEAR

9. Youth Leadership in Urban South-African Contexts..................... 151
   SHANTELLE WEBER

10. The Common Priesthood and Swedish Church Politics:
    An Analysis.. 169
    THOMAS GIRMALM

11. Pre-Military Academies and the "Making" of Religious-Zionist
    Communal Leadership Capital.. 186
    UDI LEBEL

Epilogue: Back to the Roots. Paradoxes in the Development of
Leadership Theories.. 208
JOKE VAN SAANE

Bibliography

    Book and Article References 217
    Webcontent References 246

    Index of Modern Authors 251

List of Contributors

JAN-ALBERT VAN DEN BERG (1970) (PhD, University of Pretoria) is a member of the Department of Practical and Missional Theology, Faculty of Theology and Religion, University of the Free State, Bloemfontein, South Africa. Initially, his main publications were about narrative pastoral care. He is currently doing research on the role of social media in articulating the Christian faith.

REIN BROUWER (1962) (PhD, Utrecht University) is Senior Lecturer in Practical and Empirical Theology at the Protestant Theological University, Amsterdam. His publications are based on research in the fields of Religious Leadership and Congregational Studies, and also of Religion and Arts.

JOHN ELIASTAM (1967) (PhD, University of Pretoria) is Research Fellow in the Department of Practical Theology at the University of Pretoria. Field of interest: Prejudice and Intergroup Relations.

LESLIE J. FRANCIS (1947) (PhD and ScD, Cambridge University; DD, Oxford University; Dlitt, University of Wales) is currently Professor of Religions and Education and Director of the Warwick Religions and Education Research Unit at the University of Warwick, UK. He is an Anglican priest serving as Honorary Distinguished Canon at Manchester Cathedral, UK, and Canon Theologian at the Cathedral of St John the Baptist, Newfoundland. He researches in the fields of practical theology, empirical theology, and religious education.

THOMAS GIRMALM (1968) (PhD, Umeå University) is Senior Lecturer at the Department of Historical, Philosophical and Religious Studies at Umeå University, Sweden. Field of interest: Historical and Practical Theology.

DAVID W. LANKSHEAR (1943) (PhD, University of Wales) is Research Fellow at Warwick Religions and Education Research Unit, University of Warwick, and Visiting Professor at the University of Glyndŵr. His fields of interest are Congregational Studies and Christian Education.

UDI LEBEL (1973) (PhD, King's College London) is Associate Professor in the Department of Sociology and Anthropology at Ariel University, and Senior Researcher at the Begin-Sadat Center for Strategic Studies at Bar Ilan University, Israel. His main research interests are Sociology of Trauma and Bereavement, Civil-Military Relations, and Post-Heroic Leadership and Communities.

JOHANN-ALBRECHT MEYLAHN (1970) (PhD, University of Pretoria; PhD, Vrije Universiteit Amsterdam) is Professor at the Department of Practical Theology, Faculty of Theology, University of Pretoria, South Africa. His research interests are in Philosophy of Religion and the ethical challenges of living in a global village.

IAN NELL (1961) (PhD, University of Pretoria) is Professor in Practical Theology at Stellenbosch University. His field of interest is Leadership and Congregational Studies.

JOKE VAN SAANE (1968) (PhD, Psychology of Religion, Vrije Universiteit Amsterdam) is Professor of Education Theology and Religious Studies at the Vrije Universiteit Amsterdam. She is a specialist in the Psychology of Religion. Her research interests are the psychological processes in the interrelationship between religion and spirituality, especially in leadership.

SHANTELLE WEBER (1981) (PhD, University of Stellenbosch) is Senior Lecturer in the Department of Practical Theology and Missiology at the University of Stellenbosch. Her research interests include Youth Ministry, Faith Formation, and Religious Education. Weber is the Director of Uzwelo Youth Development, an organization for mentoring and training youth workers in South Africa.

THEO ZIJDERVELD (1983) is a PhD student at the Vrije Universiteit Amsterdam. His field of study is Digital Media, Religion, Culture. He is finishing his thesis on 'The Personal Branding of Religious Leaders'.

Introduction

The Future of Lived Religious Leadership

Rein Brouwer

*Like religions themselves,
religious leadership is a dynamic entity*
(Gallagher, 2014).

1. Introduction

"Not another book on leadership! What could possibly be added to the proverbial library on leadership?" Good question, but still. This is a book on leadership, on religious leadership to be specific, leadership exercised by men and women in a religious context. "Religious context" as such is not a very accurate concept. It comprises more than one phenomenon. In this book, it involves leadership by pastoral professionals in religious communities, as well as leadership through communicating religious context via television broadcast, internet and social media to a mostly indistinct audience, and religiously motivated leadership exercised by people who are not ordained by a religious denomination but who play a pivotal role in promoting a religious cause. This book presents in-depth examples and cases of religious leadership which raise several challenging questions. What can we learn from these cases about the development of leadership in religious contexts? What new shapes of religious leadership seem to appear in the rural, urban and virtual spheres of our network society? And how is leadership in society and politics related to religious leadership?

By themselves, these questions already warrant another book on religious leadership. However, the main reason why we decided to work together on this book, as scholars in practical theology and religious studies from different countries and continents, is the way we perceive leadership in culture, society, politics and religion. While working on this book, and supported by the Netherlands Organisation for Scientific Research

(NWO), we organized three meetings (Durham 2013, Amsterdam 2014, Pretoria 2015) out of which the coherence of this book developed. We created a threefold structure that is recognizable in the overall frame of the book chapters, although it is more implicit in some chapters than in others. To identify this threefold structure, we used the following topics, on which I will elaborate below: Difference in Contexts, Lived Religion, and Engaged Research.

Besides agreeing on the importance of a threefold structure for the book chapters, we also decided to be explicitly aware of a meta-theoretical perspective on leadership. During the meetings that preceded the writing of the book, we distinguished two meta-theoretical aspects. The first one raises the question of how we position ourselves within four acknowledged leadership paradigms: the classical, the transactional, the visionary, and the organic paradigm (Avery, 2004). The classical paradigm is focused on the essential characteristics of the leader, on which his position and power are based. The transactional paradigm concentrates on the relation and communication between the leader and the followers, and on how the leader influences the followers. The visionary paradigm is centred on how leaders transform organizations by projecting an appealing and inspiring vision. And, finally, in the organic paradigm, leadership is not seen as vested in individuals; as a group process, it is based on the continuous exchange of a shared vision and core values. All four paradigms are visible in the chapters.

Another meta-theoretical aspect follows from the statement that leadership is part of a specific narrative. According to a social constructionist approach, there is no such thing as leadership separate from a particular paradigm. If so, it becomes important to ask who decides on the paradigm, who scripts the narrative, and who constructs leadership? Leadership is an essentially contested concept. What counts as the right way of leading in a situation is a question of interpretation, and not an issue that can be decided by objective criteria. Leadership is in the "eye of the beholder"; leadership is attributed, according to social constructionists (Fairhurst and Grant, 2010). In religious contexts, highly charged with religiously motivated norms, values, and ideals, it is evidently significant to know in whom, or what, the power of definition lies. Which institutional body determines the confines of leadership? Who sets the rules and regulations for the exercise of leadership? What are the possibilities and limitations for leadership in a given community or organization? The chapters in the book document the authors' awareness of the meaning of a social constructionist approach.

In general, all of the chapters reflect on the issues regarding either one or both meta-theoretical aspects. Furthermore, writing on religious leadership always implies referring to topics like authority and power (in society and religion), identity (relating to groups, congregations, communities), and social cohesion (embrace, exclusion). The chapters also show ample proof of that. But mainly we find the book structured by the already mentioned three categories.

2. Different Contexts

What we knew from theory and research, we experienced first-hand during our meetings in preparation for the book, namely that the different contexts in which leadership operates (geographical, organizational, cultural, "real" or "virtual") influence the shape of leadership. Acknowledging "Different Contexts" is an important notion for understanding leadership. There is a difference between reflecting on the value of "democracy" in the representation regulations in the former Swedish state church (see the chapter by Girmalm) and observing the leadership capital that is established by pre-military Zionist academies in Israel (see Lebel), like there is a difference between contributing to the work-related psychological health of professional leaders in the Church of England (see Francis) and exploring new expressions of digital leadership on Twitter (see Van den Berg). The authors in this book cover three continents (Europe, Africa, Asia) and five countries (UK, South Africa, Israel, Sweden, The Netherlands). And the topics of research vary from pastoral professionals and lay leaders in religious communities (see Brouwer, Lankshear, Weber) to religious entrepreneurs in the virtual world (see Van den Berg, Nell, Zijderveld) and the discourse of religious leaders in politics and society (see Eliastam, Lebel, Meylahn).

This book presents a contextual approach to leadership. It offers insights into the contextual uniqueness of leadership and the contextual differences between leadership situations. Because leadership is transforming in accordance with the changing societal structures, there are shifting trends in leadership. And these shifting leadership paradigms consequently affect the way we perceive religious leadership, because societal leadership influences religious leadership. That is the reason why some of the chapters reflect explicitly on the societal challenges that question our thoughts on leadership. For example, violence against foreign migrants in South Africa evoked interest in the social construction of discourse in leadership (religious) (see Eliastam). Another example is the new positioning in Israeli society acquired by the religious Zionist movement through aggravating leadership capital (see Lebel). One of the chapters starts with the leadership crisis in postcolonial Africa and proposes a deconstructionist approach to leadership (religious) (see Meylahn). Furthermore, there are several chapters that ponder how the digital revolution affects our perceptions of leadership (see Van den Berg, Nell, Zijderveld).

Religious leadership not only mirrors the societal challenges and impact of political and secular institutional discourse on leadership, leadership in religious denominations and communities also influences what we expect from leaders in our daily life. The scholars from South Africa, in particular, show how in the African reality, religion is integrated (still) in society and culture. Churches and other religious communities are often (still) the only institutions that are appreciated because they are different from secular institutions regarding the formation of social capital, integrity, and lack of corruption. But even in secular Europe we find traces of religious discourse and practices that affect (or try to) democratic policy and decision-making (see Brouwer, Girmalm).

3. *Lived Religion*

A second category that structures the books is the concept of "Lived Religion." This concept is connected to an empirical perspective on leadership, to getting a grasp of leadership by building on empirical research. All of the chapters are based on an empirical methodology and refer to a broad scope of research methods, like survey research (see Francis, Lankshear), narrative approaches (see Meylahn, Eliastam, Lebel, Weber), qualitative methods (see Brouwer, Girmalm), and some new ventures in analysing digital information (see Van den Berg, Nell, Zijderveld).

Taking an empirical perspective means that we, following the intention of this book, are not interested in biographies (nor hagiographies) of great men who inspire us by their exemplary leadership in recent history. Of course, we all could probably learn something from Donald J. Trump,[1] but that is not what we have in mind with this book. We do not want to impress our readers by exposing the great qualities of charismatic leaders, like for example Obama, Nixon, or Gor-

---

[1] Donald J. Trump, *Crippled America: How to Make America Great Again*, 2015.

bachev,[1] because the "strong leader" is a myth.[2] We also do not have any affinity with writing a "how-to" book, or a "getting" book, with "two-minute" rules for managers.[3] Nor are we interested in presenting a new philosophy, or theory of leadership. There are many books that deal with theories and explain the nuances of a leader's traits and roles, contingency and situations, transaction and transformation, or try to integrate these theoretical approaches.[4] Some of these theories will play a part in this book, but we do not focus exclusively on one such theory (see Van Saane).

The main incentive to take an empirical perspective on leadership is the notion of "Lived Religion" and its prevalence in practical theology (Failing and Heimbrock, 1998; Gräb, 1998; Streib, Dinter and Söderblom, 2008; Ganzevoort and Roeland, 2014) and religious studies (Orsi, 1997; MacGuire, 2008; Ammerman, 2014). In general, when religion is mentioned in conjunction with the adjective "lived," we are referring to the religious practices of people in everyday life rather than just focusing on official, institutionalized religious traditions. In the German language (as in Dutch) there is the play on words between *gelebte* ("lived") and *gelehrte* ("learned" or "traditional") religion. Lived Religion implies an academic interest in how people experience life and find subjective meaning, as individuals or in groups, in religious practices within specific contexts and cultural settings. Hence, the concern with empirical research on leadership, as disclosed in every chapter of the book. By writing about "Lived Religious Leadership" we intend not just to contemplate leadership that is prescribed by religious institutions and defined by church law, for example. Instead, we embrace empirical research on leadership phenomena that defy the well-trodden paths of vested authorities, or theories, or expectations, and offer a new perspective on leadership and its future. The reader will find in this book not only how Lived Religion shapes the leadership of professional clergy, but also how lay people in the Church of England exercise lead-

---

[1] David Garrow, *Rising Star: The Making of Barack Obama*, 2017; John A. Farrell, *Richard Nixon: The Life*, 2017; William Taubman, *Gorbachev: His Life and Times*, 2017.
[2] Archie Brown, *The Myth of the Strong Leader*, 2014.
[3] E.g. *Getting Things Done* by David Allen, 2015, or *Getting More* by Stuart Diamond, 2012, or *Getting to Yes* by Roger Fisher, William Ury, and Bruce Patton, 2011.
[4] E.g. Peter Northouse, *Leadership: Theory and Practice*, 2015[7]; Nitin Nohria and Rakesh Kurana, *Handbook of Leadership Theory and Practice*, 2010; John P. Dugan, Natasha T. Turman and Amy C. Barnes, *Leadership Theory: Facilitator's Guide for Cultivating Critical Perspectives*, 2017; and of course, Bernard M. Bass, *The Bass Handbook of Leadership: Theory, Research, and Managerial Applications*, 2008[4].

ership (see Lankshear), the importance of youth leaders (non-academically trained) in evangelical churches in South Africa (see Weber), the emergence of leadership in a fresh expression of church (see Brouwer), and the role of Religious Zionist-inspired officers in the Israeli Defence Forces (see Lebel), to give just a few examples.

4. *Engaged Research*

The third, and final, category that structures this book and its chapters is related to the authors' engagement with the future of leadership. Besides our personal involvement in religious affairs, all of us are deeply invested as researchers and scholars in research on leadership. Whether we focus on the health of clergy (see Francis) or on how social media and the internet are changing leadership (see Van den Berg, Nell, Zijderveld) or reflect on the political situation in our country (see Eliastam, Lebel, Meylahn), we are doing empirical research from a normative orientation (Van der Ven, 2005).

Of course, much could be written about "normativity" in practical theology and religious studies, but as authors of this book we agreed from the beginning that the rhetoric of "strong leadership" demanded some deconstruction. Our intention was not only to be aware of its contextual dimensions, but also to expose the "vulnerability" of leadership (for example, the abuse of power, but also the predicament of leadership in the face of complexity) and to reveal again its salvific potential. The chapters reflect critically on what presents itself as "leadership" in the managerial literature and/or different political and cultural practices, which are often quite influential on religious practices of leadership. The aim of this critical deconstruction of what presents itself in contextualized theory and practices as leadership was to reconstruct creatively the possibilities of healthy leadership in the domains of the urban, rural, and virtual worlds we live in. With this as our objective, we reflect in this book on the transformation of leadership, and on a suitable research methodology for that purpose. The chapters show proposals for new ways of thinking about religious leadership, and reconstructing sound theory and practices for leadership in church and society (see Van Saane). The book suggests, for example, coordinates of degrees of longitude and latitude to lead in new spaces of a digital existence (see Van den Berg), characteristics of virtual leadership (see Nell), an ethos of listening to those who suffer the consequences of political leadership (see Meylahn), revisiting the robust criticism of Martin Luther on the power structures of papal supremacy in order to confront the political systems in place today (see Girmalm), and the introduction to new stories of leadership that not only have the potential to create new identities, but are able to create new communities and new cultures (see Eliastam).

5. The Future of Religious Leadership

To conclude, there were sound reasons for another book on religious leadership. Starting this book project was just as ambitious as the title we provide the book with, "the future of." Leadership exists given the existence of social beings. Likewise, religious leadership exists in every culture and society of which religion is a constituent element. There is a future for religious leadership, full stop, because being a "dynamic entity," it will change, transform, and adapt, to emerge time and time again in a new framework or configuration. So there definitely will be another book on religious leadership after this one, as the author of *Ecclesiastes, Qohelet* (12:12) already said, "there is no end to the crafting of many books," in particular books about leadership in religious contexts.[1]

---

[1] I would like to thank Esther van Bijsterveld, student at the Vrije Universiteit Amsterdam/Protestant Theological University, who assisted me in editing this book.

Chapter One

Postcolonial Leadership between the Sovereign and the Beast[1]

Johann-Albrecht Meylahn

Abstract

There is a crisis in leadership throughout the world, but the focus of this article is on the crisis in postcolonial Africa. How is this crisis constructed within the politics of the global village? The leadership crisis in Africa is often portrayed by Western-influenced media as leaders being characterised as beasts if they do not comply with the wishes and dictates of Western capital, or as puppets of Western capital, of the Western sovereign. Is there a way beyond these characterisations, or is it a political necessity to divide the world into friends and enemies, as Carl Schmitt would like us to believe?

Taking Derrida's thoughts into consideration, a way will be sought beyond this characterisation. Derrida's ideas concerning the sovereign pose the question: can leadership move beyond being either a puppet of a Western sovereign or the beast of darkest Africa? I shall argue that the political will not be destroyed if this distinction disappears, although the distinction will be ruined. Yet these ruins offer space for the possibility of something other, an impossible possibility – the madness of the impossible possible, or the madness of holy folly and the hope and dream of leadership still to come.

1. Introduction

The purpose of this chapter is to examine theories on leadership within their worlds-of-construction and thereby offer a deconstructive reading of them. The chapter will not specifically focus on leadership in the church, but leadership in general. By offering a deconstructive reading on leadership theories, it offers a theology of hope within leadership studies, without necessarily focusing on leadership in the church. The

---

[1] This chapter is an edited version of my article "Postcolonial leadership between the sovereign and the beast," *Verbum et Ecclesia* 38, no. 1 (2017), https://doi.org/10.4102/ve.v38i1.1784.

chapter is not based on empirical data concerning various practices of leadership, but on the theory that makes such empirical studies possible. The basic argument is that leadership theories are constructed within specific worlds, and therefore this chapter reflects on leadership as such on a meta-theoretical level. Yet I believe that the deconstructive reading of leadership theories can also offer important insights into leadership practices in churches. This chapter is written from a specifically South African perspective with the general opinion, mainly a Western one, that there is a leadership crisis in Africa. I will use this apparent crisis in leadership in Africa to illustrate a deconstructive reading of leadership theories, by placing the various theories into their respective narrative contexts. I will illustrate such a deconstructive reading of leadership by using two dominant discourses concerning leadership in Africa as the material for this chapter, without personally taking sides in these two opposing views. These two dominant views are characterisations of certain leadership trends rather than empirically verifiable leadership styles.

2. *Leadership Crisis in Africa: Two Dominant Narratives (Characterisations)*

There is a crisis in leadership in Africa, and this raises the question of can Africa be saved? This question can only be answered if we know what Africa must be saved from. According to the dominant media, specifically after the latest immigration or refugee tragedies in the Mediterranean ocean (2015), Africa needs to be saved from wars, corrupt leaders and extreme poverty. Africa needs to be saved from being hopeless Africa as *The Economist*[1] describes it, or the lost continent as World Socialism[2] describes it. There are so many crises facing Africa, and the general opinion is that their cause and their solution are to be found in leadership (Matsengarwodzi, 2013).

The cause for the crises is bad, incompetent and corrupt leadership. The corrupt leaders are driven by self-enrichment, thereby abusing their subjects' trust. Their goals are limited: If they are not war mongers, they are consolidating absolute power oblivious of the route they take.

---

[1] "Africa: The Hopeless Continent," *The Economist*, May 11, 2000. http://www.economist.com/node/333429.

[2] "Africa: The Lost Continent?" The Socialist Party of Great Britain. http://www.worldsocialism.org/spgb/education/depth-articles/politics-and-conflict/africa-lost-continent.

In the process they utilise force that their atomic minds can assume to turn their agendas into immortal theories ignoring glaring resistance (Matsengarwodzi, 2013).

This leadership crisis is playing well into the hands of Western capital, as it allows the West to keep their hands deeply buried in the mineral and natural wealth of Africa.[1] Therefore, the West is often interpreted as being part of the problem, as certain Western states support corrupt leaders,[2] helping them and keeping them in power to insure their influence and thereby protect their economic interests. The West's help in solving the leadership crises is often in the form of funding and developing leadership academies. The leadership theories and management theories developed and proclaimed by these leadership academies are all designed and developed in the West and thus are part and parcel of the Western world.[3] Keep in mind that most leadership theories and management theories are designed not to transfer skills to Africa but

---

[1] "The food giants, Nestlé and Cadbury, buy only cocoa beans from Africa, at prices fixed by them. Cocoa beans from Ghana, Cote d'Ivoire, Nigeria, Cameroon and Sao Tome and Principe come to processing plants in Europe, thereby denying these countries the profits they would have otherwise have accrued from exporting finished cocoa products. Ghana has been cultivating cocoa for over a century now, yet we can only boost of one cocoa processing plant at Tema. African leaders have every right to blame colonialism for the continent's problems," George Bob-Milliar, "Re: The Failure of African Leadership, Cause of Africa's Problems," Modern Ghana, 2005. https://www.ghanaweb.com/GhanaHomePage/diaspora/Re-The-Failure-Of-African-Leadership-Cause-Of-Africa-s-Problems-81437. See also Belinda Coote, "The Trade Trap," in *Introductory Reader on North-South Issues for the Autumn University "Play Fair Europe!" Aachen, 25th of September – 8th of October 1995*, edited by S. Hernandez, 75–104 (1995).

[2] "Most of the African dictators … were and are in power because of the support they enjoy from western governments," Bob-Milliar, "Re: The Failure Of African Leadership." 'Africa has been deprived of some of its most charismatic, able and independent minded leaders (Dr. Kwame Nkrumah, Patrice Lumumba etcetera) by the direct involvement of Western governments in African affairs,' Bob-Milliar, "Re: The Failure Of African Leadership."

[3] "Leadership theory emanates primarily from the United States based on studies of American leaders. Yet, leadership theory is largely represented as universal and scholars often do not notice the 'universal' is indeed specific," Stella Nkomo, "A Post-colonial and anti-colonial reading of 'African' leadership and management in organization studies: tensions, contradictions and possibilities,' *Organization* 18 (2011): p. 371, doi: 10.1177/1350508411398731. "Corporate culture as experienced in South Africa is very Eurocentric. Business practice as currently conceptualised in most South African corporations is generally cast in a Eurocentric mould, in fact, worse, an Anglo-Saxon mould," R. Khoza, "The need for an Afrocentric management approach. A South African based management approach," in *African management. Philosophies, concepts and applications*, edited by P. Christie, R. Lessem and L. Mbigi (Pretoria: Sigma, 1994), p. 121. "Therefore, because it is created in a different world, it cannot be imposed on another culture that is seen to be essentially different to the world in which the theory originated."

to help "Western managers to do business in Africa" (Bolden & Kirk, 2009, p. 73). A good example that illustrates this point is how the Aspen Academy interprets the problem of the leadership crisis and offers a typical "Western solution":

There is a crisis of leadership in Africa. The result is continued poverty for millions of men, women and children. The causes of this crisis are numerous. But high among them is the fact that many African countries lack a broadly shared vision of the future that effectively melds the demands of globalisation with local values. For there to be progress, the next generation of leaders in all three sectors must come together:

- to identify and address their personal strengths and weaknesses as leaders;
- to understand the challenges they face as participants in a rapidly globalising society;
- to share and refine their respective visions of the society they would like to live in, and
- to lead by example in building this society.[1]

The dominant interpretation of the leadership crisis in Africa is that Africa or African leaders are backward, and Africa does not really have what it takes to become a "civilised" continent, so it therefore needs Western aid in the form of leadership theories and management skills. This attitude can very easily lead to what has been called Afro-pessimism, as no solutions to the problems are foreseen, and Africa is presented as a failure (Ayittey, 1998; The Economist, 2000). It is a failure because Africa is portrayed as corrupt, hopeless, criminal and ungovernable (Andreasson, 2005; DeMaria, 2008; Harris et al., 2004; Martin, 2008).

If Africa is a failure, what test has it failed? Who set the test, and who set the standard and the norms? To counter, there are those who argue that this is not necessarily a true reflection, but only how the West portrays Africa, and then they offer an "explanation" for this "failure," but they thereby agree that it is a failure (Bob-Milliar, 2005). For example, in response to Afro-pessimism, there is the New Partnership for Africa's Development initiated by the African Union, which calls for an African Renaissance – a renaissance where Africa solves its own problems and looks for answers not in Western theories and ideas, but from within the African culture or world-view. The slogan, Africa will solve Africa's problems in an African way, tries to counter the Western Afro-pessimist view.

---

[1] "South African Fellows Fight on in the Name of Mandela," The Aspen Institute, December 10, 2013, http://www.aspeninstitute.org/leadership-programs/africa-leadership-initiative/south-africa.

How will Africa solve Africa's problems in an African way? Is there an African way and is there a Western way? The idea of an African way is based on the conviction that there is an African way that is fundamentally and essentially different from the Western way. To be able to find and develop this African way, the mind or soul of Africa must be liberated from the shackles of imperialist or colonialist Western epistemologies and world-views, and then Africa's own unique voice and contribution must be sought. These ideas link up well with most postcolonial (Bhabha, 1994; Said, 1979; Said, 1993; Spivak, 1988) and/or anti-colonial (Césaire, 1972; Fanon, 1967, 1968, 1990; Senghor, 1964, 1994) or nationalist (Appiah, 1992; Mbembe, 1992, 2001, 2002a, 2002b; Mudimbe, 1988) approaches. The problem with these movements is their essentialist understanding of race or culture and/or a glorification of Africa's undocumented past. The idea that Africa has something unique to offer the world is found in various forms of African nationalism, such as: Négritude, Pan Africanism, African Socialism, and African Humanism (Nkomo, 2011, p. 368), and we could add Ubuntu.

Such nationalist theories lead to a clash of essentialisms, as the West is portrayed as being essentially this or that, and Africa is portrayed as being essentially something other than the West. The West is generally portrayed as having all the characteristics which Africa either lacks or essentially does not subscribe to. African nationalism agrees that Africa lacks that which makes the West "successful," but that which the West sees as a lack or as a stumbling block to successful leadership and management in Africa is interpreted as something positive and unique to Africa, which could offer a cure for some of the challenges that the "successful West" faces. For example, the idea of Ubuntu is something that Africa can offer the world to make it more humane and transform the individualistic West into something more communitarian.

Examples of the negative essential characteristics of Africa, which were interpreted as the cause of management and leadership failures (sensuality, rhythm, earthiness, mysticism, communalism), are therefore transformed into positive markers for humanity. Another example of such a re-interpretation of African essentialism is Senghor's negritude (Nkomo, 2011, p. 368). The main criticism of African nationalism and anti-colonialism is that it transforms race and/or culture into something essential and static, which is somehow inherent to a race. Part of this cultural or racial thinking is a call for a return to a time before this race or cultural group was influenced by the other races, that is to pre-colonial Africa, where apparently there were no problems, and the whole of Africa lived in peace and prosperous harmony. Obiakor argues, for example, that there was pre-colonial African capitalism that worked (Obiakor, 2004, p. 406). This pre-colonial time also saw strong patriotic leaders, who developed from within the community and for the community (Obiakor, 2004, p. 407). These ideas argue that there was a time when Africa did not fail the test set by Western standards, but these theories still accept the test as universal and valid.

In the above paragraphs, I have tried to sketch two dominant narratives in which leadership and the leadership crisis in Africa are embedded. It is the struggle between these two narratives, which is possibly best characterised by President Robert Mugabe (often portrayed in Western media as an ape in cartoons), whilst his counterpart Morgan Tsvangirai is often portrayed as a puppet of Western capital[1] in Zimbabwean nationalist media. In this article, I will not argue my opinion on these leadership "styles," nor will I argue for one or the other of the current dominant interpretations, that African leaders are either corrupt and incompetent or puppets of Western capital, but place these characterisations in their particular narrative contexts.

These narratives are dominant and influence many of the comments made about African leaders as being backward or wayward or primitive while on the other hand being a puppet of the West. For example, in a recent quote from the media on President Zuma, the vice-chancellor of the University of the Witwatersrand, Adam Habib, recently argued that "Zuma's idea of leadership is that of a "chieftaincy" in which he provides from the government largesse and expects something in return." This means we are stuck with selfish leaders who are ready to stick to their wayward behaviours despite their glaring failures (Matsengarwodzi, 2013).

Interpretations and/or critique of leadership are always emplotted within a narrative. In other words, the styles or characteristics of leaders are emplotted into a narrative, to use a term from Ricœur (1984, 169), and in and through that narrative the ideas concerning leadership make sense and have meaning. Each of these above-mentioned leadership challenges are placed into different narratives. There are the generally accepted dominant interpretations of what is happening in Africa, which in turn depends on the context of interpretation. One such dominant interpretation, or emplotment, is the Western criticism of these backward leadership styles (Afro-pessimism), and the other is

---

[1] "Tsvangirai: Puppet on a string," The Herald, August 9, 2013, http://www.herald.co.zw/tsvangirai-puppet-on-a-string/.

the African nationalist response, arguing that they will refuse to submit to the neo-colonialism of Western morals or ethics and world-view, and rather seek an African solution to African problems. There are numerous other narratives, for example, those that seek to explain these events or practices within the light of the global-political or geo-political narrative, namely that both these characterisations are just part of a game-plan of global capital to insure access to important natural and mineral resources.

3. *Leadership*

What is leadership? Well, it is many different things, depending on the narrative it is part of, or the context in which it is spoken of. For example, at a conference on leadership, leadership could be a hot topic, and if you add Africa to it, it becomes an even hotter topic. If "African leadership" is in the title of a research project, it will probably guarantee good funding, which is becoming very scarce in faculties of the humanities. There is a proviso, though: your interpretation of leadership must coincide with the ideas of leadership formulated by the leading leadership experts of the West, such as Leadership Magazine[1] or Forbes.com's interpretation of leadership[2] or the Aspen Institute's[3] understanding of good leadership or the African Leadership Academy's[4] ideas, because all these ideas are believed capable of saving Africa from itself.

A different narrative is being truly interested in leadership, and concerned (*Sorge*) about this beloved continent and her people. This article is about deconstructing the narratives of leadership by reading the various concepts of leadership within their world-constructions. This deconstruction is dependent on the thoughts of both Heidegger and Derrida, and therefore I shall use various German terms linking these thoughts to those of Heidegger.

There are different narratives in which leadership is my *Sorge* – the academic world with its funding opportunities and the life-world of this continent and my existential being-there (*Dasein*) in this context. In all these worlds, leadership plays a role, which explains my concern (*Sorge*) with the topic. This *Sorge* for this continent is not neutral or objective, but one's *Dasein in this Mitsein* is part of a particular *Austrag* of a particular world.

---

[1] *Leadership Magazine,* www.leadershiponline.co.za.
[2] Forbes Media, www.forbes.com/leadership/.
[3] The Aspen Institute, "South African Fellows Fight on in the Name of Mandela."
[4] African Leadership Academy, www.africanleadershipacademy.org/.

The method employed in this article is to read the various theories on leadership in Africa in their specific narrative contexts, whilst seeking that which is forgotten or not said, and thereby witnessing a certain auto-deconstruction of these various leadership theories or ideas. The intention of such a reading is not to arrive at an understanding of leadership, or to develop the theory of leadership, but to create a certain democracy of thought (Laruelle, 2013, p. 187) concerning leadership in Africa. My suspicion is that there is no democracy of thought, not just the obvious domination of the thought on leadership by two differing paradigms, but that there are numerous voices that are not heard, and perhaps space can be created to hear them. These voices are not the truth about leadership, but they might challenge the dominance of certain voices and thereby create a sense of justice, by giving other voices a platform to be heard. Such a democracy of thought could possibly open a more inclusive space, allowing ever more voices to be heard and specifically also the voices of the vulnerable and marginalised.

4. *The Narratives of Leadership Theories or the Differing Worlds of Leadership Theories*

Every theory on leadership is emplotted within a specific narrative, and these narratives create (*Austrag*[1]) a particular world. Or, one could say, create various differing worlds, as there is a world believed to be behind the text, a world implied in the text, and a world created in front of the texts on leadership. There are no universal ideas or theories on leadership, as each theory is embedded in a particular narrative, and leadership is disclosingly appropriated into a particular world through the narrative (language) (see Hofstadter, 1971, p. xxi; Heidegger, 1971, pp. 202–203). The author of a particular leadership theory, with his or her text, wishes to convince the reader that these differing worlds all refer to the same world, the one we all share, and because we all share the same world, it is believed possible to formulate a universal theory on leadership. The two dominant ideas mentioned above are both emplotted into narratives that create a particular world, either the world of Western management and leadership or the world of African nationalism. In these two differing worlds, leadership is either seen within the Western world, which is stereotypically interpreted as being individu-

---

[1] See Caputo's interpretation of Heidegger's literal translation of the Latin *dif-fere* (J.D. Caputo, *Heidegger and Aquinas: An essay on overcoming metaphysics* (New York: Fordham University Press, 1982), 151152.

alistic, goal-driven, etc. whilst African leadership is stereotypically presented as being human-orientated, consensus-driven, etc. In one sense, these differing views are good as the difference breaks the hegemony of the single universal idea of leadership. Numerous studies have been done taking these cultural differences into consideration. One of the main theorists concerning cultural differences in leadership studies is Geert Hofstede (1980; 1993). Other studies that have focussed on cultural differences are House (1993; 1996), House et al. (1997; 1998) and Triandis (1995). There is also a South African study (Booysen, 2001) which focusses on cultural differences in leadership, namely the differences between black and white leadership styles.

What is forgotten (*Seinsvergessenheit*) is that each of these theories on leadership is emplotted within a particular narrative that in turn is embedded within a particular world or culture. I do not want to argue for cultural essentialism, where distinct, essential characteristics are identified with different race groups as, for example, Booysen (2001, p. 47) does.

The texts on leadership often imply that the world in front of the text is the same as the implied world of the text as well as the world behind the text, and because it is the same, the reader can pass judgement on that which is supposed to be happening behind the text through the author's "world." Out of fear of over-simplifying, the author, the text and the reader generally presuppose that there is only one world (the real world) that is being talked about, and that the language (text) is the medium that communicates a truth about this one true world. On the basis of this truth, the leaders and leadership styles can be judged or criticised. What is forgotten is that there is not only one world, but differing worlds. What is forgotten is difference.

What is necessary is to think the following, if one wishes to think what is forgotten:

> 1. There are different world-creations as humanity is *weltbildend*, or rather language is *weltbildend*.
> 2. The wolf and the lamb: The differing world-creations have a sovereign that has the power (is authorised and legitimated) to judge according to a "universal standard."
> 3. The peculiar similarity between the sovereign and beast (Derrida, 2011) even within the same world-creation
> 4. What if all this thinking is also *weltbildend*.
> 5. *Die Welt ist fort, ich muss dich tragen* (The world is gone, I must carry you).

The rest of the article will more or less follow these five thought-paths in the light (*Licht-ung*) of reflecting on leadership.

5. Humanity is weltbildend

Heidegger argues in *Die Grundbegriffe der Metaphysik: Welt – Endlichkeit – Einsamkeit* that humans are *weltbildend*. For him it is only humans that have the ability to create worlds, whilst animals are *weltarm*, and stones (inanimate beings) are *weltlos*.[1] This view of humanity and animals is of course also part of a particular Greek world-creation, in other words, it is part of a thinking that has been influenced by Greek thought, together with the thought-worlds of the three great monotheisms, which have influenced and shaped Western thinking. These ideas are thus embedded or emplotted within the greater Western narrative (not that there is only one Western narrative). In this particular world, humans are interpreted as sovereigns who create their own world. They create their own world mostly unconsciously, through their being in language, where language is understood as the house of Being. Humans live in their socially constructed worlds. These world-creations of humanity are worlds in which a certain logos *waltet* (Derrida, 2011, p. 42) – a logos that gathers and carries out a world into and out of the difference. Already in *Being and Time* (1996) Heidegger argued that logos, understood as speech, should be primarily understood as *apophainesthai*, as that which lets what is talked about be seen (phainesthai) as it is in itself (apo) (Heidegger, 1996, p. 280). It is this difference that is sovereign, that rules or reigns. Derrida refers back to Heidegger's use of the term *walten* when he says that it is in the *Austrag* that it *waltet* (Derrida, 2011, p. 256). Heidegger argues, "Im Austrag waltet Lichtung des sich verhüllend Verschließenden, welches Walten das Aus- und Zueinander von Überkommnis und Ankunft vergibt"[2] (Heidegger, 1957, p. 63). The *Aus- und Zueinander von Überkommnis und Ankunft* is the way in which he in his later work describes the role of language (Heidegger, 1971, p. 206). Language, in and out of difference, *waltet*, as things carry out or bear a world, just as the world (carried out) grants to things their ontological place (Heidegger, 1971, p. 200).

---

[1] "'The stone has no world,'" he says, *der Stein ist weltlos*, "The animal is poor in world," *das Tier is weltarm*, "Man is world-configuring or world-forming," *der Mensch is weltbildend*' [Martin Heidegger, *Die Grundbegriffe der Metaphysik: Welt- Endlichkeit – Einsamkeit*. Reissued by Friedrich-Wilhelm von Herrmann (Frankfurt am Main: Vitorio Klosterman, 1983), 261ff] Jacques Derrida, *The Beast and the Sovereign*. Volume II. Transl. G. Bennington (Chicago: University of Chicago Press, 2011), 6).

[2] Within the *Austrag* (Dif-ference) *waltet* a clearing (Lichtung) of what veils and closes itself off, which *Walten vergibt* [gives, misgives, forgives] the being-apart and being-related, the one to the other, of Supervening and Arrival [thus Being and beings as such]. See Derrida, *The Beast and the Sovereign*, 256.

Language, in and out of the *Austrag*, creates (poiesis) a world. These are the language-worlds (narratives) into which events, like those mentioned above, are disclosingly appropriated. Each of these different world-creations are made up of the *Geviert* (four-fold: earth-sky-mortal-divinities) (Heidegger, 1971, p. 191ff).

Thus, each world-poiesis contains some form or other of divinity. The divinities can be understood as the theo-ontological-political constitution of these worlds or their Logos; the divinities or the sovereign principle that is seen to be beyond the world, but that which not only gathers, but binds (*religare*) a world into a comprehensible whole. The divinities are the sovereign of that particular world. This has been interpreted as the religion or metaphysics of the particular world – religion understood as the ultimate meaning of that world (Berger, 1967, p. 32; Geertz, 1995, p. 90).

Thus, humans, who live in the house of being (language), which carries-out their world, a world that includes some idea or other of sovereignty, find themselves under the power of that sovereign, which is part of the carried-out world of the speaking of their language. This sovereign Logos, in turn, also gives them the power or sovereign right (legitimate authority) to judge others in the light of this Logos. It gives them the sovereign right to judge and declare who is beast and who is not, as well as the sovereign power to declare what makes the beast a beast (backward or primitive).

There are different interpretations of leadership according to different narratives, which in turn are embedded in different world-creations, gathered together by different logoi. There are the two dominant interpretations mentioned above, one that is embedded in the Western-world-creation and the other that is embedded in an African-world-creation. Bolden & Kirk (2009) seek to go beyond this simple dichotomy towards a more differentiated understanding of differing leadership styles. They identify four distinct categories of leadership theory, namely: essentialist, relational, critical, constructionist (Bolden & Kirk, 2009, p. 71). Each of these four differing theories has its logos that binds the theory together into a comprehensible whole. For example, the essentialist theory is based on an objectivist or positivist world-view, the relational is based on a more social-constructionist view of leadership, the critical model focuses on the underlying powers at play in leadership, and the constructionist focuses on "facilitation group processes."

Each of these theories has this underlying logos (objectivism, social-constructivism, power, constructivism, deconstruction). The logos is the gathering or binding principle that gives birth to a particular world, by gathering the things of that world together and giving the things of that world their rightful place (ontology). It is because of this gathering logos that leadership styles can be understood and therefore also judged. If one is at home in a constructionist paradigm, then most leadership theories will be interpreted as being essentialist and therefore backward, as they would be judged to be part of the modernistic paradigm. The essentialists would in turn argue that the constructivist argument is useless as it is too relativistic and will not solve any of the problems facing Africa.

Each theory (logos) co-creates a particular world and/or is part of a particular created world, and in that particular world, certain leadership styles are classified as ungovernable, chaotic, corrupt, or the other culture is classified as individualistic, self-centred and goal-driven. To get involved in the battles between these theories, with their respective worlds, would only make sense if we still believe that one true and correct theory can be found, or that we have found it.

There are battles between these different leadership theories and worlds because there is power and there is interest – both interest in the sense of *Sorge*, as well as interest in the sense of capital gain. In a global context of different worlds, the question arises of who or what decides what leadership is? Who decides what is proper to leadership, and whose interests does this interpretation of leadership serve?

From the above it is clear that it is the *Walten* of the Logos that has the sovereign power to bestow the qualification "good leadership" on a particular leadership style or theory. It is the Logos, which is the metaphysical principle (beyond the norm and law, yet instituting the norm), and therefore the sovereign that decides what is proper and right. Thus, the question is: What Logos *waltet* in these differing worlds? Each of these differing worlds has a different logos, which determines and by "walting" gathers and carries out a particular world.

6. *The Sovereign and the Beast or the Wolf and the Lamb*

Who or what is the sovereign able to declare what is good leadership? The question in the context of sovereignty is: can the subaltern speak (Spivak, 1988)? Can s/he be heard? In whose voice does s/he speak? If they speak in their own voice, this becomes a tendency to essentialise "African" culture or the culture of the Other (Nkomo, 2011, p. 377). As a result, "In their efforts to cancel the negative images and/or invisibility of Africa, African management proponents often end up repeating the very errors they hope to erase" (Nkomo, 2011, p. 377). To argue that Ubuntu can not only solve the African crisis (see Mangaliso, 2001, p. 32), but can also be a product to be exported from Africa to the rest of the world, that is, be a lesson the world can learn from Africa, does not question the basic managerial assumptions that underlie the "universal" theory to which Ubuntu would add value. In these essentialist theories, African culture is portrayed as a homogeneous whole, thereby not taking into consideration that Africa is a vast continent with numerous distinct cultures and traditions.

Instead of the binary between Africa and the West, we could move away from pure (Bhabha, 1994) and essential interpretations of culture towards interpretations that appreciate the mutual effects of colonizer and colonized in what can be described as post-colonial thinking. The challenge is not to create a binary, but to create space for democracy of thought. To create the necessary space for democracy of thought, the power games in the space need to be understood.

Who or what or where does the power come from, "the power that gives itself its own law, its force of law, its self-representation, the sovereign and reappropriating gathering of self ..." (Derrida, 2005, p. 11)? Derrida argues that "The sovereign, in the broadest sense of the term, is he who has the right and the strength to be and be recognized as himself, the same, properly the same as himself" (Derrida, 2009, p. 66). The sovereign is he or she or that which has the power (*Gewalt*) to gather together a world, granting each thing (being) in that world its rightful (normative) place so that the world, as such, can come to self-consciousness.

And again he argues, "[T]he concept of sovereignty will always imply the possibility of this positionality, this thesis, this self-thesis, the autoposition of him who posits or posits himself as ipse, the (self-)same, oneself" (Derrida, 2009, p. 67). Sovereign is understood as that which has the power to declare that which is proper to oneself or to someone. It declares what is proper to leadership. What is true of oneself, this ipseity includes the power, the force to proclaim that (Derrida, 2005, p. 17). Who is the sovereign, who is the one who is above the law, outside the law, who has the ability to dictate what is right, proper and lawful? And therefore the ability to declare what is outside of what is right and proper, to be labelled backward, wayward or rogue (Derrida, 2005, pp. 1920)?

The United Nations believes itself to have the duty to oversee the various sovereign nation-states of the global village, and yet it does this on the basis of something that is beyond the particular laws and sovereignties of the various nation-states. The United Nations was given the right, the sovereign right, to judge the laws and leadership styles of particular sovereign nation-states, on the basis of what it believes to be universal human rights and universal good governance. If a particular nation-state contravenes or abuses human rights, the United Nations can impose economic sanctions, for example. What logos gives (*vergibt*) (Heidegger, 1957, p. 63) the right to be beyond the law (sovereign law) of the various nation-states to these universal rights, so as to be in a position to act as a universal judge?

Derrida refers to Carl Schmitt, who argues that universal rights, which are believed to be above the particular nation-states, is a form of neutralising, de-politicising (*Entpolitisierung*) of the state (Derrida, 2009, p. 71). Yet Schmitt argues that this so-called de-politicising is in actual fact a hyperpoliticity (Derrida, 2009, p. 73). Universal human rights, which pretend to de-politicise, in actual fact hyper-politicise in the name of the Western state, declaring all those who do not uphold human rights, who do not subscribe to universal (Western) standards of governance, as being outside the law and therefore as beasts or backward in need of Western intervention. In declaring the other as beast, the other may be treated as beast (outside the law). To accuse someone of being a beast (backward) means "basically, of being virtually deprived, as is the beast, of all that is supposedly proper to man, beginning with language, but also reason, logos, as language and reason, the sense of death, technique, history, convention, culture, laughter, tears, etc., ..." (Derrida, 2009, p. 167). This is exactly what happens. Africa is considered to be backward, and therefore it does not have a logos. Its peoples do not have the necessary theory and skills to solve their problems and therefore are in need of Western aid in the form of various leadership academies. If they are beasts, they can be treated as such. But in treating the other as a beast outside the law, you become a beast yourself, which the story of neo-colonialism clearly reveals. There is no sovereign beyond the sovereign of the various worlds, be they nation-states or not. The so-called sovereignty of universal human rights is just a universalisation (neo-colonisation) of a particular Western nation-state.

The fable concerning the sovereign, La Fontaine's the Wolf and the Lamb, reveals that the sovereign is always the beast. "The reason of the strongest is always the best" (Derrida, 2009, p. 7). The logos of the stronger is always the best, is always what is right. The sovereign, in always being right, is the wolf in the fable, yet the wolf is the beast.

7. The Beast is the Sovereign

This is perhaps what Derrida argues in *The Beast & The Sovereign Vol I*, that the beast and the sovereign are the same. In French, it is just the absence of one letter between the beast and [*et*] the sovereign and the beast is [*est*] the sovereign (Derrida, 2009, p. 18). In this onto-zoo-anthropo-theologico-political copulation between sovereign and beast, we cannot distinguish the one from the other, as the one is the other.

It is within this context, this onto-zoo-anthropo-theologico-political context, that there is a sovereign and [*et*] a beast. Yet it is also in this context that the beast becomes the sovereign and the sovereign becomes the beast: beast is [*est*] sovereign, and sovereign is [*est*] beast. Derrida refers to Kant's distinction between warfare (*Krieg*) and conflict (*Streit*) (Derrida, 2009, pp. 166–167). Conflict calls for a rational and institutional arbitration as opposed to war – "the accusation of bêtise is a warlike response, an act of war that would achieve the rational status of conflict only on the hypothesis that someone, a third party or an institution, could determine both the meaning of the word bêtise and the justness, justice, justification or not of the accusation" (Derrida, 2009, p. 167). Who can determine that meaning? There is no transcendent rule, no transcendent inalienable human rights or universal theory of leadership that can arbitrate between these different worlds. These different worlds can be thought of as different ecologies of thought (worlds of a particular logos) or ethologos as Laruelle (2013) argues, which could be developed into something like etho-spheres, or bubbles as Sloterdijk (2011) might argue. Each sphere has its own ontology and ethics, based on its own conscious or subconscious metaphysics, the logos (*ethologos*) that *waltet* over that particular world (*ethosphere*). Maybe it would be useful to introduce a term of lived-metaphysics or lived-logos, that is the logos that *waltet* in a particular world.

The metaphysics or the sovereign divinities of these spheres (worlds) can be compared to Aristotle's Prime Mover. There is no escaping this metaphysics to a place from which we could compare and judge these different world-creations carried out by differing logoi. There is no beyond metaphysics, only a closure or enclosure within metaphysics (see Derrida, 1981, p. 13).

8. What if This Thinking is Also weltbildend?

The infamous statement by Derrida that there is nothing beyond the text (Derrida, 1997, p. 158) might help in this regard. There is nothing beyond the text, in other words, there are no universal leadership theories, but neither are there particular cultural-religious pre-colonial essentialist leadership theories either, as both are part of a particular world-creation.

Can there be no absolute sovereign? Heidegger, according to Derrida, argues for the *Walten der Differenz* (Derrida, 2011, p. 207). Is this *Walten der Differenz* a new absolute sovereign, beyond the sovereigns of the various worlds? Is the *Walten der Differenz* not just another logos that gathers together a world by carrying it out? Or is this *Walten der Differenz* something different, something sovereign beyond the sovereignty of the onto-theological sovereignty of the different worlds?

Walten der Differenz is different and cannot be equated with the various sovereign logoi. "Walten would be too sovereign still to be sovereign, in a sense, within the limits of the theologico-political. And the excess of sovereignty would nullify the meaning of sovereignty" (Derrida, 2011, p. 279). It is different to the onto-theological God as causa sui, as one cannot dance and sing and make sacrifices to this onto-theological God (Heidegger, 1957, p. 70). Maybe the God of Abraham and Jacob can offer an alternative sovereignty that is not sovereign in the metaphysical sense. If we take a step back (Heidegger, 1957, pp. 71–72), one that brings us back from forgetting of Differenz, if we take that step back and no longer forget the *Walten der Differenz*, but remember it, what then? Then the world as such is gone. *Die Welt is fort, ich muss dich tragen.*

9. *Die Welt ist fort, ich muss dich tragen* – Christian Servant Leadership

Die Welt ist fort, ich muss dich tragen, ich muss dich Austragen, ich muss dich ertragen! The world is gone, and I must take responsibility for you and for it. I must carry it, take the burden of it upon myself, take the responsibility for you and for it upon myself (see Derrida, 2011, p. 268). The world is gone, the world must be carried out. This opens the way for an ethos of responsibility for the other, whoever or whatever the other is.

The God, the sovereign onto-theological God, has been crucified, and we are left with a God to whom we can dance, sing and above all pray. The God of faith revealed to the faith of the fathers, Abraham, Isaac and Jacob. The world-creating logos, the world-forming logos became flesh, the New Testament states in the Prologue to the Gospel of John. The logos entered into the world-creation, entered history, and in history, was crucified, accused of blaspheming the onto-theological gods. The world-creating logos was crucified, and thus the world is gone with the crucified logos, *die Welt ist fort*. We are all like stones, *weltlos oder weltverlorene* – unchained from the world or from the sun, the logos-light which creates the world is dead. The world has been unchained from its sun (Nietzsche, 1974, pp. 181–182). Unchained from the sovereign logos that has the power to *Walt* over the world. That leaves us as a child, the last *Verwandelung*[1], without a world, besides the world that one has co-created: a temporal and spatial world, as it is a world-creation within a very specific Zeit-Spiel-Raum (see Caputo, 1993, p. 30). Nietzsche's last *Verwandelung* into a child is a child who needs to be carried, both carried to be born and carried until it is grown up enough to stand on its own feet: *ich muss dich tragen*.

Die Welt ist fort, ich muss dich tragen. Who is authorised to say these words and to whom are they said? Who carries whom in this *weltverlorene, weltlose Welt* of the child without a sovereign Father? We could carry each other, carrying each other's worlds by respecting each other's worlds. All the different worlds would stand next to and thus equal to each other, yet without a universal Logos by which to compare or even judge or evaluate the different worlds. Such a situation would be absolute relativism, and the result would be a total breakdown of communication in the global village. Are all these worlds equal? They are equally created and, as created equally, haunted by *différance*. Maybe the ethos that I am proposing is not an ethic of *Streit* and *Krieg* on the basis of some arbitrating principle or other, but rather an ethos of listening to the haunting cries of those who are *weltarm* or even *weltlos* in these various worlds. The stones who are *weltarm* and *weltlos* will cry out, as Luke 19 says, to prepare the way for a king, a sovereign who is different, to whom one can sing, sacrifice and pray. It is an ethos of listening to those who carry the burden of their particular worlds. They who are *weltarm* or even *weltlos* carry the burden of the *weltbildenden* sovereigns or leaders. Listen to their stories, not because their stories are truer or better, but because only they can tell us the weight, the weight in gold, of the world they carry.

It is not the Western world with its sovereignty and leadership theories that can judge the leaders in Africa, nor the religious/cultural world of Africa with its sovereignty of African nationalism which is

---

[1] "Drei Verwandlungen nenne ich euch des Geistes: wie der Geist zum Kamele wird, und zum Löwen das Kamel, und zum Kinde zuletzt der Löwe," Friedrich Wilhelm Nietzsche, *Also sprach Zarathustra. Ein Buch für Alle und Keinen* (Köln: Anaconda Verlag, 2005). Project Gutenberg, 2005, www.gutenberg2000.de/nietzsche/zara.also.htm.

better, as both are world-creations. Often these world-creations are embedded in different global-political or geo-political world-creations. All these worlds are equally *weltbildend* and therefore *weltlos* as such. From no point or point of view would we have a better view, except maybe from the view of those who suffer the weight of these worlds. An ethos is offered, of listening to the cries of the destroyed lives that haunt these world-creations. These cries of those who are truly *weltlos* because they are either dead or treated like stones (objects) offer a perspective (hauntology) by which to weigh the weight of these worlds. This offers these crying-out-stones[1] and restless souls, the living dead, a place in a world where they can rest: be at home and no longer *weltlos*, as they pray to the sovereign of the world still to come. Not a Western world nor an African traditional world, but a world to come, a world of the child, beast and stone: where the wolf shall dwell with the lamb, and the leopard shall lie down with the kid; and the calf and the young lion and the fatling together; and a little child shall lead (carry) them.[2] Such an ethos of listening to the cries of those who are truly *weltlos* could be the task of the church, and as such the church can lead the way towards a leadership that is to come.

---

[1] Luke 19:37–40.
[2] Isaiah 11:6.

Chapter Two

Discursive Leadership and the Other

John Eliastam

A significant leadership challenge for the 21st century is the shaping of relations between groups characterised by difference, whether this difference is ethnic, cultural or religious. This chapter takes a discursive perspective on leadership to explore the role of leaders, including religious leaders, in shaping inter-group relations between South Africans and foreign migrants.

Leadership studies have typically focused on the individual and psychological characteristics of leadership rather than investigating it through a social and cultural lens. The term "Discursive Leadership" is used for a body of work on the social, linguistic, and cultural aspects of leadership. Rather than attempting to explore the attitudes, thoughts and other characteristics of leaders, discursive leadership explores the actual interactional processes and linguistic patterns that constitute leadership (Fairhurst, 2007).

This chapter examines the role of leadership discourse in violence against foreign migrants in South Africa. The first section of this chapter outlines my research approach. The next section explores the social construction of meaning that has resulted in violence against foreign migrants in South Africa, and how this process has been influenced by leaders. The concluding section will discuss discursive approaches to leadership in order to highlight possibilities for religious leadership discourse to shape new meanings and generate new options for action.

1. Research Approach

I conducted empirical research into the social construction of meaning that resulted in what has been termed xenophobic violence against foreign migrants in South Africa (Eliastam, 2015). Within the broader framework of qualitative research, I utilised a specific narrative approach. Müller points out that a postfoundationalist approach forces us to listen to the stories of people in a particular context (Müller, 2009, p. 204). A narrative approach recognises that as a researcher I am an active participant, not merely an observer, in the research process. The research is therefore a co-production of knowledge that involves the researcher and the participants. Thus, I refer to the participants in this research as co-researchers (Burr, 1995, p. 160). I use pseudonyms for the co-researchers in order to maintain anonymity, but also to maintain a sense of personhood.

I conducted a series of unstructured interviews with people living in a rural and an urban community in the Eastern Cape province of South Africa between 2013 and 2015. The co-researchers included seven men, between the ages of 18 and 15, and five women, between the ages of 18 and 55. Some of the co-researchers were unemployed and dependent on social assistance from the government, some worked part-time in the government's Community Works Programme, and one was a student.

The aim of the research was to understand how meaning was being constructed in order to develop insights into possibilities for shaping the creation of new meaning. Stories from within the context were listened to and described, and then interpretations were made and developed with co-researchers. These stories were explored in order to discover how they reflected dominant Discourses in South Africa, and how these Discourses were being harnessed in the leadership discourse, the media, and people's stories to produce certain meanings in relation to foreign migrants. Following Alvesson and Kärreman, I use discourse (lower-case "d") to refer to discourse as language used in ordinary social interaction and Discourse (capital "D") to refer to the systems of thought that provide the linguistic resources for communication (Alvesson & Kärreman, 2000).

Most studies that explore xenophobia in South Africa focus on offering explanations for the eruption of overt violence against foreign migrants and on identifying specific triggers for it (Misago et al., 2010; Landau, 2012). The weakness of this approach is that it problematizes the violence rather than the causes of the violence (Kerr & Durrheim, 2013). The deployment of a reified notion of xenophobia to account for the violence against foreign migrants in South Africa is problematic. While the label of xenophobia may provide an accurate description of the symptoms of this social malaise, there are risks that it may obscure problems or over-simplify them.

Postfoundational Epistemology

My research followed Van Huyssteen's postfoundational epistemology. A postfoundational approach offers the possibility of avoiding the naive realism of foundationalist approaches, without surrendering to the absolute relativity of non-foundationalist approaches. It is suspicious of foundationalism's claims of objectivity and representational knowledge, and of non-foundationalism's assertion of complete relativity (Van Huyssteen, 1997, 1999, 2006). In Van Huyssteen's words, it seeks a balance between "the way our beliefs are anchored in interpreted experience, and the broader networks of beliefs in which our rationally compelling experiences are already embedded" (Van Huyssteen, 2006, p. 22). Van Huyssteen's notion of rationality is central to his epistemology.

Rationality and the Rational Agent

Rationality is the human capacity to construct beliefs about reality. This is something that all humans do. It is a product of human evolution and is rooted in the need to survive or adapt to the environment. Van Huyssteen argues that the ability to interact with the world and understand it is fundamental to human intelligence. Rationality is the product of context, interpreted experience, and tradition. Its goals are intelligibility and optimum understanding. More than this, rationality is the ability to propose suitable solutions to problems in a specific context. All forms of human knowledge are attempts to grapple with different but equally real aspects of the human experience (Van Huyssteen, 1997, pp. 13–14).

Rationality and Transversality

Van Huyssteen borrows the mathematical concept of transversality from Calvin Schrag and explains that it refers to the point of intersection between one line and a system of other lines or surfaces. Transversal rationality is an intersection of different disciplines or Discourses (Schrag, 1992). Van Huyssteen describes it as a lying across, an extending over and linking together. It is a place of convergence in space and time where multiple beliefs, practices, habits of thought and assessments come together. Van Huyssteen locates claims of reason "in the overlaps of rationality between groups, discourse or reasoning strategies" (Van Huyssteen 1999, pp. 135–136). There is a similar production of meaning where narratives overlap and intersect. I will return later in the chapter to this notion of transversal narrativity and the possibilities it presents for addressing the violence against foreign migrants.

2. Violence against Foreigners in South Africa

The South African Social Context

Despite considerable progress made by the post-apartheid South African government in addressing the injustices and inequality produced by colonialism and apartheid, the country faces numerous challenges. South Africa is a society characterised by systemic poverty and inequality, rampant unemployment, and huge challenges in the areas of health and education (Woolard et al., 2009; Spaull, 2013; Cronje, 2014). There are also high levels of crime (Altbeker, 2007), much of it violent. The significant progress in providing housing and basic services to the poor since 1994 has increased expectations of further service delivery. This has been the cause of severe frustrations in areas where service delivery has been poor (Managa, 2012), and sometimes leads to violent protests (Alexander, 2012).

South Africa has a long history of violence. From the violent dispossession of colonialism and apartheid, to the violence of the struggle against it and the violent repression of that struggle, to the violent crime and interpersonal violence that is recorded daily, violence is endemic to South African society and its history (Von Holdt, 2013). This broader culture of violence has included ongoing violence against foreign migrants from other parts of Africa.

Violence against Foreign Migrants

Foreign migrants started to arrive in South Africa after 1994. Their number increased in the late 1990s around the time of the passing of the Refugees Act in 1998, and again around 2005 with the collapse of the Zimbabwean economy. Census data from 2011 shows a dramatic increase in the number of foreign migrants living in informal settlements since 2001 (Monson, 2015). This influx resulted in South Africa being the number one host of new asylum seekers in the world between 2006 and 2011 (UNHCR, 2012). According to the South African Department of Home Affairs, there were 889,943 documented foreign migrants living in South Africa between 2010 and 2015 (Davis, 2015). It is impossible to get accurate figures for the number of undocumented migrants living in South Africa, with estimates ranging from 200,000 to 8 million (Eliastam, 2015). The Southern African Migration Programme argues that South Africans show levels of hostility and intolerance to foreign migrants that are virtually unparalleled elsewhere in the world. Foreign migrants were perceived to be involved in crime, taking economic opportunities from South Africans, and placing an undue strain on government resources (Crush, 2008).

In 2008 violence broke out against foreign migrants living in townships and informal settlements around South Africa. While such incidents were not new, the intensity and pervasive nature of the 2008 violence were unprecedented. In the period between 11 and 26 May, 62 foreign nationals were killed, around 700 injured, and an estimated 35,000 foreigners were driven from their homes. A detailed account of the May 2008 violence is provided by Misago, Landau and Monson (Misago et al., 2009, pp. 24–28).

There was a decline in anti-foreigner sentiment between 2008 and 2010, but continuing instances of violence against foreign migrants have been documented, which suggest that the issues that were catalysts in 2008 are far from resolved. The authors record a staggering number of xenophobic incidents and attacks between July 2008 and the beginning of 2013 (Crush et al., 2013, pp. 52–69). Violence against foreigners continued to simmer in settlements around South Africa in 2013 and 2014, sometimes escalating into organised attempts to force foreign migrants to leave communities, often by attacking their businesses or taking their possessions from them. Violence against foreign migrants increased in 2015, particularly after a speech given by the Zulu king, Goodwill Zwelithini (The Herald, 2015).

3. The Stories that Construct Xenophobia

The themes that emerged from the stories of co-researchers reflect certain dominant Discourses within South African society. Discourses, narratives, as systems of thought and ways of thinking about things, function as linguistic resources for people when they communicate (Foucault, 1972, p. 1984).

Narratives of Difference

Co-researchers articulated perceptions of difference, in which foreigner migrants were described negatively. In his explanation of the term *amakwerekwere*, a derogatory name for migrants, Luvuyo explained that, "Something smells, something does not smell right. You cannot even sit alongside that person." Such negative descriptions of other Africans are said to be a product of self-hatred and reflect Discourses of Afrophobia or negrophobia (Mngxitama, 2008; Matsinhe, 2011). The violence against foreign migrants is problematized as a product of historically and structurally produced identities that are the result of the racism of apartheid. This presents itself as Afrophobia, from a loathing of blackness that is the result of the oppression of colonialism and apartheid. It is an externalisation of self-contempt that projects the negative feelings one has about oneself onto others.

Narratives of Competition and Threat
There are dominant Discourses on foreigners that focus on crime, illegality and "the image of a subtle invasion of South African territory" (Vigneswaran, 2007, p. 144; Landau, 2012). Andile explained, "They are a threat to all of us, these foreigners. They bring crime, they bring drugs. These people are undermining our economy."

The presence of foreign migrants also constitutes "illegitimate" competition for scarce resources and opportunities, such as jobs, businesses, houses, social services and women (Misago et al., 2009). Liso explains, "They are stealing our jobs and shutting down our shops." Buntu points out, "Those guys, they work for peanuts. They will take a job for little money. Then you see we can't get jobs because these foreigners have them."

Narratives of Displacement
The dispossession of colonialism and apartheid has created landlessness and poverty that are sources of pain and frustration. Land reform has been slow and largely ineffective (Walker, 2006; Ntsebeza & Hall, 2007). Co-researchers spoke of being marginalised and pushed aside. Andile described this experience, "We have already lost so much; now we are losing even more because of these foreigners."

Within this context of dispossession there is a dominant Discourse about a massive influx of illegal foreigners as a result of the government's failure to control its borders (Crush & Ramachandran, 2009). This is seen to impact negatively on already marginalised people. Hlonelwa described the pain that this causes. "The displacing of people, even if it's now their businesses, it kind of feeds into the pain of apartheid. It's become a monster. We've been pushed from our community, and we're always losing out. We're the losers. We just keep losing. Your land, you've lost respect, all of that, and it just keeps happening, even in freedom."

Narratives of Dependence
There is a dominant Discourse in South Africa that regards the state as the primary agent responsible for the protection, advancement and

realisation of rights (Thomas, 2010, p. 32). The South African Constitution guarantees rights to housing, food, water, and social assistance, but recognises the constraints placed on the realisation of these rights by the availability of state funds. This leads to a passive dependence that is captured in Busisiwe's statement, "We are waiting for the government to give us houses. We are still waiting for the government to provide jobs." Extravagant promises of a better life are made before elections, but delivery is increasingly impeded by inadequate resources and corruption. A lack of delivery leaves South Africans feeling angry and frustrated (Managa, 2012).

Narratives of Belonging
There are increasingly dominant Nativist/nationalistic Discourses on who "belongs" in South Africa. These contribute to a construction of national subjectivity based on whether people are indigenous. Odwa's statement reflects this, "This is our country, and we must put our people first. They do not belong here. They must go." Busisiwe expressed similar sentiments, "Our community is flooded with Zimbabweans and Nigerians and Congolese. This is our country. They must go or there will be problems." These nationalist and nativist discourses, through their construction of citizenship as autochthony, are contributing to a discursive creation of foreigners that is becoming increasingly broad in scope (Comaroff & Comaroff, 2001; Mbembe, 2006; Neocosmos, 2008; Nieftagodien, 2012; Monson, 2015).

These narratives of belonging are located within a broader Discourse of South African exceptionalism that views South Africa as being more like a European or Latin American country because of its greater levels of industrialisation and its liberal democracy (Mamdani, 1996; Neocosmos, 2008).

Narratives of Frustration
A ubiquitous feature of all co-researchers' stories was that of frustration: frustration that their lives had not changed since 1994; frustration that they lived in poverty; frustration that they had not received houses and other services; frustration that they are unemployed and that prospects of employment are remote; frustration at the levels of crime in their communities; frustration that they feel neglected by a government that had promised them a better life; frustration that their voices are seemingly not heard by those in power.

Foreign migrants were perceived to be the cause of many of these frustrations and disappointments. Although there was no suggestion that migrants were the only problem, in a context where people felt powerless in the face of multiple problems, there was the sense that action could be taken to address this problem. This was captured in a statement by Bongani. "We cannot live like this. People are getting angry. People they are sick and tired of waiting for things to improve. If things do not get better, we must take this in our own hands to take back our country."

Narratives on the Absence of Freedom
A theme that surfaced repeatedly was that of freedom: freedom as the healing of identity; freedom as the recovery of land and a place in the world; freedom as the experience of belonging in their own land; freedom as access to economic opportunities; freedom as the escape from poverty into middle class affluence. There is an emerging post-apartheid discourse in which freedom is constructed as a certain level of economic status and consumption (Cooper, 2009; Posel, 2010). Sipho explains, "After twenty years we are still not free. How can I be free when all I have is poverty?" Unathi adds, "Without economic freedom black South Africans are not free. Where are the houses? Where are the jobs?"

These narratives on freedom are shaped by discourses of comparison, in which relative levels of affluence or deprivation are compared (Pillay, 2008; Gelb, 2008). Poor South Africans, frustrated with the reality that democracy hasn't brought the expected improvements to their life situations, target vulnerable outsiders and blame them for problems and social ills (Duncan, 2012). I was curious about the origins of co-researchers' perceptions of foreign migrants as a problem. When I asked them about this, I was told by most of them that it was just something that "everyone knows." The source of this taken-for-granted knowledge invariably involved references to national leaders, community leaders, and the media. This is reinforced by studies that have shown that elite leadership discourse on foreign migrants, which is harnessed by local leaders to mobilise people against migrants, is a ubiquitous feature of the violence against foreign migrants in South Africa (Crush, 2008; Misago et al., 2010; Misago, 2012).

Religious Narratives
Interwoven with the various narratives on foreign migrants are narratives about God and spirituality. These faith discourses indicate the potential for alternative discourses to shape different meanings in relation to foreigners living in South Africa. However, most of the co-

researchers did not think God or the church was relevant to the issue of foreigners in their communities. In fact, religious leaders did not seem to address the issue at all. Thandi explained, "In our church they do not speak about this thing. The pastor he just preaches on whatever else." Churches reflect the same divisions that exist in the community. Buntu observed that, "In the churches it is the same as the community. The foreigners and the South Africans are separate."

This has resulted in a perception among the co-researchers that religion and religious leaders do not offer any solutions to the problems that they face. Luvuyo made a sceptical observation, "I don't know if that stuff can help me."

Narrative Intersections and the Construction of Meaning
The intersections between the various narratives about foreign migrants form a site for the construction of meaning. Stories of hopeless poverty, of unmet expectations created by perceived rights, of frustration at the absence of social change, of comparison with relatively affluent South Africans, of illegitimate economic competition from migrants, and of the experience of continual marginalisation and dispossession combined with a sense of helplessness create a gestalt of meaning with regard to their current circumstances and to what foreigners signify for them. An understanding of freedom – and that they are not yet free – was central to this meaning.

There is a perception that foreign migrants have skills and entrepreneurial abilities which facilitates an upwardly mobile economic trajectory that eludes the majority of poor South Africans. They are receiving the benefits of freedom that remain elusive for many South Africans. South Africans are being pushed aside and marginalised in their own communities. This touches on the pain and loss of apartheid and colonialism. Who "belongs" and is entitled to share in the country's resources becomes an increasingly important question.

4. *The Role of Leaders*

The Role of Elite Leadership Discourse
South African leaders have a history of self-serving and convenient scapegoating of foreign migrants (Hayem, 2013; Mosselson, 2010; Neocosmos, 2008; Crush, 2008). The "problem of foreigners" is created by leaders, both national and local, as well as by the media. This "problem" is offered by leaders as an explanation for their life conditions. This is

reflected in the inflation of immigration statistics (Crush & Williams, 2001) and xenophobic attitudes among the police (Vigneswaran, 2012) and Ministry of Home Affairs (Palmary, 2002). The state has tended to criminalise African foreign nationals as "illegals," "illegal aliens," "illegal immigrants," "criminals" and "drug traffickers" or claim that their presence drains state resources that would otherwise be available to improve the lives of South Africa's poor. Elite leaders scapegoat foreigners and blame them for social decay, for crime, for the government's inability to deliver promised services, and for economic hardship as a consequence of illegitimate competition. The following examples are illustrative rather than exhaustive.

Foreign migrants are represented as a threat to service delivery. For example, in 1994 Mangosuthu Buthelezi, the Minister of Home Affairs, said, "If South Africans are going to compete for scarce resources with the millions of aliens that are pouring into South Africa, then we can bid goodbye to our Reconstruction and Development Programme" (in Croucher, 1998, p. 650). In his 2004 State of the City address, Amos Masondo, the Mayor of Johannesburg, said, "While migrancy contributes to the rich tapestry of the cosmopolitan city, it also places a severe strain on employment levels, housing, and public services" (in Landau, 2012, p. 7).

Leaders also link foreign migrants to crime. In 2002, Billy Masetlha, the Director-General of Home, argued that "Approximately 900% of foreign persons who are in RSA with fraudulent documents, either citizenship or migration documents, are involved in other crimes as well" (in Misago et al., 2009, p. 16).

Leaders have repeatedly described foreign migrants as an economic threat. In 2015 the Water and Sanitation Minister, Nomvula Mokonyane, told South Africans that "Almost every second outlet (spaza) or even former general dealer shops are run by people of Somali or Pakistan origin in a yard that we know who the original owners were.... Our townships cannot be a site of subtle takeover and build up for other situations we have seen in other countries" (South African Press Association, 2015). Shortly after Mokonyane's comments, foreign-owned shops in Soweto were attacked and looted. The violence escalated and spread to other communities, albeit on a smaller scale.

The same year Lindiwe Zulu, the Minister of Small Business, argued that "Foreigners need to understand that they are here as a courtesy and our priority is to the people of this country first and foremost... They cannot barricade themselves in and not share their practices with local business owners" (in Nyembezi, 2015). Lindiwe Zulu's comments were followed by violence against foreign migrants.

On 20 March 2015, at a moral regeneration event in Pongola, the Zulu king, Goodwill Zwelithini, called for foreign nationals to be deported, arguing that locals should not have to compete with people from other countries for the few economic opportunities that are available (Ndou, 2015). Zwelethini told a crowd that "We must deal with our own lice. In our heads, let's take out the ants and leave them in the sun. We ask that immigrants must take their bags and go where they come from" (The Herald 2015). He blamed foreign migrants for crime and said they had brought untidiness and "filth" to South Africa's streets. Zwelithini's speech was followed by a large-scale outbreak of violence against African foreign migrants in the province of KwaZulu-Natal, where most of South Africa's approximately six million Zulus live. The violence spread to other parts of the country, particularly Gauteng. Not only did Zwelithini not apologise, his spokesman went on record to say the king had meant every word he said and had nothing to apologize for. He insisted that Zwelithini's words had been taken out of context and distorted. President Zuma's son, Edward, also came out in support of King Zwelithini, saying he feared that South Africa was sitting on a ticking time bomb of foreigners taking over the country (Khoza, 2015).

The Role of the Media
The media has played a leading role in constructing meaning with regard to foreign migrants in South Africa. Banda and Mawadza (2015) show how the discursive creation of Zimbabwean migrants by the media begins with the language of "us/our" and "them" that constitutes immigrants as an out-group. With this boundary in place, language is used that suggests a moral crisis. The numbers of immigrants are "overwhelming," a "flood" of them "flocking" over our border. The use of words like "exodus" evokes the biblical migration of an entire nation; the idea that this exodus is "smothering" South Africa contributes to the sense of crisis. There is a "cost" as they "compete" for jobs and other resources. Government services are "struggling to cope." Words and phrases like "taking over," "stripping us of our livelihood" are used. Headlines report that "Foreigners are looting SA coffers," and people are quoted as saying things like "foreigners are stealing our birthright." The public imagination is seized by images of the threat of floods of foreigners invading the country.

The Role of Leadership at a Local Level

Misago (2012) points to the role of micro-politics in communities where violence against foreign migrants took place, and to the role of local leaders in mobilising violence against foreign migrants in communities where there have been violent attempts to expel them, accompanied by the looting of foreign-owned businesses.

It has been shown that violence against foreigners was organised and led by local individuals and groups who saw popular frustration as an opportunity of mobilising people to commit violence. By constructing meaning around foreign migrants as a problem and a threat, local leaders were able to bolster their support and propose solutions to the problems faced by the community that served their own interests. This allowed them to usurp authority from dysfunctional local government structures and use this authority for personal, political, and economic benefits (Misago et al., 2010).

Stories from co-researchers about the role of local leaders confirmed Misago's observations. Co-researchers referred to statements made by politicians and to media reports on the impact of foreign migrants, and explained how these had ensured that they were properly informed and aware of the problem of foreigners, and that some kind of decisive action needed to be taken.

The Role of Local Religious Leaders

An examination of the public discourse of religious leaders in the churches that the participants in the research attended revealed an almost complete disconnect between what was happening in the community and the issues that were addressed from the pulpit. Recordings and written records of preaching during periods when there was violence against foreign migrants revealed that the issue of violence against foreign migrants was addressed in only one out of nine churches. In five of the other churches, the preaching focused entirely on accessing blessing and prosperity by tithing; the other three addressed issues such as prayer, repentance from personal sin, and submission within Christian marriages. Apart from the local Roman Catholic priest, there was a complete failure by local religious leaders to address the violence taking place in their community or point to different possibilities for action.

Even more revealing were reports from some co-researchers of the opinions expressed by certain pastors in private. Thandi reported hearing her pastor describe foreigners as a problem, and express support for those who had resorted to violence to eject foreigners from the community. Buntu said that at informal gatherings he heard Christian leaders from his community echo the sentiments of the political leaders described earlier in this chapter. Rather than being a vehicle for shaping new and more positive meaning with regard to the presence of foreign migrants, it seems that the discursive practices of religious leaders either ignored the violence or condoned it.

5. Leadership as Sense-Making and Problem-Solving

There are multiple, interlinked problems in South Africa: inequality, landlessness, poverty, unemployment, crime, violence, prejudice, corruption, service delivery failure, the diminishing capacity of the state to provide education and basic health services, etc. Statements by elite leaders join the dots between various problems and scapegoat foreign migrants to maintain political loyalty, account for a lack of social transformation, and ultimately avoid accountability. Elite leadership discourses provide an interpretive repertoire that is used by people to make sense of their lives and circumstances. Where dysfunctional local leadership structures are unable to solve local problems, it allows opportunistic parallel leadership structures to emerge and scapegoat foreigners to further their political and economic agendas. In both of these instances, leaders are able to offer sense-making accounts in which "reality" and "truth" are constructed through persuasive but unstable Discourses. In both situations, the "problem of foreigners" is constructed socially, and the role of leaders is pivotal.

In my understanding, rationality and narratives are the same. We tell stories to make sense of our lives, the world, and our place in the world. What we think of as "real" and "true" are really constructed narratives in which events have been linked and then interpreted to give them meaning. Our stories are attempts to understand the problems we face; they also shape the options we choose to solve these problems. Certain stories about foreign migrants are present in elite leadership discourse, in the media, and in the talk of local leaders. Leaders created new meanings with regard to foreigners by making explicit connections between various stories and constructing foreigners as a problem.

In contrast, the narratives offered by religious leaders are extremely limited in their ability to shape meaning in this context. Co-researchers experienced them as irrelevant to the problems and challenges they faced, and preferred the accounts offered by leaders and the media. The reason was because those accounts proposed solutions that were perceived to meet their needs.

6. Hegemony, Identity, and Meaning

Laclau and Mouffe's post-Marxist Discourse Theory offers insight into the construction of meaning with regard to foreigners. It provides a framework for analysing the populist political discourse that instigates violence against foreign migrants (Laclau & Mouffe, 1985). My choice for their poststructuralist political theory is informed by its sensitivity to conflict and struggle over meaning and identity within society (Walton & Boon, 2014).

Discourses are created and organised around a nodal point that represents some social ideal. Constructed ideals such as "justice," "prosperity," or "equality" function as anchors; they temporarily stabilise a Discourse, and in so doing they also temporarily stabilise other units of meaning in relation to that Discourse. These nodal points consist of what Laclau terms empty signifiers or empty universals. They function as reference points within a Discourse that bind other signifiers together. The empty universal is able to do this because it has a relation of semantic equivalence to other signifiers in the Discourse and binds them together in a chain of equivalence (Laclau & Mouffe, 1985).

A crisis of meaning has been precipitated by a lack of transformation in South Africa since 1994. This has dislocated dominant Discourses of reconciliation (Renner, 2014) and the Rainbow Nation (Gish, 2004). Structural dislocation creates the need to rearrange the social ideals around new empty signifiers, thereby making social change possible (Renner, 2014). Laclau argues that the contingency that exists with regard to the creation of a future social order means that dislocation brings about possibility and freedom. It generates "a set of new possibilities for historical action which are the direct result of structural dislocation. The world is less "given" and must be increasingly constructed" (Laclau, 1990, p. 40). The result of this dislocation can be seen in hegemonic struggles over meaning and identity within a context of competing political demands. Hegemonic practices are the means by which competing groups in society attempt to construct new collective identities based on widespread acceptance of the "concrete demands" of that group (Laclau & Mouffe, 1985, p. 120).

The process of hegemonic articulation can be viewed in three interwoven stages. In the first stage, a signifier is harnessed to refer to a possible future state that is more desirable than the current state (metonymy). Renner points out that "What makes one particular signifier credible as a potential empty signifier is its signification of a constitutive lack, something which is absent but seems highly desirable in the present" (Renner, 2014, p. 269). This signifier must be clear enough to be a motivational force, but vague enough to accommodate a variety of meanings and political claims. It must also represent something that multiple groups regard as desirable so that it can be used in a general way to represent their political claims (metaphorical substitution). This universalisation of the empty signifier leads to the exclusion of competing meanings and claims. The claims represented by the empty signifier are stabilised by antagonism towards competing claims, which are constructed as a radical "other." In the final stage of the hegemonic process, the appeal of the empty signifier binds other discourses to it through chains of equivalence. The result is the creation of a new discourse that is unified by the empty signifier and stabilised by the presence of the Other (synecdoche).

The process thus begins with metonymy and moves through metaphorical substitution to synecdoche. The meaning of the empty signifier changes during the shift from metonymy to synecdoche. Its connotations of something that is simultaneously vague and desirable give way to something more concrete; it comes to represent multiple demands that are connected by chains of equivalence. In synecdoche, the shift in meaning is complete, and the signifier now represents a collective identity that has been united by its connection of various demands.

The initial moment of metonymy creates a political frontier between "us" and "them," and this acts as a point of convergence at which people become unified in their antagonism towards "them." A collective social identity replaces particular demands (Laclau, 1988b, p. 250). The empty signifier stands in a relation of equivalence to other signifiers within the hegemonic Discourse and holds them together on the basis of similarities in identity and a common enemy. Hegemony is created by the construction of a threat. It is the presence of a threatening "Other" that gives a hegemonic discourse stability, while at the same time preventing its ultimate closure.

I have shown that the construction of meaning and identity in relation to foreign migrants in South Africa can be understood in terms of a hegemonic discourse on freedom. Attempts to expel foreign migrants were given moral legitimacy because they were usurping the rights of South Africans and impeding the attainment of freedom (Eliastam, 2015).

1. There is an initial moment of metonymy in which an empty signifier is used to represent something with which it is associated. The sig-

nifier, "freedom," is constructed in a way that represents the economic aspirations of poor South Africans. Freedom creates a political frontier between those who are not free (us) and those who are (them).

2. "Freedom" as a metaphor becomes a point of convergence for a number of other, related Discourses which unite people in their antagonism towards "them." To use Laclau and Mouffe's language, chains of equivalence link the various concrete political demands.

3. This is expressed in a synecdoche, where the part now stands for the whole. "Freedom" now represents the various and multiple concrete demands of the collective political identity that has been created by the convergence of Discourses through chains of equivalence and stabilised by the empty universal, "freedom."

This hegemonic freedom Discourse is stabilised by antagonism towards the Other – towards "foreigners." Foreign migrants are constituted as a threat, particularly because they are reaping the benefits of freedom that are still so elusive for "us." Frustration with foreign migrants becomes a focal point for the group identity that has been created by shared opposition to "them" and carries with it all of the political demands that have been connected by means of chains of equivalence.

These Discourses on freedom and foreigners are becoming increasingly dominant in social discourse. They are deployed in leadership discourses in such a way that they are constructing a particular social reality. This points to the need to understand leadership, particularly leadership as discursive performance.

7. *The Social Construction of Leadership*

From a social constructionist perspective, leadership is a product of collective meaning-making within a sociohistorical context. Leadership is continuously negotiated and co-constructed through a complex interplay among various leadership actors, including designated leaders, emerging leaders, and their followers (Meindl, 1995; Grint, 2000). Social constructionist approaches to leadership usually avoid a leader-centric approach that regards the leader's personality, style, or actions as dominant influences that determine the thoughts and actions of followers (Fairhurst & Grant, 2010). The nature of leadership is contested, and theories that essentialise leadership as something found in a leader's personal qualities, in situational factors, or as a combination of them are resisted in favour of a view of leaders as decentered subjects or thin actors. Kelly explains:

> ...leadership does not exist within a person, or even within a relationship between bounded figures called leaders and followers. Instead, leadership represents a kind of epiphenomenon that organizes and determines our experience of social reality and our experience of ourselves (Kelly, 2014, p. 908).

The nature of leadership as a reality that is co-constructed in interactions between social actors is emphasised. Leadership is socially constructed by the leaders and their followers, and influenced by intermediaries such as the media (Liu, 2010). It is not necessarily the domain of the individual, but can be distributed quite widely among members of an organisation or community (Fairhurst, 2007, p. 6). This leads constructionist approaches to leadership to emphasise the social or relational rather than the individual (Holman & Thorpe, 2003). Most constructionist approaches recognise the ability of followers to also make sense of and evaluate their experiences as being equally important (Meindl, 1995, p. 332).

Discursive Leadership
Within constructionist approaches to leadership, there is an increasingly praxis-oriented turn towards discourse (Alvesson & Kärreman, 2000). A constructionist approach to leadership brings communicative practices such as conversations, discourse, and other symbolic media to the forefront of leadership studies. Communication gives rise to leadership; it is not merely an input or an output in leadership processes. The implications of constructionist views of leadership are that leaders must constantly enact their relationship to their followers and "perform leadership in communication and through discourse" (Fairhurst, 2007, p. 5). Discursive approaches take the socio-historical and local situatedness of leadership seriously by attempting to understand the ways in which communication and language are used in the series of "doings" that construct leadership in a specific context (Kelly, 2008).

Discursive leadership explores the social, linguistic, and cultural aspects of leadership. It focuses on leadership discourse rather than the inner psychological world of the leader. There is an increased depiction of leaders as "managers of meaning" (Smircich & Morgan, 1982; Shotter & Cunliffe, 2003). An example of this is Shotter's description of leadership as "practical authoring." For Shotter this means that leaders have "formative power: the ability of people in otherwise vague, or only partially specified, incomplete situations . . . to "give" or to "lend" to such situations a more determinate linguistic formulation" (Shotter, 1993, pp.

149–150). Leaders shape history because, when they are confronted by circumstances they have not chosen, they are able to create a range of factors that limit possibilities for action, along with moral positions for them, and are able to argue persuasively for them. Fairhurst proposes that "Leadership is therefore a process of influence, through the management of meaning, that creates progress towards a goal. This may not be something done by just one person, and it can be distributed quite widely among members of an organisation or community" (Fairhurst, 2007, p. 6). Leadership occurs when people recognise the value of ideas for solving problems or achieving things that are important to them.

Discursive Leadership and Rationality
Leadership is therefore a social activity that involves defining reality and making sense of it. Leadership involves identifying what is important and finding ways to communicate about the meaning of events (Smircich & Morgan, 1982). When one conceptualises leadership as facilitating the construction of social meaning in order to accomplish shared goals, it points to a close relationship between leadership and Van Huyssteen's notion of rationality. This should not be surprising because rationality is a defining feature of humanity, it is rooted in the need to survive or adapt to the environment. Leadership, as the management of meaning, also involves optimum understanding and problem-solving. It extends beyond them to include attempts to mobilise collective action to solve the problems that have been identified – within the scope of whatever options or constraints are perceived to exist.

Discursive Intersections and "Transversal Narrativity"
Meaning with regard to foreign migrants was produced through the confluence of multiple narratives, rather than through any single narrative. Borrowing the notion of transversality from Schrag (1992), I propose that it is in a transversal arrangement of stories that new meanings emerge. The points at which narratives overlap and intersect are able to both modify the meanings of the intersecting narratives and create new meanings that arise from a combination or even a conflation of stories. The intersection of various narratives that were connected by the empty signifier "freedom" modified the meaning of freedom.

I have proposed the term "transversal narrativity" to describe this creation of new meanings at the intersection of various narratives (Eliastam, 2015). When two signifiers are combined, each modifies the meaning of the other. Since the meanings attributed to signifiers are relational, contextual, and are a product of difference rather than a product of identity, they are inherently unstable, and the combination of signifiers can either reinforce or destabilise their meanings. This instability of meaning is equally characteristic of narratives. The absence of certain narratives will shape meaning, as will the introduction of certain narratives. The different narratives reflect attempts to make sense of life and circumstances, and the convergence of multiple narratives produces new understandings that entrench previous understandings, modify them, or dislocate them.

People's identity and their reality are produced by positions that they take in various Discourses. This positioning means that "selves are located in conversations as observably and subjectively coherent participants in jointly produced story lines" (Davies & Harré, 1990, p. 48). Multiple positions modify the content of both identity and reality. Social meanings emerge and are managed as different interpretations of events compete with each other in social interaction (Weick et al., 2005). There are always a number of competing Discourses at play in any context.

Weick (1979) has argued that meanings emerge in the interplay between narratives as cognitive patterns are imposed on a multitude of flexible and disordered phenomena through processes of organising. Greater competition within the discursive field creates the possibility that people can break free from the way a particular Discourse defines them. Fairhurst writes, "The presence of other meaning potentials, in effect, dislocates a subject's identities, which opens a space for contingency and choice" (Fairhurst, 2007, p. 99).

The use of certain Discourses as an interpretive repertoire by South African leaders produces meaning in relation to identity, belonging, entitlement, and particularly freedom. These stories coalesce in sense-making processes that simultaneously construct the problem of foreign migrants and place constraints on the possible solutions to this problem. The hegemonic freedom Discourse creates an Other, and is stabilised by antagonism towards this constitutive outside.

To the extent that leaders are able or willing to offer alternative Discourses as explanations for problems, meaning around the presence of foreign migrants in South Africa could change. However, leaders seem unable to articulate alternative Discourses that are credible in terms of their ability to make sense of reality and solve problems. The absence of such alternative Discourses lends credence to the hegemonic Discourse and the political identities created by it.

Transversal Narrativity and the Other

The narrative approach has been influenced by poststructuralism's emphasis on language as an instrument of power with constitutive effects, and the deconstruction of dominant discourses which have a limiting influence in people's lives. However, a narrative approach differs from poststructuralism because it regards people as the authors of the ways in which they understand their lives (Weedon, 1987, p. 30). It offers possibilities for the construction of new meanings and identity that transcend subjectivity as a fragile, contradictory site of struggle that is constantly being reconstituted in different discourses (Weedon, 1987, p. 33).

Schrag argues that "an unavoidable task of philosophy for the new millennium is that of installing the dynamics of transversal rationality and transversal communication across the landscape of difference within an increasingly global and pluralistic world order" (Schrag, 2004, p. 80). This need for transversality applies as much to social difference as it does to academic interdisciplinarity.

Discursive leadership is a performance of transversal narrativity. Conceived this way, the task of leadership is to facilitate the social processes of meaning-making and problem-solving by telling new stories that intersect with existing dominant narratives, but simultaneously challenge or unsettle them. Leadership is concerned with the creation of new meanings and new possibilities for action. New meanings and new possibilities for action are made possible by the introduction of new stories. It is critical, however, that some point(s) of natural intersection exist(s) between narratives for new meaning to emerge. Not all narratives intersect. A complete absence of intersection will not result in any new meaning or any modification of meaning. The intersections of the narratives revealed by the interviews with co-researchers suggested that their needs and interests played a key role in the positions they took within various Discourses. A variety of needs were indicated: for meaning and identity; for personal and social transformation; to escape poverty; to experience a sense of belonging, etc. The needs of co-researchers created an affinity for particular stories in a similar way to the process in which chains of equivalence bind concrete demands to the empty signifier for Laclau and Mouffe. This suggests that if leaders are to introduce new stories to people that are able to dislocate old stories and create new meaning, these stories will have to meet some perceived need that they have.

An example of this can be seen in a brief description of an initiative developed by a church leader in Lingelethu, a community that did not experience significant violence against foreigners. The pastor of the local Roman Catholic church called a meeting to meet with residents and listen to their concerns. These concerns included fears of an "invasion," competition for jobs and resources, fears of criminal activity, and perceptions that foreigners were dirty. The pastor acknowledged these concerns, but then pointed out that the foreign migrants had valuable skills that residents lacked, and that it might be possible to learn from them in a way that produced economic benefit for local people. This led to the establishment of a forum where locals and foreign migrants met. After a process of dialogue, it was agreed that the migrants would work with locals to transfer entrepreneurial and other skills that they possessed. This resulted in increased social contact and greater integration of the migrants into the local community. The introduction of a narrative that could lead to enhanced economic opportunities shaped new meaning with regard to the presence of foreign migrants.

The intersection of this new narrative with the other narratives was transversal, in contrast to the chains of equivalence between narratives described by Laclau and Mouffe. Transversality diminished the antagonism inherent in the hegemonic freedom discourse and made it possible for the Other to be included. The new narrative satisfied a need, in much the same way that chains of equivalence connect concrete demands for Laclau and Mouffe, and this resulted in a modification of meaning with regard to foreign migrants.

8. *Conclusion*

Transversal narrativity will introduce new stories that intersect transversally with dominant stories. It will shape meaning through the intentional introduction of new narratives and the juxtaposition of these narratives with existing Discourses in a way that destabilises them or deconstructs them. Leadership as transversal narrativity is therefore invitational as well as provocative. It introduces new stories and asks for new stories. It is inevitable that narratives will reflect both the positioning and the interests of leaders, but a multiplicity of narratives in a transversal arrangement facilitates participation and collaboration. A multiplicity of connected narratives creates a need for new sense-making processes in order to assimilate the various stories. This need is rooted in the human need to survive or adapt to the environment that gives rise to rationality.

A challenge for religious leaders is to reflect on the stories they tell, and examine their ability to shape the construction of meaning with regard to social issues and problems. In what ways do our religious narratives contribute to an optimum understanding of the world in which we live? Do they offer solutions to real problems? How do these narratives intersect with dominant social Discourses? What possibilities for new meaning emerge at these points of intersection?

Transversal narrativity facilitates intentional collaborative engagement with a world that is characterised by pluralism and the ubiquity of the Other. It makes it possible for new meanings to emerge, for different ways of knowing, different ways of being with those who are different, and different ways of solving social problems and eliminating oppression and injustice. New stories are made possible that not only have the potential to create new identities, but are able to create new communities and new cultures. The stories that define who we are can be deconstructed and refabricated. Our sense of we are, and who others are in relation to us, can be unmade and then made.

Chapter Three

Leadership in a Deconstructed Church

Rein Brouwer

1. Introduction

Leadership is part and parcel of any organization or institution. Wherever people convene, working on the same goals and sharing the tasks involved, the group will develop structures of responsibility and leadership. This is a law of sociology, and this law applies even after "the subjective turn" (Heelas & Woodhead, 2005). Nevertheless, "subjectivization" affects the life of organizations and institutions, and questions the self-evidence of traditional leadership structures. Within the particular Christian ecclesial realm, we see this manifested in the phenomenon of the "emerging Church" or "emerging congregations." This chapter focuses on one emerging congregation, in the city of Amsterdam in the Netherlands, and tries to understand what the meaning of leadership is in such a "deconstructed Church" (Marti & Ganiel, 2014). Before I present my research method, and the structure of this chapter, let me start by introducing this Dutch emerging congregation.

2. Pop-up Church

In September 2013, Rikko Voorberg (b. 1980), minister in one of the smaller Reformed denominations in the Netherlands, started the Pop-up Church in Amsterdam. With a small group of about twenty people who were not familiar with church but nevertheless interested in the life-changing potential of biblical narratives, he embarked on a new community. Looking for a location to gather on Sunday mornings, Voorberg found a suitable space in a pop-up office building ("PopUpKanToren") in the Mercator neighbourhood in the western part of the Dutch capital. The adjective "pop-up" doesn't refer to the office building as such, but to the flex spaces that are rented out. Since then, the congregation has moved a couple of blocks over. In 2015, they began meeting in a building facilitated by a neighbourhood development organization ("Coop Mid-West"). This bottom-up organized initiative collects and invests in creative people (musicians, artists, performers) and ideas.

The neighbourhood where the church gathers was designed in the 1920s by the Amsterdam School architect Berlage. The area developed into a prestigious part of the city, with several characteristic squares, but deteriorated strongly in the 1980s. Drug dealing, crime, and ethnic tensions resulted in a bad neighbourhood reputation. Those who could afford it moved away to other parts of the city, or outside the capital. In the late 1990s a new chapter started. The city council made plans to revitalize the area, which resulted in a process of gentrification that is still going on. At the moment it is perceived as a young and vibrant urban area with a lot of potential (creative, social, and economic).

It was not a coincidence that Voorberg started a "pop-up" church in this creative urban area, nor that they gathered in a building with flex spaces (Marti & Ganiel, 2014, pp. 128–132). For some, the word "pop-up" is connected with annoying online advertisements. For others "pop-up" might be a pleasant memory of the three-dimensional books that enlivened our toddler years. Nowadays, "pop-up" is predominately associated with a shop, or a restaurant, or a parking space that operates only temporarily for a short period when it is likely to get a lot of customers. But it is also used, for example, to describe a building system for houses that consist of easily assembled prefab structures. In her research on American evangelicals, anthropologist Tanya Luhrmann (2012, p. 52) refers to this word by mentioning how evangelicals describe the experience of faces of people "popping up" in their minds. These faces appear spontaneously, but they are experienced as deliberately placed there by God for a reason, i.e. a reminder that God wants them to pray about these people.

Combining "pop-up" with church might suggest several things. First, it is a church that fits with the economic and social world of the people attracted to it. Younger generations are familiar with short-term labour contracts and doing flex work at flex places. Second, the importance of church in the sense of a building or an organization is downplayed by this adjective. A church can be moved to another place, or even disappear and make room for something different. Third, from a theological perspective, church is fluid and liquid (Ward, 2002). Church is not burdened by institutional structures and organizational demands, but goes with the flow and pops up where people converse about God and the gospel. Anyway, pop-up church is a catchy name for a postmodern emerging Christian congregation that wants to deconstruct what church is about.

On their website (popupkerk.nl) the church presents itself in these words (the translation is mine, RB):

> The Pop-up Church gathers every Sunday morning for a Bring-Your-Own & Share Brunch, during which we talk about a Bible passage, and discuss whether it has a thought that could change our lives. The visitors are mostly unchurched or non-religious people in their thirties who believe that things could and should change in the world, and that change starts with us. We don't believe in individual best intentions. We realize that real change demands community and rhythm. Early Christianity was a revolutionary grassroots movement already starting to shape the future world together. Since then, a lot has happened in this movement. Our society asks for a new communal commitment to change. We share the desire for a different world, and we let ourselves be challenged by the old concepts of Christianity. In this way, we really take a moment to reflect.
> We EAT, READ, and LIVE – because eating connects, because reading makes us more profound, and if it is not about our lives it is meaningless. It is a POPUPCHURCH because it dares to reinvent the notion of church as a continuous experiment in a non-churchy surrounding with non-church people. (July 8, 2013)

Voorberg might be considered the "minister" of this "pop-up" congregation because he is the instigator and facilitator of the group meetings and activities. His authority, however, is not official. He is an academic theologian and is supported by his denomination to do missional work, but the Pop-up Church itself is not part of this or any other denomination. Decisions are not made by a church board nor written down in minutes. Some people are involved in preparing the get-togethers, but nothing seems to be official, in the double sense of the word: there are no ecclesial offices, and there is no authorized structure or organization. The Pop-up Church is what we call an "emerging" Christian congregation. Nevertheless, being an emerging congregation without official authority structures does not imply that the Pop-up Church is a social group where leadership is absent. The question, however, is what sort of leadership Voorberg exerts.

To answer this question, I first looked at what we know from leadership in emerging Christian congregations. If emerging congregations are "deconstructing the church," they probably also deconstruct leadership. Second, I present the perspective on leadership from the "new psychology of leadership" based on the work of Haslam et al. (2011). This perspective implies that leadership is a group function, which also applies to small, informal groups like the Pop-up Church. And third, I want to suggest that, from a theological perspective, the leadership practised in this postmodern, emerging congregation has a prophetic dimension. The prophet-leader is a postmodern criticism of older forms of leadership, but it is also a robust theological concept for leadership. So this chapter has three interconnecting perspectives: emerging Christianity, new psychology of leadership, and a postmodern theology of the prophet.

I used a qualitative approach for the research on the Pop-up Church (Beuving & De Vries, 2015). The data were gathered in 2015 and 2016, and consisted of two interviews with Rikko Voorberg, texts published by Voorberg on the church's website and on Instagram, Facebook, and Twitter pages, a blog on the website by an intern of the church, and also some material from public sources like newspapers, radio and television (interviews with Voorberg, a documentary that features the Pop-up Church, reports on events organized by Voorberg and the Pop-up Church, and columns by Voorberg).[1]

3. Leadership in Emerging Congregations

In referring to the Pop-up Church, I prefer the notion of "emerging church," although "fresh expression of church" or "contextual church" (Moynagh, 2012) are valid descriptions as well. Michael Moynagh (2012, pp. 73–96) suggests that these new contextual churches fit the sociological trends identified as the "ecclesial turn," the "ethical turn," and the "economic and social turn." The church has become self-limiting in its relevance, availability, and organization, and that is the reason people in Western Europe turned away from it. Another turn manifests itself in the emergence of expressive selves living within an "immanent frame" (Charles Taylor), their everyday concerns dominated by hedonism with an ethical dimension and "personal communities." These turns are part of a larger turn in society characterized by networks and "space of flows" (Manuel Castells).

---

[1] See also the blog by Devika, 'self-proclaimed idealist, fascinated by justice and in justice', who visited ten churches in Amsterdam, 2015, including the Pop-up Church. The blog offers an interesting view by an outsider on what is happening on a Sunday morning, and on what Voorberg's role is in the service. She quotes Voorberg as saying, "The Pop-up Church is an experiment to reinvent the notion of church with non-churchy people in a non-churchy environment." Devika, "10 weken, 10 kerken – week 1 de Pop-up Kerk," [10 weeks, 10 churches – week 1 the Pop-up Church] Something Righteous, January 31, 2015, http://somethingrighteous.nl/2015/01/10-kerken-in-10-weken-de-popupkerk.

Moynagh's book is a comprehensive reflection on all possible aspects of the theory and practice of new contextual churches, but his take on leadership is not very extensive. Robert Doornenbal's doctoral thesis promises a deeper reflection on leadership. Doornenbal (2012) explores what he calls the Emerging-Missional Conversation, and what the implications might be of the vision on leadership in this conversation between the "emerging" and the "missional" movements for theological education in general. Exploring the literature to reconstruct this "conversation," Doornenbal hardly conjectures a straightforward definition of what leadership entails. A lot of metaphors are used for leadership – he mentions more than fifty adverbial metaphors ranging from "adaptive" to "visionary" – but there is no clear demarcation of leadership. In his reflections on church structures, authority, decision-making and leadership styles, Doornenbal discloses an "organic" leadership paradigm, implying that emerging-missional leaders are primarily facilitators, that their authority is not based on academic credentials or church office, and that decisions are made collectively. From this "organic" perspective, leadership is fluid, flexible and distributed, not bound to specific positions and roles. A network structure demands a different approach to leadership. Leaders need well-developed relational capabilities to bring people together in informal groups where they can creatively express their individual faith and life (Doornenbal, 2012, pp. 169–197).

Elaborating on this, Doornenbal presents his own definition of missional leadership:

> Missional leadership refers to the conversational processes of envisioning, cultural and spiritual formation, and structures within a Christian community that enable individual participants, groups, and the community as a whole to respond to challenging situations and engage in transformative changes that are necessary to become, or remain, oriented to God's mission in the local context. (Doornenbal, 2012, p. 200)

The obvious criticism is that his perception of leadership is solely based on what is written on leadership in books and blogs, not on qualitative empirical research on real and concrete practices of leadership in emerging or missional congregations.

An example of the latter is the seminal work on emerging Christianity by Gerardo Marti and Gladys Ganiel (2014). Marti and Ganiel base their understanding of ECM, which stands for Emerging Church Movement, on a decade of ethnographic research, making use of participant observations, focus groups, interviews, congregational survey, and textual resources. In their research methodology appendix, they also mention the use of what they call "opportunistic ethnography," indicating data gathered through everyday interactions out of personal interest (Marti & Ganiel, 2014, pp. 197–208).

In the chapter on "deconstructing congregational practices," they also reflect on leadership in the ECM (Marti & Ganiel, 2014, pp. 117–122). One of their findings is that emerging congregations resist institutionalization through flat leadership structures and an egalitarian form of government. The respondents stated that the ideal structure is "decentralized, egalitarian, spontaneous, and relational, with low overhead and an energizing atmosphere." However, this does not exclude dependence on the leader. Although some communities, like the Irish community Ikon with its leader Peter Rollins, one of the main sources for Marti and Ganiel's research, emphasize the viability of valid congregational life without a centralized leader, it is still recognized that the decentralization results in certain people having more influence in decision-making than others. Marti and Ganiel summarize their findings.

> In short, the ambiguity of structure in emerging congregations, under a supposed egalitarianism, leads to a type of oligarchy that concentrates influence and decision-making to an elite few. (...) In sum, all organizations, even those highly committed to non-hierarchical relationships, become ruled by an oligarchic structure due to the demands of keeping the organization functioning. (Marti & Ganiel, 2014, pp. 121–122)

Organizational demands, i.e. the structuring of tasks and responsibilities, always enforce a minimum of leadership. That is the sociological regularity Marti and Ganiel also discover in postmodern, anti-institutional and "clergy-ambivalent" emerging Christian congregations. Following this sociological order of organizations and leadership, it is not far-fetched to assume we could track leadership in the Dutch Pop-up Church, too. This leadership, however, is not strong, powerful, authoritarian, hierarchical, established and legitimized by an institution. It might still be rather patriarchal, even though Marti and Ganiel (2012, p. 112) state that ECM practices minimize patriarchy. Nevertheless, understanding leadership in the Pop-up Church requires a different approach.

4. New Psychology of Leadership

The discourse on leadership in the ECM reflects the disparity emerging Christians experience between life in their congregations and the hierarchical and clerical structures they perceive in regular churches. Ministers wearing colourful clerical robes or dark suits with white collars are absent in emerging congregations, at least visibly, or in an official role. Nor do we find liturgical orders, or anything else for that matter, prescribed by a denomination or a bishop. Hierarchical leadership and official structures of authority do not fit with postmodern Christians, apparently. Aversion towards institutionalized leadership is part of the desire to deconstruct the church as it is, in order to explore new shapes and forms for sharing communal faith. Still, there are leaders in these congregations, which makes it relevant to reflect on leadership, especially since the ECM intention is to deconstruct leadership, in practice.

One theoretical way of deconstructing leadership I find interesting is the work of Alexander Haslam et al. (2011), called "the new psychology of leadership." Criticizing the "old" personality model of leadership, "the great man and his charisma" approach, Haslam et al. designed an empirically tested theory of leadership that elaborates on the building blocks proposed in the recent literature: the importance of context, the role played by followers, the function of power, and the dynamics of transformation. The model Haslam et al. present is not based on the individual qualities of leaders but is founded on a social identity approach to group processes. Leadership is seen as a function of the group. When people share a sense of social identity ("we" and "us"), it affects leadership. Haslam et al. break down these effects into four rules for leadership (2011, p. 75). First, leaders need to be in-group prototypes. Their influence is proportionate to the degree of their representing the social identity of the group. Second, leaders need to be in-group champions. In order to gain the trust of the followers, leaders need to operate in the interest of the group. Third, leaders need to be entrepreneurs of identity. Leaders do not just adapt to a given group identity, they actively participate in the construction of that identity. Fourth, leaders need to be embedders of identity. There is more to it than constructing the group identity. Group members must recognize how a leader translates, credibly and faithfully, the social identity into social reality.

In sum, according to Haslam et al., leadership is a process of social identity management. In proving that their model of identity leadership is more than a theoretical exercise, the authors develop some practical principles of leadership. Practical leadership is about the three R's: "reflecting" on the culture of the group and how it relates to other groups and networks; "representing" the norms and values of the group in thoughts and actions; and actually "realizing" what is important to the group (Haslam et al., 2011, pp. 205–215).

In what follows, I want to illustrate the explanatory meaning of the identity leadership model for understanding leadership in the Pop-up Church as an example of an emerging congregation. This explication focuses on two specific cases. Both are constitutive of the social identity of the Pop-up Church. From the spring of 2014, the first case confronts us with the undeniable signs of the coming migrant crisis that still holds Europe in its grip. The second case shows how, in 2014 and 2015, Voorberg and his congregation extended their hospitality to a convicted paedophile after serving his prison sentence.

5. Boat Refugees

Even before he started the Pop-up Church, Rikko Voorberg was involved in social action for refugees. In the winter of 2012, Voorberg and several others started the Vluchtkerk (www.devluchtkerk.nl), the Refuge Church, to support a group of refugees who were living in a tent camp. Refugees whose applications have been denied are considered illegal, according to Dutch immigration policy. They were ordered to leave the Netherlands, although they had no serious alternative country to go to. However, the police did not look for them actively, so they took the opportunity to find a place to sleep and stay. After moving around like homeless people, some of them settled in an improvised tent camp in Amsterdam. For a while, the local municipality did not bother them, but in the end, they were forced to leave this camp, with no prospect of another residence. Responding to this challenge, they organized themselves under the slogan "We Are Here" (https://www.facebook.com/WijZijnHier) and were successful in drawing attention to their situation. With the winter approaching, a coalition of churches, refugee organizations and squatters started to protest against the inhuman consequences of the immigration policy. Voorberg was one of the people involved from the churches. The coalition raised a lot of public awareness for the refugees who were suffering from the cold weather and the poor living conditions. Sponsored by a mainline church's diaconal organization in Amsterdam, the network reclaimed an empty church building and started the Refuge Church. Due to the media attention, people from all over the country offered their support. The Refuge Church network collected money and food, and provided a shelter for the refugees for about four months. Ultimately, the church building was closed, and the refugees and their support network moved to, consecutively, the "Refuge apartment building," the "Refuge garage," the

"Refuge office building," the "Refuge former prison" and, in April 2016, the "Refuge Barrack" in southeast Amsterdam.

After the Refuge Church, the network remained active to protest against the consequences of the Dutch immigration policy and raise public awareness for the refugees and their "We Are Here" movement. In April 2015 the Pop-up Church people joined the protest against how European politics affected the human tragedy in the Mediterranean Sea, where boats with refugees crossed over from North Africa to Italy and Greece. Moreover, the protest also addressed the political impotence of the Dutch government to reach a viable solution for the illegal refugees who were unable (or refused) to travel to another country. The Dutch government then consisted of liberals and social democrats in a kind of political marriage of convenience. In order to save the political coalition, the parties involved negotiated an agreement. Pending their voluntary leaving, illegal refugees were allowed to stay in the Netherlands. Five locations were designated for them to stay based on a "bed-bath-bread" arrangement. Responding to this political compromise, and to the tragedy that started to unroll itself at the external borders of the European Union, i.e. the islands of Lampedusa and Lesbos, Voorberg and others covered the front of a Protestant Church in Amsterdam with a large banner, with the heading "Let's Fully Welcome Refugees" (http://www.fullywelcome. eu/; https://www.facebook.com/fullywelcome/timeline; https://twitter. com/hashtag/fullywelcome).

Following their commitment to the case of migrants and refugees, a small group of members of the Pop-up Church, Voorberg among them, visited the Greek island of Lesbos in July 2015 (popupkerk.nl> "Pop-UpReis Lesbos"), because they wanted to know what it was like to come to Europe as a refugee. On Lesbos they joined the volunteers caring for the boat refugees. The blog the group kept shows that it was an "unforgettable" experience, that they were "deeply shocked" by the "hellish camps" they saw, but above all humbled by the courage of the refugees.

In November 2015, Voorberg became a board member of a new foundation, Incubators for Immigrants.[1] The foundation encourages refugees to submit a business plan. "If a business plan is assessed as promising, the person will be included in our support program." On the foundation's site Voorberg is presented as follows:

---

[1] Incubators for immigrants, http://incubatorsforimmigrants.com, accessed March 16, 2016.

Rikko Voorberg (theologian, writer, cultural entrepreneur) is founder of the PopUpChurch and is known for articles and initiatives that raised national attention (a Lesbos travel, Fully Welcome campaign and others). He is one of the initiators of the "Vluchtkerk," the first initiative of refugees, mostly out-of-procedure, to protest their in-limbo situation. He combines performance art (Nuit Blanche, ADE, Eye FilmMuseum) with new socially engaged interpretations of Christianity. He writes for some newspapers, gives lectures and creates installations.

October 2015, Voorberg announced the release of a book, in which he would write about his travel to Lesbos and the refugee situation. But, interestingly, the book would also be about "anger," he tweeted. The book was published in 2016 and lived up to its promises (Voorberg, 2016).

6. *Hospitality for a Sex Offender*

In this book, Voorberg also writes about Benno Larue, better known to the general Dutch public as "Benno L.," a convicted child molester.[1] The relationship between the Pop-up Church and Benno Larue is on public record as part of an independent Dutch documentary, called "The Benno Tapes" (54 minutes), directed by Ton van Zantvoort and produced by Van Osch Films, September 2015. The documentary points out how difficult it was for Larue to get his life back on track. The details of the court case following his arrest shocked Dutch society. Larue was sentenced to four years in prison. In 2015 he was released on parole, which made a lot of people angry. Hunted down by the media, every time his place of residence was identified, people start protesting against Larue living in their neighbourhood, and consequently he had to move to a different area until he was hunted down once more. At the end of the documentary, just before he leaves for Germany to live there, we see Larue in a meeting of the Pop-up Church. People are sitting in what looks like a living room. Voorberg explains in a few words what the Pop-up Church is about ("this is what we do every Sunday, eating together, and reading texts from the Christian tradition about how things could be different in the world, and how we could live differently"), and we see how they share the bread that is broken in two by Voorberg. Larue visits the church for the final time. He is there to say goodbye and

---

[1] Voorberg spoke about 'anger' and meeting Larue in a sermon-column held in 'De Rode Hoed', the student church in Amsterdam, November 8, 2015. Ekklesia Amsterdam, prekenarchief, http://ekklesia-amsterdam.nl/prekenarchief/, accessed February 10, 2016.

to thank them for receiving him as a human being, instead of treating him like a monster. He starts by saying that he did something terribly wrong, for which he was rightly convicted. Consequently, he lost everything, including his family, which makes him thankful for this congregation. They present him with a family photo album and the words "You will always be welcome. There will never be a moment again that you ask for help and there isn't any, because we are here for you!" Larue laughs in a way that suggests he is comfortable with these people, and feels at home. Voorberg adds that he is grateful to Larue for asking if he was allowed to come to the church, and also that the community had the nerve to say "yes, of course." This fragment of the documentary, approximately four minutes, ends with Voorberg and Larue hugging like friends.

According to the church's website and Voorberg's book (2016, p. 55), Larue was a regular visitor for about a year. In the beginning they feared that he would be recognized and that people would come and protest, but that turned out not to be the case. It all started with Voorberg creating a new Facebook page titled "Benno L, welcome in our street" (February 2014). Voorberg's action stood out because it moved beyond public outcry, even criticizing this outcry. As a result, it became part of the huge media attention surrounding the parole case of Larue. All the national newspapers covered the Facebook page of "reverend" Voorberg, and the moral question he raised. It evoked a lot of angry reactions, even a death threat against Voorberg, but also appreciation and approval. About 1500 Facebook users liked the action.[1] In a radio interview (February 26, 2014), Voorberg mentioned that it is his job as a minister to ask the right questions.

> Is Benno L. a human being like we are? Or are we allowed to say to some people who have done bad things that they are not humans but monsters, and that we want them dead and gone? If I disagree with that, am I willing to take my responsibility and say that despite my fears I welcome him, even though it means taking a risk for myself, the people around me, and maybe also my three-year-old son?[2]

---

[1] Benno L. welkom in onze straat [Benno L., welcome in our street], Facebook, February, 2014, https://nl-nl.facebook.com/BennoLwelkom. Accessed April 11, 2016.

[2] "Rikko Voorberg doodgewenst om Benno L.," EO Visie, https://visie.eo.nl/2014/02/rikko-voorberg-doodgewenst-om-benno-l/, accessed January 20, 2016. See also Voorberg's own report in a column in NRC, Rikko Voorberg and Tjarko van de Pol, "Op de koffie bij Benno L.," NRC, May 14, 2015, http://www.nrc.nl/next/2014/05/03/op-de-koffie-bij-benno-l-1372666. Accessed February 11, 2016.

These two cases illustrate Voorberg's savviness when it comes to the media, the old (newspapers, radio and television) and the new (Facebook, Twitter) (Marti & Ganiel, 2014, p. 18). He knows how to make an argument to a secular audience and is well connected in the world of media and culture. Furthermore, he is not afraid to make a bold statement and put his money where his mouth is. Although a minister, he is easily perceived as a social activist, fitting in perfectly with a younger generation that is familiar with the force of social media to start a revolution.

7. Identity Leadership

What can we learn from these cases about Voorberg as a leader/religious leader? When we look at these practices from the perspective of leadership as a process of identity management (Haslam et al., 2011), we recognize how Voorberg is representing and realizing leadership in the Pop-up Church, and we might presume his reflecting on the identity of the congregation in its social context.

In order to realize leadership, the leader must advance the group interest in two ways (Haslam et al., 2011, pp. 212–215). The leader helps the group with acquiring the things they value, and by creating a social world in which these values influence their lives, resulting in what is termed "collective self-objectification." Group members identify themselves with the group identity (norms, values, and beliefs) that is tailored by the leader. Haslam et al. (2011, pp. 171–195) portray leaders as "artists" and "impresarios" of identity, and also as "engineers" of identity. Leaders create a compelling vision of identity using language and other forms of communication, based on an adequate analysis of culture. As a minister, Voorberg chooses the scripture passage that is read in the meeting, he reflects on the meaning of the text, and he also suggests creative activities to incorporate or familiarize oneself with the Bible story. In this sense he is an artist of identity, which fits extremely well with his abilities as a performance artist and writer. As a servant of the Word, he is a man of words and narratives (Marti & Ganiel, 2014, pp. 85–86). But he not only reads and talks, he also stages activities and events, organizes meetings and visits where people get to know and learn from each other, and invites the participants to move beyond their comfort zone. In this sense Voorberg is an impresario of identity. If the Pop-up Church is about the desire for a different world, Voorberg embodies this desire in words and actions. Besides creating and moulding the group identity, he is also the main facilitator of the church. He is the administrator of the website, he organizes the meetings, he is the public face of the church, and he coordinates everything. In this sense he is an engineer of identity, by initiating and embedding a structure that realizes the communication and transmission of group identity.

Haslam et al. stress the importance of practices and the material dimension of successful leadership, which we observe in Voorberg's leadership. The authority to realize the group identity is based on him being the champion of the in-group, the prototype of the Pop-up Church identity. He embodies the identity and the interest of the group when he invites a convicted sex offender to the Church, when he organizes a visit to the isle of Lesbos, when he inspires others to meet illegal refugees, but also when he invites them to break the bread they share on Sunday morning in church. Being a minister is part of representing leadership. Although reading from the Bible and breaking bread are ecclesially not the same thing as ministering the Word and serving the Lord's Supper, as a symbol and ritual it is unquestionably recognized as part of the Christian tradition. Besides his personal charisma (Marti & Ganiel, 2014, p. 117), it is fair to say that Voorberg's ministry adds up to his leadership in representing the group identity.

I have not found data that corroborates if and how Voorberg reflected on the identity of the group. This is probably because he did not become a leader of an existing group but "planted" his own church. It would be interesting to go back in time and reconstruct the previous initiative of Voorberg to think about new ways of being a church. In 2011, Voorberg brought together a group of artists, filmmakers, and performers in a collective called StroomWest (StreamWest). They created installations and interactive performances, of which Voorberg was the artistic leader. On the collective's website, Voorberg wrote about the art they made (the translation is mine, RB).

> The work is always an autonomous experiment with maybe the final taboo in art: faith. Believing or not believing is no longer relevant. We break open the no-man's-land between art and church, because of our culture that is shaped by it, because of the rawness of the stories, and because of the deep impact that arises from this work.[1]

Voorberg himself said he learned three things from this project: the meaning of community, the importance of confrontation and unmask-

---

[1] Stroomwest, http://www.stroomwest.nl. Accessed March 16, 2016.

ing, and the significance of doing good things.¹ In 2014, the collective reached the end of its life cycle. It would be meaningful to reconstruct how these experiences affected the identity of the Pop-up Church, because some of the people of this creative collective are participating in the Pop-up Church. But that would be another story.

8. *The Deconstructing Prophet Leader*

In a column he wrote for a nationwide secular newspaper (NRC), titled "Rolling Goddamns" (September 4, 2014), Voorberg suggested we need to swear and curse after being silenced by the news from Gaza, Syria, and Ukraine, in particular the shooting down of the Malaysia Airlines flight 17 in July 2014, killing all 298 passengers and crew, 193 of which had the Dutch nationality.²

> And now it's time to swear. There is no better remedy for our ingrained cynicism than righteous and whole-hearted cursing. As minister of the Pop-up Church and a Reformed theologian, I would like to introduce you to the power of deeply felt swearing, pure goddamns. Because there is nothing worse for humanity than not believing that something can be cursed. It is an antidote to our debilitating relativism, and to the discomfort we feel proceeding to business as usual. We can change things if we learn, again, to swear and curse, pure and wholeheartedly.³

After the publication of his column, Voorberg was interviewed by two Dutch Christian newspapers about his passionate call to swear.⁴ In another, rather orthodox Christian newspaper, he was questioned about a different ambition, i.e. "causing confusion."⁵ Confronted by the news-

---

¹ "Rikko Voorberg," Lazarus.nl, http://www.7keer7.nl/portfolio/rikko-voorberg. Accessed April 30, 2015.

² "Investigation crash MH17, 17 July 2014 Donetsk," Dutch Safety Board, October 13, 2015, http://www.onderzoeksraad.nl/en/onderzoek/2049/investigation-crash-mh17-17-july-2014. Accessed January 10, 2016.

³ Rikko Voorberg, "Rollende godverdommes," *NRC*, September 4, 2014, http://www.nrc.nl/next/2014/09/04/rollende-godverdommes-1416050. Accessed October 14, 2015.

⁴ Daniël Gillissen, "Vloekende Rikko Voorberg vraagt om kwaad weg te werpen," Nederlands Dagblad, September 5, 2014, https://www.nd.nl/nieuws/geloof/vloekende-rikko-voorberg-vraagt-om-kwaad-weg-te.433511.lynkx; Robin de Wever, "Dominee wil meer 'God verdomme' horen," Trouw, September 4, 2014, http://www.trouw.nl/tr/nl/4716/Christendom/article/detail/3737316/2014/09/04/Dominee-wil-meer-God-verdomme-horen.dhtml. Both accessed December 10, 2015.

⁵ Albert-Jan Regterschot, "Spreker EO-Jongerendag wil 'voor verwarring zorgen,'" Reformatorisch Dagblad, May 30, 2013, http://www.refdag.nl/kerkplein/kerknieuws/spreker_eo_jongerendag_wil_voor_verwarring_zorgen_1_742281. Accessed September 13, 2015.

paper with a comment by an orthodox colleague, stating that causing confusion is the work of the devil, Voorberg defended himself by pointing at Jesus, "who always did unexpected things."

Above, I mentioned how Voorberg recognized the importance of confrontation and unmasking everything that presents itself in the name of God, or of Christian values and traditions. Perhaps it is part of his character, or the outcome of his biography (Marti & Ganiel, 2014, p. 91), but Voorberg has a predilection for provocation (Marti & Ganiel, 2014, p. 116). But it is more than a particular habit, it is a calling or, to phrase it in a secular manner, a responsibility to life. His task as a minister is to raise difficult questions, and definitely not to provide easy answers. Like old wine in a new skin, there is a kind of Old Testament prophetic dimension to Voorberg's leadership in a postmodern appearance. In this respect, there is a similarity with Peter Rollins.

When I asked Voorberg about Rollins (January 8, 2015), he indicated being inspired by him in a way. According to Voorberg, Rollins addresses people who need to get rid of their bad experiences with the church, which is not Voorberg's motive. It is too close to the church for Voorberg's taste, too much about changing the church. Voorberg needs non-Christians to be able to change the world. They ask the questions that are important to them, which help him to understand the Bible texts. It is not about the church but about the Kingdom (N.T. Wright), about the desire for a different world. "When I start a church with atheists, then it is no longer about keeping up an ideal, but about what is really important in life," Voorberg states.

Nevertheless, despite the differences, I see a connection between Rollins and Voorberg, which was confirmed by Voorberg.

> He (Rollins, RB) was the only one who worked with the same kind of language and from the same sort of notions, like "everything may be destroyed" in order to find out what is there. Really trying deconstruction as an important tool to discover what remains in the end. And also with a kind of faith that the story (of the Bible, RB) is able to prove itself. (Interview January 8, 2015)

Voorberg not only has the same hipster haircut as Rollins, but these leaders of emerging congregations also share a prophetic inkling to deconstruct religion and church. As a leader who "engineers" the identity of the Pop-up Church, Voorberg defies what pretends to be holy and sacred, in quite a rough manner, to get at the core of things, which is obvious in the cases I described. This rather provocative way of communicating and performing sounds a lot like Rollins's notion of "a/

theism" (Rollins, 2006) and his call for "insurrection," elaborated in his "pyro-theology," which sees the truth of faith not nestled "in any positive claims to reality but in the ongoing testing and transformation of those claims through the fires of passionate, loving debate" (Rollins, 2011/2012, p. 173).[1]

From referring to deconstructing the church, provocative performances, and radical theology, it is a small step to the work of John D. Caputo (Brouwer, 2015). Marti and Ganiel (2014, p. 26 n. 88) mention Caputo as the authority for a critique of conventional Christianity through the lens of deconstruction. Caputo can be perceived as one of the important thinkers and theologians behind the emerging postmodern church. Deconstruction and prophetical vision come together in the work of Caputo (1997; 2006). Although Voorberg claims never to have read Caputo's work, Caputo is one of the main inspirations for Rollins.[2] Caputo uses an Ikon service as a telling example of how his vision for a postmodern church could be worked out in practice (2007, pp. 129–134), but it is conceivable that Caputo would have made a reference to Voorberg's performative leadership if he had known about it. We can even envision how Voorberg's prophetic leadership could benefit from Caputo's poetic and radical theology, as Rollins's has done. In any case, Caputo helps us to understand the prophetic dimension of Voorberg's leadership.

Caputo's Derridean-inspired theology is deeply influenced by the voice of the biblical prophets because "the voice of deconstruction is not far from the voice of the prophets" (Caputo, 2007, p. 65). The prophets do not belong to the order of being "but to the order of the event of the call, not to presence but to provocation, as one who speaks for (prophetes) justice, who calls for justice, who warns us about ignoring justice" (Caputo, 2006, pp. 30–31). For Caputo, God is primarily manifest when justice is done. Where Derrida said "justice," Caputo says "God" (Caputo, 2013, p. 9). Justice is always to come. It belongs to the vocative order. Caputo relates this prophetic call for justice to the "sacred anarchy" of Jesus: "there is something deconstructive about the New Testa-

---

[1] See P. Rollins, *The Idolatry of God. Breaking the Addiction to Certainty and Satisfaction* (London: Hodder & Stoughton, 2012), 184–190, for how the notion of pyro-theology is communicated in an Ikon gathering in a bar in Belfast, Northern Ireland. See also Patreon, Peter Rollins, https://www.patreon.com/peterrollins. Accessed February 12, 2016.

[2] Peter Rollins, "'You're Looking For Nothing': John Caputo Responds to My Work," Goodreads, https://www.goodreads.com/author_blog_posts/8653298-you-re-looking-for-nothing-john-caputo-responds-to-my-work. Accessed April 2, 2016.

ment, where the same madness for the impossible and love of paradox scrambles the laws of worldly common sense and submits them to the foolishness of the cross" (Caputo, 2007, p. 86). Deconstruction is set in motion by a prophetic aspiration, according to Caputo (1997, p. xix), a movement of "transcendence," a passion and prayer for the impossible, "the provocation of something calling from afar that calls it beyond itself, outside itself."

Haunted by the fate of refugees, illegal migrants, and a sex offender on parole, Voorberg shows prophetic leadership with a passion for justice that the "political" Jesus had, as portrayed in the Emerging Christian Movement (Marti & Ganiel 2014, p. 144; Claiborne & Haw, 2008). In realizing the identity of the Pop-up Church, Voorberg is not only deconstructing the Christian tradition and the notion of church with a prophetic vigorousness ("anger"), he is also deconstructing religious leadership as such by leading with the weakness of a prophet, as Caputo teaches us. Of course, whenever a leader is deconstructing himself, he is also constructing himself, co-creating a place where he is at home, and where he himself can identify with other people and with a cause. Nevertheless, leading a "pop-up" church, for as long as it lasts, implies that the leader always must be prepared to "break down his tent" and leave. That is part of the identity of the group, which might even reflect the weakness of God, but it is certainly part of the prophetic vulnerability of leading the Pop-up Church or, presumably, any religious leadership for the future.[1]

---

[1] I would like to thank my colleague Mirella Klomp for her thoughts and comments on this chapter.

Chapter Four

Virtual Leadership?
The e-Church as a South-African Case Study

Ian Nell

1. Introduction

Frits Gaum[1] conducted an interview with the leader of the e-church,[2] Dr Stephan Joubert, which was published in Die Kerkbode (the official newspaper of the Dutch Reformed Church) on 3 December 2014. Gaum reports as follows:

> Joubert's other "day job" is his involvement in the e-church. It started 12 years ago when he was living in New Zealand and initiated a ministry through email. It wasn't long before he had a list of more than a thousand people. A group of friends that supported his ministry and also wanted to help him to enlarge it convinced him to return to South Africa. The ministry was formalised and became known as the e-church, a non-profit organisation with a board exercising control. The e-church operates on different fronts. There is an electronic ministry making use of the webpage www.ekerk.org, where people can subscribe to the weekly newsletters. Another way in which the e-church is operative is by equipping leaders through a learning community, where they arrange day seminars, often inviting visitors from overseas who are considered the pioneers on being a church in the 21st century. Research is another part of the work of the e-church. But the part of their work about which they are surprised by God's work is what they call the give-away ministry. They give away more than 50% of their income from donations from individuals and businesses. For free, just like the grace of God is for free. They support orphanages and many projects helping poor people.[3]

---

[1] Frits Gaum is an emeritus Dutch Reformed minister who was formerly the editor of *Die Kerkbode*, the official newspaper of the Dutch Reformed Church. Currently, he still contributes to the newspaper through interviews with public and influential figures in the Reformed tradition.

[2] In Afrikaans it is called the "ekerk," referring to the fact that it makes use of electronic media. The content of this reference is explored in more detail in the rest of the chapter by making a distinction between 'online church' and 'church online'.

[3] This was translated by the author from the original Afrikaans.

Reading this interview on the life and work of Joubert generated some questions concerning my research interest in leadership studies. Linking with the overall theme of the TRIC project, with a specific focus on the virtual sphere, the question arises: Can we speak about something like virtual leadership? In other words, is it possible to exercise some form of leadership online and does it have an influence on the lives of people? If so, what might be the nature of this kind of leadership and in what ways can it be exercised? These are the basic research questions that will be addressed in this chapter.

I endeavour to answer these questions in the following way. First, I take a closer look at what is meant by leadership in the literature on the topic. Second, the focus shifts to different aspects concerning the virtual world before discussing the e-church as a case study. This is done by reporting on empirical research conducted by qualitative methods consisting of document analysis and a semi-structured interview that I conducted with Joubert. Third, I examine virtual leadership specifically, and the different components of this form of leadership are discussed utilising a theo-dramatic approach. In the final part, a critical discussion makes use of some recent literature on the topic of entrepreneurial leadership.

2. Theoretical Perspectives

Leadership

Reading through the literature on the topic of leadership, the name of Garyk Yukl (2010) appears as one of the leading scholars in the field. He has written many books on the topic of leadership and developed a wide variety of theories in the field. In his book *Leadership in organizations* (2010), his focus is mainly on leadership within professional organisations. Taking many different contexts into account, he developed the following definition of leadership: "Leadership is the process of influencing others to understand and agree about what needs to be done and how to do it, and the process of facilitating individual and collective efforts to accomplish shared objectives" (Yukl, 2010, p. 26). It is obvious that leadership is about "influence" as well as the different ways of exercising this influence through individual and collective facilitation of shared goals.

The Dutch scholar Joke van Saane (2012, pp. 13–14) built on this definition of Yukl and developed her own definition of leadership:

> Leadership is the dynamic process whereby the leaders and followers influence one another, so that (1) agreement develops about the purpose

and means of the group, (2) individual members and the group are optimally facilitated in an attempt to achieve the goals of the group, and (3) the welfare of the group and the members is enhanced.[1]

Van Saane (2012, p. 14) therefore distinguishes between three dimensions of leadership: (1) the person of the leader, (2) the individual followers, and (3) the group as a whole. According to her, these three are in continuous interaction with one another and in each situation create a unique dynamic that can at times be very complex. The specific context is of special importance and, therefore, when it comes to religious leadership, we move to another level of complexity.

In concentrating on religious leadership, the insights of Michael Jinkins in his chapter "Religious leadership" in *The Wiley-Blackwell Companion to Practical Theology* (2012) point to the contested nature of leadership language within religious discourse. "Though leadership has been an essential aspect of religious life from antiquity, its precise role and significance remain contested to this day in the academy and the church" (2012, p. 308).

In his opinion, one of the main reasons lies in the very definition of the term and the fact that the ways the concepts and forms are utilised in many churches "[bear] the marks of secular ages, especially derived from business, social sciences, and political studies" (Jinkins, 2012, p. 309). When reflecting on the place and role of religious leadership in practical theology, Jinkins (2012, p. 310) writes:

> It remains an open question whether leadership as a field of study benefits from being understood as a discipline per se. At present, it appears more likely that leadership should be viewed as a subject matter, an area of specialization, or a field of study within practical theology, though its disparate core concerns may make it more difficult to describe its disciplinary subject definitively than other specializations (such as homiletics, liturgics and pastoral counselling). However conceived, religious leadership tends to focus on concerns such as leadership proper, organizational behaviour, management, stewardship, finance, conflict, power, change, and professional ethics.

From Jinkins's (2012) reflection on religious leadership we gain the impression of the contested nature of the concept because of a number of factors that relate to aspects such as management, behaviour, conflict, power and change, which all belong to the leadership discourse. The contributions of Yukl, Van Saane and Jinkins led to the development of a number of concepts that can be used as heuristic devices when taking

---

[1] This was translated by the author from the original Dutch.

a closer look at the way in which leadership functions in the e-church. Before a closer investigation is done of the descriptive-empirical aspects of the ministry of the e-church and the type of leadership operative in the organisation, it is important to ascertain a better picture of the so-called virtual world or the digital era. Some concepts in the virtual world and digital era are discussed and used together with the insights on leadership to analyse the leadership of the e-church.

The Virtual World and the Digital Era
Most people live in a virtual world, and technology[1] plays a central role in this so-called digital era.[2] According to Cloete (2015, p. 1), excellent research has been done in the fields of sociology and communication science, but the problem is that not enough theological reflection has been done on the way the digital world influences our lives. Therefore, it is important to try to gain a better understanding of what is known as the virtual or digital world or the digital era.[3] Trying to figure out what role leadership can play in this world is also part of this endeavour. Nancy Baym (2010, p. 1) makes the following remark in her book *Personal connections in the digital age* when she writes:

> There have never been more ways to communicate with one another than there are right now. Once limited to face to face conversation, over the last several millennia we have steadily developed new technologies for interaction. The digital age is distinguished by rapid transformations in the kinds of technological mediation through which we encounter one another.

Miller (2011, pp. 12–22) helps us to understand something more about the digital era in his discussion of certain key elements of the digital

---

[1] For a discussion of the role of technology in our lives, see also the contribution of Elaine Graham, "Being, Making and Imagining: Towards a Practical Theology of Technology," *Culture and Religion* 10, no. 2 (2009): 222–227, who believes technology operates according to its own set of values that relates to the unique nature of what it means to be human. Therefore, according to Graham, technology is not a luxury any more and not only forms part of our daily survival, but is also the vehicle of transformation that is changing the world around us and directly impacts the way we are thinking about ourselves.

[2] See also the chapters of Jan-Albert van den Berg and Theo Zijderveld in this volume.

[3] Anita Cloete describes the characteristics of the digital age "as 'networked' via different forms of media like telephones and the Internet. Digital media are also interactive in terms of its responsiveness between the user and media object. The different media forms are composed of nodes and blocks which are connected by different links between them, which make the text hypertextual." See Anita Cloete, "Living in a Digital Culture: The Need for Theological Reflection," *HTS Teologiese Studies/Theological Studies* 71, no. 2 (2015), doi: http://dx.doi.org/10.4102/hts.v71i2.2073.

media and the way they relate to the network society, the interactivity of communication, the hypertextual nature of the internet and the important role that big data are playing. According to Miller (2011, p. 12), the three basic elements of the digital era can be described as "technical processes (the technological building blocks), cultural forms (the way in which digital media objects are created, encountered and used) and immersive experience (the environments that digital media create)."

To live in this so-called digital era is not without its problems. Cloete (2015, p. 2), concurring with the thoughts of Miller, asks serious questions, *inter alia*: "How can we be absent yet also present?" and "What is the self if it is not in a body?" In other words: "Where and how is the real self in digital communication?" Baym (2010, p. 3) also asks penetrating questions in this regard, for example about the difference between the online and the offline self and whether they might not be in contradiction to each other. According to Baym (2010, p. 4), the borders between a human being and a machine can even collapse, with the result that the body and the self can be thrown into a situation of flux. This can lead to the situation where the borders between personal and mass communication can fade even to the point of becoming disruptive for both. Therefore, the question that belongs to the heart of these fluid borders is: "What is real and what is considered virtual?" Baym (2010, p. 5) describes the challenge this situation poses in the following way: "Digital media calls into question the very authenticity of our identities and relationships and practice" (2010, p. 5).

Baym's question leads to the question about the unique nature of what we can call virtual leadership. Kerfoot (2010, p. 117) uses the insights of different scholars and writes that virtual leadership entails exercising leadership in a community that differs from the physical environment in that leaders communicate and interact, even coordinate people through the electronic media. According to her, successful virtual leaders learn how to cross the boundaries of time, space and culture in exercising their leadership roles. Therefore, skills and capacities that virtual leaders need include aspects such as the following:

- "Listening to see" – because of the fact that there are no physical spaces where one can observe people's behaviour, with the result that one has to use one's imagination and concentrate to listen with attention.
- "Creating aliveness" – which entails creating a "community of practice" with a feeling of aliveness. "Virtual leaders must use evolving social media technology to create a virtual sense of aliveness and a high-performing virtual community within the organization" (Kerfoot, 2010, p. 118).
- "Communicating effectively" – from the previous it is obvious that the

virtual leader is dependent on diverse forms of technology (email, webpages, blogs, etc.), which also means that one has to do sound preparation before starting to communicate.

She concludes with the words:

The evolution into virtual leadership is one of the requirements for evolving a career in leadership. Fortunately there is more information available as this discipline evolves. As technology is developed and utilized, virtual leaders will have many ways to "listen to see" (Kerfoot, 2010, p. 119).

Caulat (2006, p. 6) identifies in her research a number of factors that are expected of a virtual leader:

Building and nurturing relationships where social aspects are essential, maintaining presence in spite of being remote, generating information as an act of co-creation rather than a content, co-creating shared realities, allowing for planning and emergence, monitoring what people achieve rather than what they do, bringing the informal into the formal, redefining the "etiquette" for their own specific team, project managing, managing conflict, working with diversity, establishing the context, managing workload in relation to time available and time zones, managing own and others' stress.

Indeed a long list ... With a bit more insight into what is understood when one uses the concept of virtual leadership, it is now time to take a closer look at the e-church as a case in point.

3. A Description of the e-Church

A descriptive-empirical approach in describing some aspects of the e-church was undertaken by making use of two main sources. The first was a semi-structured interview[1] that I conducted with the leader of the e-church, and the second was a document analysis of the information on the website of the e-church (http://www.ekerk.org/). In the interview, I posed the following questions to Joubert, and what follows are excerpts from the transcriptions of the answers he gave.

"Tell me something about the origins and history of the e-church and some of the people and interest groups involved."

From the interview it became clear that the e-church has now (2015) been in existence for 13 years. It started as a dream of Joubert in New

---

[1] The interview took place on 30 April 2015 at 15:00 in Stellenbosch, during a visit of Dr Stephan Joubert to the Western Cape.

Zealand after he left the University of Pretoria and thought about a digital ministry while abroad. Individuals bought into his dream, and they started out with nothing. In his own words, "It was a kind of faith ministry with knowledgeable people from different backgrounds that came to offer their help. It started to grow and we established a board, a full-time woman to handle the website and some more people later. It was and still is an independent ministry that relies on donations."

Everybody working at the e-church who receives some money also has other sources of income in order to serve in the Kingdom, and to keep costs lower than most other ministries that drown under the burden of salaries.

Among the group forming part of the team are people who act as managers, manage the finances, handle the e-church Bible School, coordinate projects and leadership tours, take responsibility for the webinars, organise leadership development (also known as "learning communities") all over South Africa, and handle webpage design, creativity and the general "look and feel" of the e-church. There are also people who are responsible for the technical "hosting" of articles and material on the Afrikaans webpage, handling the English blogs and translating Afrikaans content into English.

"How do you understand the culture and context?"

The vision of the e-church is described by Joubert as: "Jesus visible, touchable and understandable." They focus on the following areas: *Spiritual growth* via a website and digital newsletters. The e-church sends out newsletters with the titles "Goeie Nuus" and "Kernkrag" (Good News and Core Power) twice a week. Together the subscribers to the weekly newsletters and emails constitute just under 50,000 individual email addresses. Two years ago they established a large research department producing a report every six weeks on the newest trends in the postmodern world that they think Christians should take note of, from bio-technology to "selfies." They also have regular live webinars where Bible schools and some of their trend reports are presented, which is a growing part of the e-church.

Equipment of leadership takes place on the grassroots level through learning communities with leaders from many different churches. They invite visitors from abroad such as Alan Hirsch and Leonard Sweet. A person makes his lodge in the bushveld available, where they conduct the development of their spiritual leaders. During the past couple of years they have equipped more than a hundred ministers and pastors through these sessions. They also organise two annual tours for leaders – one to Leonard Sweet and one to other innovating people in the USA, to which they invite up to 20 ministers as well as people from the business world. They also have a "blessing ministry" for spiritual leaders, where they annually sponsor two students studying theology at the University of Pretoria by paying them a small salary. They want to give these students the opportunity to enjoy their studies and to have enough time for study and thinking. Another interesting part of their ministry is the "Day of sages." In Joubert's own words: "Every year we organise a "Day of sages" in the Atterbury Theatre in Pretoria. We invite wise leaders to come and share their insights with us. This year we invited Pik Botha, Brand Pretorius, Theuns Eloff and Naas Botha."

For the past five years they have also had weekly conversations over a cup of coffee every Friday at 09:00 in the Basiliah Restaurant at the Moreletapark Church. The e-church uses the facilities for an hour and approximately 120 to 150 people normally attend these occasions, which entail Bible teaching accompanied by drinking coffee. All the funds gathered during these sessions are deposited into the account of the diaconal ministries of the e-church.

Involvement in need. They are very involved in a number of need (diaconal) ministries. The e-church's board of six members expects that they should give away close to 50% of the income they annually receive. In Joubert's own words:

"Currently e-church is involved with PEN action in the city centre of Pretoria, the Echo Youth movement, the Mosaic ministry in Potchefstroom, working amongst children with Aids, therapy at Louis Botha orphanage, Morester orphanage in Rustenburg, Herfsland home for the elderly in the East Rand where we provide meals and other forms of life support to 40 elderly people, "Word for word" in Cape Town and a few other ministries on an ad hoc base in the Western Cape."

"How do you understand the audience that you want to serve?"

They focus on Afrikaans-speaking people and also a smaller English audience in terms of their vision. Church affiliation is not important to them. Joubert made the following statement about the e-church audience. "We also realised that many of the members participating in e-church are somewhat disillusioned and unchurched, but most of them are not prepared to leave the church permanently or are extraordinarily angry at the church." The vision of the e-church is a Kingdom-orientated ministry that is not a substitute or surrogate ministry for their local congregations. They are not an "online church," but part of the "church online."

"In terms of the structure of the leadership, how do the leadership, processes and organisation of the e-church operate?"

According to Joubert they are following an organic model. Although he sees himself as the designated leader, he believes in organic leadership, where different people are supposed to take the lead at different times. He admits that he does not exactly know how everything works in the e-church and describes it in the following way:

"Person A for example is responsible for the finances. We do have a board because we are an Article 21 organisation and two of our board members are supporting Person A with the finances. We have a 120-seconds rule when it comes to the distribution of funds and I am also involved in that. If we are not sure after two minutes what to do, we leave it for the next meeting. Our organisation is very strong on relationships."

"How do you see the e-church's impact and efficiency?"

Joubert is of the opinion that this is difficult to measure and mentioned some statistics already referred to. They send messages and newsletters weekly to approximately 50,000 individual email addresses. Their webpages, blogs and Facebook page attract quite a number of visitors. Their leadership training via learning communities had more than 800 attendees during 2015, mainly because of the presence of Leonard Sweet.

4. Data Analysis

During the content analysis of the data, a number of interesting topics related to the e-church context, technology and digital communication, different forms of ministry, spiritual growth and the equipment of leadership were identified. Looking at these concepts, we could say that the e-church is a dramatic new way of performing church in contemporary society. In concentrating on this performative aspect of being church, I therefore make use of "theo-dramatic lenses" to take a closer look at the data. Working with this approach, it was possible to identify at least four aspects that constitute the main components of the drama, namely the stage, the plot, the audience and the role of leadership.

Before discussing the different aspects, it is important to provide some clarification on what is understood as a theo-dramatic approach.[1] A theo-dramatic paradigm is an approach in which drama and the art of the theatre provide a paradigm for the task of reflecting on some faith practices, in this case the practice of virtual leadership. The use of

---

[1] Theo-drama is a term that was developed by Hans Urs von Balthasar in a series of books published in the early 1980s. Theological dramatic theory takes seriously the narrative or dramatic way that God reveals Godself. God is acting first within the inner relationships of love inside the Trinity, but then also in relation to the world through acts of creation, redemption and glorification. Theo-drama also implies that we, God's creatures, are invited to find our own stories taken up into the larger Story of the Trinity. According to Von Balthasar, it is an approach that has the potential to combine several theological methods by making use of dramatic categories. Seen from this perspective the world becomes the stage on which God's story is dramatically performed with the faithful having the responsibility to act with integrity in a community of love and justice. See Hans U. von Balthasar, *Theo-drama: Theological Dramatic Theory*. Volume 1: Prolegomena. Transl. by Graham Harrison (San Francisco: Ignatius Press, 1988).

drama as an image of God's activities is not new.[1] Karl Barth, following in the footsteps of John Calvin, described the creation of the cosmos by God as the *Theatrum Gloria Dei* in which the created reality was seen as the theatre for God's great deeds and also as part of his grace and salvation (Thompson, 2006, p. 5). In this paradigm, drama (a text-centred concept) and theatre (a performance-centred concept) become analogies through which one can understand history in its relationship to the author of this drama. In this regard, creation is indeed the theatre of God's glory and finds expression in the drama of Jesus, the main character who appears on the stage. With this in mind, the following aspects were investigated.

The Stage and the Role of Technology and Digital Communication
Little doubt exists that the stage looks quite different in the case of virtual leadership than in an institutional context or within the context of a normal congregational ministry. Van den Berg (2012, p. 3) illustrates in his research that the postmodern person is not only surrounded by technology, but is also very dependent on it. At the same time we are not yet sure what the effect of all this might be on people's lives. That the nature of technology and digital communication is contested is undisputed. As already referred to in the section on the virtual world and the digital era, more research is needed on different aspects concerning the stage of the e-church before we will be in a position to develop a more balanced perspective.

On the positive side concerning virtual leadership, it is quite apparent that there are a number of advantages when reflecting on the role of technology and digital communication. In this regard, we can think

---

[1] There is an interest in the potential of drama from a diversity of backgrounds, not only in practical theology, but also in most of the disciplines within theology. For example, in the New Testament: Tom Wright, *The New Testament and the People of God* (Minneapolis: Fortress Press, 1992) and Bernhard Anderson, *The Unfolding Drama of the Bible*. Fourth edition (Minneapolis: Fortress Press, 1988); church history: Ben Quash, *Theology and the Drama of History: Cambridge Studies in Christian Doctrine* (Cambridge: Cambridge University Press, 2005); systematic theology: David Brown, *God and Mystery in Words: Experience through Metaphor and Drama* (Oxford: Oxford University Press, 2008), Kevin Vanhoozer, *The Drama of Doctrine: A Canonical-linguistic Approach to Christian Theology* (Louisville: Westminster John Knox, 2005), and Von Balthasar, *Theo-drama*; and practical theology: Richard Osmer, *The Teaching Ministry of Congregations* (Louisville: Westminster, 2005), Nicholas Healy, *Church, World and the Christian Life: Practical-prophetic Ecclesiology* (Cambridge: Cambridge University Press, 2000), and Jana Childers and Clayton J. Schmit, eds., *Performance in Preaching: Bringing the Sermon to Life* (Grand Rapids: Baker Academic, 2008).

of aspects such as "connectivity," which not only refers to speed, bandwidth or connection capability, but especially to the participants' needs for interconnectivity in this new reality, as is evident from the data. We also find language in which concepts such as "links, social networks, followers, friends" are used (Joubert, 2010, p. 52). This kind of language in the digital world makes it possible to participate in international meetings, group discussions and even PhD thesis defences with people from different continents. According to Rice (2009) and Friesen (2009), it also relates to people's intense search to escape from their enclaves of loneliness and is deeply about the core of psychological wellbeing that one finds in healing relationships. Facebook is a good example of this through the possibility of connections with different friends, creating for many a feeling of "home." It is indeed a place where people can keep everything together that they deem important, such as photos and a life narrative. It is also a place where people find and inform their families and exercise some sort of control over their environment and just be themselves. These thoughts are found in Joubert's reflection on the audience the e-church wants to serve, as quoted above.

Dawson (2004, p. 6) makes an important distinction in this regard between "religion online" and "online religion." He describes the difference in the following way: "Religion online ... invites internet visitors to participate in religious activities" that can be understood as a variety of activities, such as prayers, Bible studies, counselling and even church services. On the other hand, "[o]nline religion ... is the provision of information about and/or services related to various religious groups and traditions." In reality, many different forms of religion on the internet fit somewhere in-between these two categories as both information and participation are offered. It is interesting to hear that Joubert is of the opinion that the e-church is not an "online church" but a "church online."

These insights should not blind us to a number of dark spots found on the stage of virtual leadership. The instruments or tools that we use are not neutral, and Hipps (2009, p. 45) writes in this regard, "The tools we use to think actually shape the way we think. The same applies to our faith as well." The virtual world undoubtedly places great emphasis on the role of the visual, and Hipps (2009, pp. 76–77) indeed stresses the fact that images play on our feelings rather than stimulate our thoughts. Images do not invite arguments, but stimulate experience. These ideas have important consequences for the practices of Bible reading and interpretation within digital realities. A situation that is closely related to the previous one concerns the absence of specialists who can encourage critical thinking. Leadbeater (2009, pp. 32 ff.) is of the opinion that it can easily turn to manipulation, where a reality is created in which all views, opinions and ideas are on the same level; therefore, a re-evaluation of specialists and scholars within cyberspace is of the utmost necessity. A last blind spot on the stage concerns the accusation that one often comes across about the superficiality of the different forms of connections in the virtual world. Hipps (2009, p. 107) talks about "the near become far, and the far are brought near," while Siegel (2008, p. 6) even goes as far as calling cyberspace "the first social environment to serve the needs of the isolated, elevated, asocial individual," meaning that relationships, emotions and experiences can be managed and controlled at a safe distance. According to Joubert (2010, p. 55), these aspects can quickly make individuals dull to real caring and selfless servitude towards other people struggling with personal suffering and sacrifice.

A last comment about the virtual stage relates to what Joubert (2010, p. 58) calls "the philosophy around ministry in the digital era." According to him, the typical question that emanates from the printing culture is: Can it be that the use of digital media is a stumbling block in the way of the message? This question is stated differently in the digital world that entails narratives and an "image-driven culture." The question is rather: Which forms of communication are we convinced are worthy to communicate the message of the gospel? The informative work of Wilson (2008) shows how the digital media can be understood in four different ways within faith communities, namely: "media as the arts" through artistic beauty and different aesthetical forms, also in the history of the church; "media as information" where the media can act as a medium for the transformation of the image of Christ; "media as mission and evangelisation" where digital media endeavour to invite people into the family of faith; and "media as cultural language" where the purpose is the transformation of culture through the mediation of the presence of the church in the world. Taking a closer look at the data through these lenses, it seems as though the e-church is making use of all four forms of the digital media in the service of the Church and the Kingdom. More explanation is given below.

The Plot Consisting of Different Forms of Ministry
In my analysis of the data from both the interview with Joubert and the information on their website, it becomes clear how they structure the

plot of the ministries of the e-church by making use of three basic activities, namely spiritual growth, equipment of leadership and involvement in need. Spiritual growth relates to the digital newsletters that are distributed through the webpage and in different formats. Their content is normally reflections on passages from Scripture in conversation with everyday experiences. For example, the theme of Joubert's most recent article (2016) is: "God is altyd tuis" (God is always home), which is actually part of a quote from Meister Eckhardt: "God is at home, it's we who have gone out for a walk." In this article he reflects on the different ways many people blame God for what is happening in their lives, without any consideration of personal responsibility. Spiritual growth is also effected through the work of the research department, webinars, Bible schools and trend reports, as discussed earlier in this chapter.

The processes of equipment of leadership are facilitated by the learning communities with different leaders from different denominations, the face-to-face opportunities presented across the country, presentations by visitors from abroad, the annual tours for groups of leaders to the USA, Bible School tours to Israel, the so-called blessing ministry for spiritual leaders, the support to students studying theology and the "Day of sages."

The last component of the plot of the e-church is involvement in need, known as the need (diaconal) ministry. This refers to the 50% of the annual income donated to projects helping people in need.

From the above description it is clear that the plot of the ministry in the e-church consists of a combination of virtual and face-to-face spaces and places. Although Joubert belongs to the Dutch Reformed Church, he steers away from confessional choices for the plot of the e-church, and the choice for specific ministries by the board of six members focuses on nurturing the faith of individuals, development of leadership capacities and the different forms of need in the world.

The Audience, Their Participation and the Challenges of Community
With the focus on the audience and their participation in koinonia (community), we again face one of the most teasing questions concerning faith and cyberspace: What entails participation and community in cyberspace?

In the reflection on the audience or the "community" under discussion here, little consensus exists on the precise meaning of the concept (Campbell, 2013, p. 59; Miller, 2011, p. 184). According to Baym (2010, p. 74), it remains a useful concept relating to the interaction among each other and social relations between people. I already referred to the crucial role of connectivity in a digital culture because it consists of different forms of communication among people. However, not everyone is convinced that community in a digital culture is really still community. According to Miller (2011, p. 97), the original understanding of community is being replaced by different networks to which people belong according to their different interests. It is also clear from the data that people "choose" to belong to the e-church's network. Baym (2010, p. 9) speaks about "networked individualism" that one finds in these kinds of communities, meaning that participants create their own communities, causing a shift in the nature of community.

It is also interesting to find in the data that the focus of the e-church is on an Afrikaans audience for whom church affiliation is not important and who may even be "unchurched and disillusioned." There is certainly a disappointment with the institutional church, but not a total unfamiliarity, while at the same time there is a pursuit of "being church" in the virtual world.

Estes (2009) summarised this development in the following way. "[A] virtual world is a created space where people can interact as if in the real world, but through some kind of technological medium." It is important to understand that the virtual world is not a fictional world and therefore not only a possibility, but also a mode of reality.

Campbell (2013, p. 63) points out that research confirms that a greater integration of online and offline communities is taking place in spite of the fact that online communities are often not seen as authentic and realistic. He concludes that one should rather see offline and online communities as complementary, where the one acts as an extension of the other without excluding the other. It looks to me as though this description can be successfully applied to the circumstances of the e-church. The fact that Joubert himself refers to the e-church as "church online" implies that they want to give the members the opportunity to participate in Christian practices by making use of electronic means, as also became clear in the description of the plot.

The Role of Leadership and the Rise of the So-called Entrepreneurial Pastor
In answer to the question of the structure of the leadership of the church and the processes and organisation, Joubert explained the organic model of the church. There are different roles and responsibilities for the people serving on the board.

What is clear at first glance is that another kind of leadership exists in this situation than is associated with the traditional offices normally found in the mainline churches. Joubert refers to himself as the designated leader, but it is clear that his style of leadership and the initiative he took because of the vision he received are functioning in a different way than is the case in the average Dutch Reformed Church, of which he is a member.

In a recent contribution by De Wet (2015, pp. 129–141), he discusses what he calls the "rise of the entrepreneurial pastor." When studying the origin and development of leadership in the e-church, entrepreneurialism and its relationship to leadership help us to make sense and find words for what is happening in the e-church. According to De Wet (2015, pp. 130-133), four different factors can be identified that gave impetus to the development of this kind of leadership in South Africa, which can be applied to the situation of the e-church.

First, there is what he calls "the force of globalization" (De Wet, 2015, p. 130), where churches are challenged by the dramatic changes in the socio-political context. These processes also call for a more holistic approach to the identity and ministry of the church. Second, there is what he calls "the entrepreneurialisation of the pastorate" (De Wet, 2015, p. 131), which directly links to the rise of the information era and the important role that technology has started to play. The mega-churches in some of South Africa's suburbs are examples of this development. Third, there is "the tide of materialism and its responsive proliferation of managerialism and business education" (De Wet, 2015, p. 131). Neoliberalism was not only the basic philosophical choice of the government since 1994, it also became part of many churches' ministerial philosophy. Many churches and congregations function like cooperative organisations that endeavour to be socially relevant and also economically viable. Last, he refers to "the critical change in the cultural fabric of society" (De Wet, 2015, p. 132), resulting in the change of many of the fundamental aspects of our reality. He writes, "it is introducing new epistemologies, thereby changing the very nature, structure, and dynamic of knowledge; new spatialities – "space" and "place" is no longer a constant, and the defining characteristic of these new geographies is mobility" (De Wet, 2015, p. 132). As part of this last factor he refers specifically to what he even calls "e-architecture," indicating that churches do not need physical spaces to gather anymore and have started to create semi- or fully online opportunities to meet for worship. He also refers in this case to Joubert's e-church.

Although Joubert refers to the e-church's model of leadership as organic leadership, it becomes clear from the thoughts of De Wet that the so-called entrepreneurial pastor plays an important role in this development and acts as a kind of precondition for the organic model. This brings us to the last section, where a number of evaluating comments on virtual leadership are made.

5. *Critical Evaluation of "Virtual Leadership"*

In approaching the task of a critical evaluation of the e-church as a form of "virtual leadership," I make use of the three categories or streams that De Wet (2015, pp. 133–136) distinguishes when he discusses the topic under the heading "The development of a theology of entrepreneurial pastoralism." He distinguishes between the following three streams that have had an influence in South Africa and that have been heavily influenced by the North American context:

- Classical entrepreneurial pastoralism (De Wet, 2015, p. 134) is the first stream and is characterised by the work and ministry of people such as John Maxwell, Robert Schuller and Rick Warren, who all popularised leadership and leadership development in ecclesiastical circles in the USA. Leadership models are often seen by them as universally applicable in different contexts.
- Prosperity theology and televangelism (De Wet, 2015, p. 134) is the second stream in which one finds the names of people such as T.D. Jakes, Joyce Meyer and Joel Osteen. This is also a more Pentecostal-charismatic stream that is characterised by televangelism and the prosperity gospel. In this stream leadership and especially financial management are important characteristics. The underlying theology of this stream is often very biblicistic and fundamentalist.
- Postmodern and neo-orthodox entrepreneurial pastoralism (De Wet, 2015, p. 135) is the last stream, characterised by the work of people such as Bill Hybels, Leonard Sweet, Brian McLaren and George Barna. According to De Wet (2015, p. 135), this is a popular group "who have formulated a postmodern and neo-orthodox entrepreneurial pastoralism." Two of the central concepts found in the work and theology of this group are "seeker-sensitive" and "missional," with considerable attention being paid to public theology. It is especially Hybels, Sweet and McLaren who are quite influential in the South African context as all of them have visited some of the mega-churches in South Africa from time to time, with Sweet having done so a number of times. In the data we also saw references to Sweet's influence on the e-church. It is interesting to see how many of the churches in South Africa took over their kind of theology and ministerial philosophy. Furthermore, it is among this group that one finds the development of the so-called emergent church, with considerable emphasis on missionality, inclusivity and a participating spirituality.

When analysing the data by making use of the above distinctions of De Wet, it is very obvious that the e-church of Joubert can be seen as belonging to the third stream. As mentioned, Joubert himself refers to the important role that the representatives of the third stream play in their ministry and theology, with specific reference to Leonard Sweet. Not only do they invite him annually to South Africa, but Joubert also takes a group of South African church leaders to the USA on a regular basis to get to know Sweet better in his own context.

The way in which Joubert and his leadership team developed their vision for a digital ministry evolving into the shape of the e-church with a specific style of leadership deserves much respect and appreciation, as it could not have been done without courage and endurance. In light of the fact that the vision of the e-church supports an organic form of leadership where participation and dialogue play an important role, I think it is important to formulate a number of points and questions for discussion concerning the form and meaning of being a virtual church and the kind of entrepreneurial leadership that one finds in its approach.

The first point relates to whether the choice for the "grassroots level of church activity" and the theological grounding of this popular form of theologising was a conscious decision by the leadership team. The question is, will it be possible to name it as some kind of "theology from under" and even a form of liberation theology, or do we find here something different, motivated by other reasons or even another ecclesial epistemology? It is in other words a question about their hermeneutical choices, points of departure and theoretical underpinnings operating in their process of theologising. Do they see themselves as part of a bigger tradition or do they see themselves as belonging to the many independent traditions?

The second point is that it is quite obvious that the majority of participants in the network of the e-church originates from the Afrikaans-speaking community. Many of them have become disappointed in the church and stopped attending, even giving up their membership. Most of them grew up in a theological background where a Reformed ecclesiology was the frame of understanding. We could ask: What is the underlying ecclesiology at work in the e-church and in what ways does it find expression in the different kinds of ministry of the movement? An important part of Reformed ecclesiology revolves around the ministry of Word and sacrament, and we could wonder how the e-church facilitates this important aspect of ministry considering the different traditions, all of them with different interpretations of the role and function of these symbols of faith.

The third point is that it is quite obvious that what has been described as entrepreneurial leadership cannot be understood without referring to the dangers of a consumer culture and the role of materialism. The question is, how does the leadership of the e-church handle this challenge? Joubert himself is a seasoned academic and a New Testament scholar, and therefore further conversations with him on this important topic could lead to interesting perspectives on the meaning of being church.

6. *Conclusion*

In the introduction to the chapter, it was stated that one of the basic understandings of leadership relates to the fact that it is seen as the involvement of a person, group or organisation that influences and empowers enough people to follow and bring about change in that area of life. The basic assumption in this understanding of leadership is that this kind of influencing and empowerment takes place in real-life situations and with face-to-face contact between the leaders and the followers. The question that I wanted to investigate was whether, considering these basic assumptions about leadership, we can speak of "virtual leadership" where there is not necessarily face-to-face contact between the leaders and the followers.

Given the evidence of the empirical data that I gathered through a personal interview with Joubert and also some literature and the website of the e-church, I want to conclude that it is indeed possible to speak of virtual leadership with certain specific characteristics. By making use of a theo-dramatic paradigm, I discussed the stage and the role of technology and digital communication, the plot consisting of different forms of ministries, the audience and their participation as well as the challenge of community, and lastly the characters with a special focus on the role of leadership. In the last section of the chapter, the concept "entrepreneurial leadership" was developed as one way of understanding this form of leadership as part of "online religion," in which we can see the development and encouragement to participate in different Christian activities summarised as spiritual growth, equipment of leadership and involvement in the need of the world.

Chapter Five

Tweeting God: Redefining Future Christian Leadership through Twitter?

Jan-Albert van den Berg

1. Introduction

The well-known entrepreneur and futurist, Sir Richard Branson (Branson, 2014a), recently sent a message – better known as a tweet – on the social-media platform Twitter, in which he shared his 10 most popular quotes on leadership with his followers. This is remarkable in itself. As a well-known and influential leader with approximately 6 million followers on Twitter (@richardbranson, 2015), he used this platform – with 140 characters – to share aspects of leadership with a potential audience of 302 million users.

One of the wisdoms included by Branson in his list is the following quote by the late Steve Jobs from Apple: "Innovation distinguishes between a leader and a follower" (Branson, 2014b). These words of Jobs – who became known through computer innovations – appeal to Branson who, as an entrepreneur, has a strong focus on the future, such as the development of a programme dealing with tourism in space.

In itself, the example from the Twitter world elicits important questions such as how the use of social media can influence and change leadership perspectives. It also questions the relevance and meaning of current and traditional leadership practices, as well as the way in which they should be adapted in a dynamic social-media environment and world.[1]

The relevance of this question for leadership practices is further emphasised through the evolutionary, dynamic and even disruptive character of a growing virtual world, and its impact on communities. The world-famous internet psychologist and philosopher, Sherry Turkle,

---

[1] See also the chapters by Ian Nell and Theo Zijderveld.

pointed out in her book, *Alone together* (2011), that what is becoming visible in the growing virtual environment is none other "than the future unfolding" (Turkle, 2011).

In exploring these perspectives, I have a strong affinity with some of the meta-theoretical perspectives referred to in the Foreword to this issue. With reference to sensitivity for the future (Van den Berg and Ganzevoort, 2014, p. 166), I have an affinity with a visionary leadership paradigm. It is, therefore, assumed that, in seeking innovation and leadership in the digital age, note should be taken of more than just what is presently happening in a specific domain. We should also venture to seek possible and tentative perspectives for an unfolding future. In previously published research, it was argued, specifically within a practical theological inquiry, that there should be sensitivity for a research agenda for the future (Van den Berg and Ganzevoort, 2014, p. 181). This research endeavour to explore, embedded in a dimension of being geared towards the future, is characterised by the metaphor of tracing, in which meanings of traversing, tracking and sketching are articulated (Ganzevoort, 2009, p. 5). The aim of this contribution lies in a critical-evaluative description of practices associated with Christian leadership on Twitter. A deconstruction of these existing practices provides building material for possible future development. The study of these practices conveys and emphasises the threefold structural orientation of the issue, namely the emphasis on different contexts, lived religion and engaged scholarship.

By tracing the outlines of Christian leadership on Twitter, an effort is made to further contribute to the movement from "a practical orientated theology towards a practice orientated theology" (Hermans, 2014, p. 126). This practice-oriented theology is, therefore, sensitive not only to official institutionalised religion, but also to "the turn away from institutes and (cultural) texts to the everyday social and cultural practices of ordinary people" (Ganzevoort and Roeland, 2014, p. 93). This orientation implies that leadership is to be understood in the broadest possible terms. Within this reading, it is assumed not only that the pastor of the congregation is to be regarded as the leader, but also that leadership is to be understood as a relationship- and community-oriented concept.

This understanding is also emphasised in a world increasingly defined through the use of social media. The question is then not just how do these new forms of expression influence the experience and description of religion, but for the purpose of this contribution, which manner are they used in by leaders (especially those leaders known for their Christian orientation) and how may these activities inform future leadership practices. In this instance, I acknowledge and find an affinity with topics such as authority, identity and social cohesion that are implicitly associated with leadership. Therefore, embedded in the search for expressions of lived religion, the aim of this research is to explore and map out innovation, with specific reference to Christian leadership in the Twitter world. These exploratory perspectives provide a framework for further research on and the development of existing practices.

2. Traversing the Twitter Landscape: An Orientation

With a view to defining the research in this article, the focus is on the social-media platform Twitter, with special reference to the tweet messages of Christian leaders. Currently, Twitter is one of the most rapidly growing social-media platforms. At the end of October 2015, Twitter had 320 million monthly active users out of a total of 1.3 billion registered users with a Twitter account (Smith, 2015). Twitter is generally known as a microblog, as it provides the user an opportunity to send a message within the scope of 140 characters (Van Dijk, 2012, p. 333; Wagner, 2012, p. 120) providing "… at best eloquently terse responses and at worst heavily truncated speech" (Murthy, 2013).

The use of Twitter revealed an important communication medium that would change the world on numerous levels. For example, this platform played an influential role in political events such as the Arab Spring (Emiroglu, 2013), the Occupy-Wall-Street movement (Fuchs, 2014, p. 196) as well as in the past two American presidential elections (*The European Business Review* 2013). An even more recent and contextual example of the use and impact of Twitter, and specifically the use of the so-called "hashtag" symbol, in mobilising socio-political change was the so-called "#feesmustfall" campaign by students in South Africa (Nicholson, 2015). Conventions, including the "hashtag," which are strongly associated with the Twitter platform are an indication of the multidimensional influence of innovative symbol and language use within this new sphere of human existence (Van den Berg, 2014). Naturally, all these factors provide the elements, with an exceptionally dynamic interaction, leading to the following possibility:

> Twitter has the potential to increase our awareness of others and to augment our spheres of knowledge, allowing us to tap into a global network of individuals who are passionately giving us instant updates on topics and areas in which they are knowledgeable or participating in real-time (Murthy, 2013).

The functioning and effectiveness of traditional leadership practices are being questioned and disrupted by the acknowledgment of the capacity of social media to connect, inform, empower and transform (Phillips, 2014, pp. 76–80). This observation serves as motivation for exploratory and experimental research, tracing possible new articulations of practices of Christian leadership within social media. The search for Twitter messages, specifically those associated with Christian leaders, is not meant to emphasise exclusivity, but rather to provide a specific focus for the research. The rationale for choosing Twitter is motivated by the association of the platform with the actuality of news. Due to the 140 characters allowed by Twitter per message, the messages are concise and can be used easily for evaluation. In the evaluation of possible new expressions of the Christian faith on Twitter posted by Christian leadership, and for the structuring of the article, the American practical theologian Rick Osmer's use of four spiritualities of congregational leadership as an expression of a practical theological investigation resonates with me. In his book *Practical theology: An introduction* (2008), Osmer indicates that the four spiritualities, namely attendance, thoughtfulness, discernment and strategy, are directly related and relevant to the four tasks associated with practical theological research (Osmer, 2008, p. 4).

The use of these four spiritualities as guiding metaphors, provide a practical theological orientation towards the tracing and description of lived religion as expressed in life's practices. Associating the four spiritualities of congregational leadership, as indicated by Osmer, with each of the four tasks is not only a description for a practical theological inquiry, but also a methodological structure for investigating expressions of Christian leadership on Twitter. Embedded within this structure of inquiry, the interplay between empirical data and theory provides for classical practical theological movements.

3. A Spirituality of Presence and the Task of Attending

In his first task in a practical theological inquiry, Osmer distinguishes a leadership position which can be described as a "spirituality of presence." In conceptualising the relationship between a spirituality of presence and the descriptive-empirical task of practical theological interpretation, emphasis is placed on a continuum of "attending" (Osmer, 2008, p. 37). Being attentive to the character and dynamics of the Twitter platform, the words of Leonard Sweet, a popular theologian and leader active on Twitter, are appropriate:

> When I look for something to tweet about, I find myself paying attention to life in heightened ways. With Twitter, every day is an awakening to things that never would have registered before. Twitter gives me openings through which I can dive into newly discovered depths (Sweet, 2012).

Using attending as part of the leading metaphor of tracing described earlier, I will map out initial descriptions regarding expressions of Christian leadership on Twitter. As in the art of tracking, where the terrain is scanned for various clues and possibilities, the same critical-evaluative *modus operandi* applies in a spirituality of attending, scanning for expressions of Christian leadership on Twitter.

As background in their book *Understanding social media* (2013), Sam Hinton and Larissa Hjorth write that social media, as a collective term, influence all levels of society. They form an integral part of the lives of a significant number of people worldwide; a dynamic and constant meaning is created through the use of different forms of social media (Hinton and Hjorth, 2013, p. 2). In this regard, Michele Zappavigna (2012, p. 193) correctly assumes that "most forms of social media, such as Facebook and other general social networking services, incorporate significant multimedia content, with images and video playing a significant role in meaning making." However, for the purpose of this research, the emphasis is on the expression of Christian leadership on Twitter. In a process of "informal attending," basic investigative research – using the search engine Google – confirms that several Christian leaders already have a presence on Twitter by way of profile accounts. This search can be identified, among others, by creating a search phrase "Christian leaders with the most supporters on Twitter." Well-known names such as Rick Warren, Bill Hybels and Max Lucado count among the top 25 Christian leaders with the largest following on Twitter (Orme 2013). Although this may be true and acknowledge the fact that numbers indeed play an important role in aspects of influence and networking, this is not the only measurement to map out Christian leadership on Twitter.

In this regard, Osmer assumes a quality of attention, which originates from sensitivity to the meaning of everyday events and patterns (Osmer, 2008, 37–38). In the quest for deeper expressions of Christian leadership, the hashtag "#ChristianLeadership" could, for example, be used to search on the Twitter platform. This presents the immediate possibility to trace relevant tweets, which have a bearing on the theme of Christian leadership associated with expressions on Twitter. The specific question could even be refined further by investigating, among others, how many times the original tweet was "retweeted" by other users and/or indicated as a "favourite" tweet. Specifically, the use of the hashtag symbol and retweet function could later be used in a more formal and structured way as part of the movement of spiritualities of discernment and strategy.

A formal empirical enquiry and description are used to attend formally to expressions of Christian leadership. With regard to this specific research, the formal empirical observation was carried out with the assistance of a specialist social-media consultation company *Fuseware* (2015), using sophisticated software computer programs, which enable access to the daily Twitter stream of all tweets as an expression of so-called Big Data.[1] The search words "Christian leadership" initiated an inquiry into all tweets sent over a set period (September 1, 2013 to May 18, 2015), but specifically including important times associated with the Christian religion, namely Easter and Christmas. Through the use of what is commonly known as "Twitterdata mining," access was gained to 100% of the so-called Twitter "Firehose," enabling the viewing and analysis of public-generated tweets every "streaming second" for the indicated period (Lutz and Du Toit, 2014). In order to map out the relevance of Christian leadership in everyday life, descriptive of the notion of lived religion referred to earlier, a further search was carried out regarding Christian leadership and its relevance towards the so-called Charlie Hebdo attacks in Paris, France, earlier in 2015, which resulted in substantial media attention internationally. The following summary of the research report by *Fuseware* (2015), after conducting the harvest of Twitter data, provides an overview of the empirical research data specifically obtained on Christian leadership:

- Across all tweets, specifically those containing the search phrase "Christian leadership," observed for the period 1 September 2013 to 18 May 2015, a total of 9,976 individual posts or tweets were collected on Twitter.[2]
- The majority of the posts originated from the USA, with Sundays as the top days for posting content, thus reflecting the religious bias of this day of the week. Mondays were the second most popular day for posting religious content, indicating a follow-through trend from the previous day that becomes linearly smaller as the week progresses.
- Analysed content trends throughout each year tended to spike in fair-

---

[1] The concept "Big Data" generally refers to substantial amounts of data being generated by computing activities such as social media (Paulus, Lester, and Dempster, 2014, p. 193).

[2] As part of accepted research practice, a random sample technique (Vogt and Williams, 2011, p. 467) was used to obtain a more manageable number of tweets from the initial Big Data list consisting of 3 million harvest texts.

ly predictable areas around Christian holidays, the most predominant being Christmas and Easter, with a nearly double average volume over those periods.
- Twitter users often use hashtags as keywords to tag content in their tweets. The top tags used are #jesus, #god, #faith, #bible, #christian and #leadership, indicating a clear intent to express specific messages in terms of Christianity and leadership.

Preliminary empirical descriptions that embodied different levels of observation documented a "spirituality of presence" in the search for expressions of Christian leadership on Twitter. From an initial informal scanning of Christian leadership, using Google, to more specialised Big Data analysis, the focus was on innovation in experimental methods of observation. Examples of a preliminary tracing of expressions of Christian leadership were provided in the first movement of a practical theological inquiry. It is, however, also important to acknowledge that, in merely seeking the possible expression of Christian leadership on Twitter, I subjectively presuppose and express a specific image of innovative Christian leadership. This presumption may not be entirely positive since, by merely tracing tweets containing the search phrase "Christian leadership," there is no guarantee of innovative, meaningful and sustainable practices contributing to quality interaction between individuals and communities.

The content of the various tweets, therefore, needs to be analysed in more detail. Building on this first task, Osmer's model leads to a practical theological search for a deeper interpretative task, making inquiries into the meaning of greater and underlying movements in tweets. This is addressed and embodied through leadership of "sagely wisdom," encapsulating a spirituality of thoughtfulness, providing an orientation for the next research movement.

4. "A Spirituality of Sagely Wisdom" and Thoughtfulness on Twitter

Osmer (2008, p. 82) rightfully describes a spirituality of sagely wisdom and thoughtfulness, as follows:

> They want leaders whose wise guidance helps them make sense of the circumstances of their lives and world. The spirituality of such leaders is characterized by three qualities: thoughtfulness, theoretical interpretation, and wise judgment, which may be viewed along the lines of a continuum.

With regard to the research in tracing expressions of Christian leadership on Twitter, an orientation of "thoughtfulness" does, in fact, suggest an acknowledgement of the underlying dynamics and implications of the digital era. The implications of the digital era assume that the identity, mobility and speed whereby information is facilitated should be re-defined. As background to the interpretation of the reality of a digital world, various scholars (Hassan, 2008; Flew, 2008; Campbell, 2011; Wagner, 2012; Campbell, 2013; Campbell and Garner, 2016) point out at least three driving factors currently leading to further development and demarcation of the digital landscape:

- First, the continuing development and evolution of the Internet.
- Second, the connectivity and mobility brought about by the Internet and specific apparatus such as cellular telephones and tablets.
- Third, the dynamics, influence, magnitude and disruptive effect of social media.

All three of these factors are addressed in the focus on the use of the social media platform Twitter. An orientation of "thoughtfulness" means that cognisance is taken of the greater movements underlying expressions of Christian leadership on Twitter, but they should also be described further in greater detail. This takes place in the next movement on the continuum of "sagely wisdom," namely "theoretical interpretation." Daniel Gruber, Ryan Smerek, Melissa Thomas-Hunt, and Erika James (2015, p. 164) have emphasised the relevance of this quest due to the need of "organizations [that are struggling] to make sense of how to manage and lead in this new ecosystem." This observation is indeed also true for religious communities, and the challenge is how to respond to these issues. As it is naive to think that the tracing of existing expressions of Christian leaders on Twitter would provide all the answers to these complex challenges, mapping out some of the signs of a possible articulation of Christian leadership on social media would indeed be useful for future paths.

Assuming that the current scientific world has the sensitivity to not be able to simply explain complex issues, a great premium is placed on interdisciplinary research in the investigation of issues underlying the expression and meaning of Christian leadership on Twitter, accommodating economic, philosophical and psychological issues as well as information and communication sciences. Theories by international theorists such as Manuel Castells (2006), Sherry Turkle (2011) and Heidi Campbell (2011; 2013; 2016) could provide a lens for interpreting expressions of Christian leadership on Twitter. However, central to this exploration is the orientation of not being fixated on a singular linear description, since "[t]here are many definitions of leadership ... However, leadership in the world of social media is a bit different. Leadership in social media includes all of the ideas" (Ingerson and Bruce, 2013, p. 74).

Acknowledging the opinion and perspective that social media is a disruptive force impacting on traditional theories of leadership as well as the fact that religious leadership theory is still a relevant young and developing discipline (Jinkins, 2012, p. 308), theory development based on empirical data and evidence seems to be imperative and important. Using the analysed data supplied by the specialist social-media monitoring company *Fuseware* (2015) not only provides a good example of interdisciplinary collaboration, but also facilitates further discussion on the analysis of the dynamics of Christian leadership following the Charlie Hebdo attacks in Paris, France, early in January 2015. All keywords relating to the Charlie Hebdo attacks and associated hashtags, namely #charliehebdo and #jesuischarlie, were searched in the context of the previously identified Christian-related keywords of Christian leadership. This, therefore, represents a Christian-biased subset of the Charlie Hebdo conversations. The *Fuseware* (2015) report provided the following research summary for this inquiry:

- In terms of volume, 9,998 individual posts or tweets were collected for the period January-February 2015. Nearly all of the conversations occurred in early January 2015 after the attacks. By February, conversations had sharply declined to a small fraction of the initial spike, indicating how quickly conversations on topics get stale on social media.
- The automated sentiment was, as expected, identified to be mainly negative, with 48% of the content having negative connotations, and 50% of the content remaining neutral. The content originated from a 66% male audience, mainly an older 35+ demographic. Most of this content originated from the USA and Europe, with a small fraction from Africa. Besides the main hashtags on the event, the top words used were "faith," "God," "Christian," "Pope" and "Jesus."
- In terms of authoritative content from influencers, the top post from the *Washington Post* shared an article on the Pope's remarks on Charlie Hebdo: "[Y]ou cannot insult the faith of others." This received widespread criticism, as it seemed to go against the fundamental tenets of free speech. Other authoritative posters included AP, *Huffington Post*, Time.com and WSJ – mostly all posting about the Pope's remarks on the subject.

The last remark is especially interesting since, on the one hand, it emphasises the authority and influence of specific leaders on Twitter, which very often also equals their influence in the offline world (Campbell and Garner, 2016). On the other hand, it illustrates the democratic character of Twitter and social media, providing the opportunity for even the most influential leader to be immediately and directly repudiated. Osmer points out that an orientation of "wise judgement" is central to good leadership. I would like to argue that it is, in fact, from a position of "wise judgement" that the essential leadership skill of steering into the future is facilitated. The development by leaders of a memory for the creation of alternative futures (Adam, 2004, 300) thus calls for a creative, innovative, but also sustainable approach to various possible future scenarios. Wise judgement fosters an approach seeking alternative routes into the future, steering away from previous tracks of thought and action that have proven inapt for meeting present or future challenges (Reader, 2008). In considering the possible opportunities provided for leaders in a digital era by a platform such as Twitter, a possible alternative route towards redefining leadership is mapped out, thoughtfully contributing to a sagely wisdom of creating alternative futures.

It is in the deconstruction and interpretation of existing practices that coordinates are mapped out for future actions. With this emphasis, the ability for wise decision-making is overtly addressed, as well as the capacity to develop inherently in contributing towards future practices. This implies that existing expressions of Christian leadership on Twitter can be investigated theoretically, but that the research also maps out future perspectives for additional use and development. The relevance and importance of this research quest have already been indicated in the economic and management environment, with Katharyn Ingerson and Jaclyn Bruce (2013, p. 76) stating that:

> [t]he need to understand what leaders are posting is great because it will allow researchers to understand how people are being influenced by what business leaders are tweeting. This will also lead to a deeper understanding of leadership in the social media world, which is important because of the numerous amounts of people influenced by social media today.

The third research movement is supported by a spirituality of discernment, seeking normative and accountable perspectives to engage with available perspectives.

5. "A Spirituality of Prophetic Discernment" on Twitter

Sending and reading tweets could be described as part of the dynamics of the endeavour of theological and, specifically, practical theological hermeneutics (Stiver, 2003, p. 178). First, as indicated earlier, we need to interpret our daily world in order to compose a tweet, and then we need to have the ability to interpret tweets that were sent. In this understanding, tweets are part of the interpretation of written texts, as presented, for example, in the documents associated with the Christian tradition, as well as that of "the living text of human action" (Brown, 2012, p. 112).

This aligns well with practical theology's interest in practices confirmed by newer developments that emphasise an interest in practically driven events that are contextually and concretely placed within everyday life, referred to as expressions of lived religion. In exploring the art of hermeneutics with a view to tracing new expressions of Christian leadership on Twitter, I proceed from the assumption that "[t]heology is not for Sundays only ... Theology is an everyday affair ... Theology not only articulates beliefs but suggests 'designs for living'" (Vanhoozer, 2007, p. 7).

Underlying this acknowledgement is the conviction that practical theology encapsulates a hermeneutics of the lived religion, in which preference is given to the praxis itself and to the knowledge concerning God that is being developed, found and lived within this praxis (Ganzevoort, 2008, pp. 11–12). Osmer indicates that, in this specific task, the "spirituality of prophetic discernment" should be distinguished (Osmer 2008, p. 136). Therefore, and as a third task of a practical theological enquiry, emphasis is placed on the normative, with the objective to describe what should be happening ethically. In this movement, the focus comes from a practical theological orientation, in particular on the interpretation of events as understood from a theological and ethical perspective.

Underscoring the perception that the culture in which we live is shaping us (Sweet, 2012) is the belief that the hermeneutics of popular culture hold the promise of pointing beyond, as Kelton Cobb (2005, p. 294) aptly indicates:

> Theology of culture depends upon this kind of trust that our cultural expressions can testify to a reality that transcends them – a reality that is really there, that matters, and in which providence is at work. Theology offers a language to speak about this reality, and can help articulate what is going on in the depths of popular culture ... it is wise to remain open to the more discerning markers of culture. Even of popular culture.

Twitter provides an excellent opportunity and platform to do just that within the scope of 140 characters. With this as a background, attention was paid to the way in which this aspect of normativity regarding theological and ethical interpretation was portrayed in the analysed tweets of the Christian leaders as well as regarding the Charlie Hebdo attacks. The hashtag symbol was used as a window to examine the most prominent themes. Zappavigna (2012, p. 1) describes the *hashtag* symbol as "an emergent convention for labelling the topic of a micropost and a form of metadata incorporated into posts." The functionality of this symbol is found in the common practice of sorting and selecting thematically related information from a torrent of messages within the context of social media platforms (Murthy, 2013).

Dominant themes were critically evaluated, as well as the background and motivation for the presentation of the relative subjects. In the research, two tracks of analysis regarding normativity were used. In terms of content trends, the most popular Christian-related content regarding Christian leadership, as indicated by the use of the hashtag symbol, typically (and except for the keywords "Christian" and "leadership") included words such as "relationship," "kingdom," "apostolic," "bible" and "Jesus" (*Fuseware* 2015). A similar analysis was done regarding the Charlie Hebdo data and, besides the main hashtags on the event, the top words used were "god," "faith," "Christian," "pope" and "Jesus" (*Fuseware* 2015). These key hashtag words serve as a summary of the dominant themes of the conversation.

By evaluating the hashtags used most often in a specific period, an overview of the main themes of the conversation(s) can be provided. These markers can, in turn, provide direction to forming a strategic positioning and participating in the conversation. Once again, the opportunity is provided in an ongoing and future conversation for anyone to contribute to the conversation by not only formulating a tweet, but also creating their own hashtag, emphasising a key aspect(s) of the specific message.

In seriously considering and interpreting events, "discernment" is indeed orientated towards drawing a conclusion that the will and presence of God are actively sought. Together with the previous two orientation points, namely spiritualities of attending and thoughtfulness, a deep awareness is set that focuses on the use of Twitter in the expression of Christian leadership. Consideration is then given to the development of a spirituality of discernment from the leadership of tweeting. Ingerson and Bruce (2013, p. 82) correctly indicate that, due to the power of Twitter's instant connection, positive and negative experiences are indeed possible. They describe various possible outcomes as follows:

> Leaders have the chance to improve the world by tweeting encouraging words or discussing positive activities they are taking part in, but the polar opposite could happen as well. One negative tweet from a leader could have devastating effects on the person, organization, or action they

are tweeting about. Precautions must be taken when powerful leaders have access to so many constitutions. Conversely, because these business leaders CEOs are so influential and have such a high amount of followers, the chance for them to improve the world is great.

In the orientation of discernment, investigative perspectives are mapped out for possible use during the last pragmatic task of a practical theological inquiry. Considering "… the real-time power of Twitter: the ability to listen and learn as decisions are made, by monitoring reactions and directing the appropriate course of action" (Gruber, Smerek, Thomas-Hunt, and James, 2015, p. 164), action can then be taken. In the following and last movement of this practical theological research endeavour, the plotting of some coordinates for a pragmatic spirituality are mapped out.

6. "A Pragmatic Spirituality": Christian Leadership Defined through Twitter?

In the last movement of Osmer's practical theological research, the specific trajectory of the search focuses on what could possibly be done and supported by a pragmatic or strategic spirituality. This is indicated by Osmer as an orientation of spirituality of serving leadership (Osmer 2008, p. 193). The research not only acknowledges the concept of serving leadership, but is also interested in the pragmatic possibilities and contributions of Christian leadership on Twitter. Within this context, a broader understanding of leadership is emphasised; the description of this does resonate with Osmer's continuum of movement within which the following three poles can be differentiated.

In the first movement, establishing a pragmatic spirituality, "task competence" is assumed. Gruber, Smerek, Thomas-Hunt and James (2015, p. 164) stated the following:

> The microblogging site Twitter has become one of the most powerful platforms through which organizations communicate with stakeholders. Therefore, it is critical that scholars and practitioners understand the real-time power of Twitter and its implications for crisis management and leadership.

The question remains, however, in what way Christian leadership on Twitter can make a pragmatic and strategic contribution towards facilitating deep change. By using existing examples of Twitter messages from Christian leaders, it can be shown how the process of deep change is facilitated, demonstrating strategic advantages flowing from it. To illustrate this, the empirical data from the *Fuseware* (2015) research report served to illustrate how original tweets of Christian leaders on Twitter for the indicated period were retweeted, reaching and influencing a large audience. In this regard, Ingerson and Bruce (2013, p. 75) correctly state as follows:

> Because of the high dissemination rate, Twitter has been thought of by many as electronic word of mouth ... Because word of mouth is a powerful influencer tool, Twitter therefore could be viewed as a powerful electronic influencer tool.

Specifically, if a tweet is retweeted often enough or by the right person(s), it gathers momentum that can emulate a snowball effect (Murthy, 2013). Thinking beyond the formal use of, for example, hashtags and retweets, Pearson rightly indicates that "[h]ow a tweet is heard and received points to what lies beyond that which is online" (Pearson, 2015, p. 192).

In future research, the underlying dynamics associated with the action of retweeting should be investigated further by asking about the reasons for messages being retweeted and the impact of retweeted messages. This could indeed link up well with a second movement on the continuum of a pragmatic spirituality, namely the dynamics of "deep change." Part of the last movement on the continuum of pragmatic spirituality is the search for the possible future meaning of existing practices of Christian expressions on Twitter. The research, although with a focus on existing practices, is simultaneously sensitive to the dynamic development of future practices.

Providing examples of pragmatic Christian leadership practices already present on Twitter for the indicated period, the 10 most retweeted messages were analysed from the data sets for "Christian leadership" as well as for the Charlie Hebdo attacks. From the indicated tweets, I have omitted all the messages that included any web references and have focused only on the typical ordinary 140-character messages. Following these criteria, the following message by @amalphurs, on 12 January 2014, regarding "Christian leadership" was retweeted more than a 100 times: "Christian leadership is servant leadership, and any definition of a Christian must include the concept of servanthood." Using the same criteria regarding the Charlie Hebdo attacks, the following message by @chrchristensen, on 7 January 2015, was retweeted nearly 10,000 times: "Breivik killed 77 in Norway & no-one asked me as a white male of Nordic Christian background if I felt the need to condemn it. #charliehebdo." Although this most retweeted post was unrelated to the Charlie Hebdo attacks, it put things into perspective with another situation earlier in Norway.

7. Summary – New Vistas Opening up …

Changes currently experienced by the world are like the movement of tectonic plates, resulting in earthquakes and tsunamis (Clayton, 2010, p. 9), the size and extent of which were never experienced by previous generations (Gore, 2013). In order to steer through these challenging times, the words of Ingerson and Bruce (2013, p. 74) serve as further motivation for this quest regarding future Christian leadership: "The use of social media via social networking sites has played a key role in leadership in the 21st century." In the preceding movements of a practical theological spirituality, a preliminarily tracing of Christian leadership on Twitter was mapped out. It was shown how expressions by Christian leaders on Twitter could not only contribute positively to existing practices, but also map out important perspectives for development and use in the future.

In terms of research, the phenomenon of "tweeting" was sketched and possibilities emphasised of how this specific form of social media can be put to use for Christian leadership practices. This orientation can accordingly lead to sketching perspectives for the development of future research possibilities. To be able to lead in new spaces of a digital existence, it seems that the following coordinates of degrees of longitude and latitude are required.

As far as longitude is concerned, thought should be given again to the type of theological discourse. The articulation of public theology, where acknowledgement is accorded to dialogic, practical, integrated, specialised and culturally oriented theological emphasis of e.g. empirical truths, seems important in order to be able to create a new and fresh style of inspiring theology (Ganzevoort, 2014, pp. 20–30). In order to develop a vocabulary for a fresh theological discourse, the focus of a public practical empirical description should not only encompass church practices, but also daily life, in particular. In this regard, Ganzevoort and Roeland write:

> The concepts of praxis and lived religion focus on what people do rather than on "official" religion, its sacred sources, its institutes, and its doctrines. As such, practical theology has much in common with what in disciplines like anthropology, sociology, and media studies, is known as "the practical turn": the turn away from institutes and (cultural) texts to the everyday social and cultural practices of ordinary people (Ganzevoort and Roeland, 2014, p. 93).

As far as latitude is concerned, it seems that the following markers could assist in establishing coordinates for future leadership. In mapping out the coordinates, I dovetail with the contributions of Philip Clayton (2010) and Len Sweet (2014). First, the theological audience has changed. This has specific results for the formulation and method of work of Christian leadership. Second, theology is not experienced in a centralised manner, but rather created in a cooperative way in which emphasis of context, relevance and actuality, as well as a dynamically changing character and connectivity are definitive. Third, theology, created after Google, is not authoritarian, but rather personal, biographical and autobiographical. By implication, theological truths are thus not presented in a linear fashion, but spaces are facilitated towards the creative articulation of a variety of perspectives.

A continuing sensitivity for these perspectives and growing developments may, in fact, lead to the strategic use of new, unexplored possibilities in the creation of innovative leadership practices, opening up new future vistas on Christian leadership and communities.

Chapter Six

The Pastor as a Brand? The Use of Social Media by Pastorpreneurs for Personal Branding

Theo Zijderveld

1. Introduction

This chapter shows how so-called pastorpreneurs employ social media to reinforce their personal brand, using the example of Joel Osteen. The phenomenon of personal branding will be embedded in the discussion about mediation and mediatization. What is the relationship between the transformation of the media landscape and the way pastors and religious leaders can position themselves on social media?

The importance of social media for religious leaders is the primary concern of this chapter. Religious leaders need to consider how they position themselves online, and what this means for the character of their leadership in their religious communities and in networks and spheres beyond local boundaries. Fortunately, in this volume, Van den Berg discusses the role of Twitter for Christian leadership, which contributes to further thinking about the role of social media for religious leaders.

In the spiritual marketplace, new requirements are emerging for leadership. Pastors of mega-churches have become charismatic media personalities. Denominational ties increasingly fail to function as identity markers. Brands, though, have become part of the system by which we order the world (Rakow, 2015, p. 218). It is not just big corporations like Nike, Apple and Coca Cola that behave like brands; religious organizations are applying the same strategies in order to compete.

Mara Einstein claims that religious organizations are marketing their message in the same way as consumer goods (Einstein, 2008, p. 78; see also Hoover, 2016). Leaders like Joyce Meyer, Joel Osteen and Rick Warren have become "faith brands" with their own mythology, central message and media channels, adapted to the styles and symbols of popular culture. They appear regularly on television, in newspapers and magazines, and they promote themselves online, often supported by media and communication professionals. Many religious leaders and their organizations have successfully used social media to gather millions of followers, "likes" and "shares."

During the Great Awakenings, pastors like George Whitefield became widely popular and attracted great masses. Nowadays, pastors like Joyce Meyer, Rick Warren, and especially Joel Osteen have been extremely successful in creating large mega-churches and employing mass media to generate a worldwide audience. The way religious leaders use media to promote themselves and their message has been studied extensively (Einstein, 2008; Hoover, 1988; Lee & Sinitiere, 2009; Moore, 1995). However, the implications of social media for the branding of religious leaders have, to the best of my knowledge, barely been analysed (Codone, 2014; Hope Cheong, 2014, 2016).

Joel Osteen is one of the most successful and also one of the most frequently analysed American pastors of the moment (e.g. Lee & Sinitiere, 2009, p. 25–52; Rakow, 2015). We will take him as a case study. He is represented on almost all important social media platforms and has millions of followers.

Already in 2004, two-thirds of Americans were using the Internet for religious and spiritual purposes (Hoover, 2004). Moreover, the use of social media has been expanding rapidly. In 2015, Facebook had 1.39 billion active users, YouTube 1 billion with 4 billion videos being watched every day, and Twitter had 288 million users.[1] Many of the most popular preachers have millions of followers on social media: Rick Warren has 2 million followers on Facebook, Joyce Meyer 9.1 million, and Joel Osteen beats them all with 10 million followers. Clearly, these American pastors have an enormous potential reach on social media. The emergence of the Internet and social media raises questions about the connection between the use of online media and the construction of religious authority (Campbell, 2012, p. 76). Religious communities are much more fluid online, and these environments pose challenges both to traditional structures, roles and tools and to the position of religious leaders.

I present the results of an analysis of the biographical information about Joel Osteen on his social media profiles and his Facebook posts

---

[1] J. Bullas, "33 Social Media Facts and Statistics You Should Know in 2015," Jeffbullas.com, http://www.jeffbullas.com/2015/04/08/33-social-media-facts-and-statistics-you-should-know-in-2015/. Accessed May 30, 2015.

in the month of June 2015. In the conclusion, I will relate the notion of personal branding to the development of leadership theory and discuss whether the use of social media for personal branding is applicable for pastors in general.

2. Who Is Joel Osteen?

Joel Osteen (born in 1963) is senior pastor of Lakewood Church in Houston, a church with approximately 43,000 attendees, which makes it the largest church in the United States.[1] His televised sermons attract millions of viewers weekly. His website claims that he has written several New York Times bestsellers. Numerous elements in the life of Joel Osteen are narrated in his stories and sermons, which have become part of his brand mythology. Key to this brand mythology is the story of his vocation. His father, pastor John Osteen, founded Lakewood Church in 1959. Joel dropped out of university in order to devote himself to television promotion of the church's ministry.

In 1999, his father became ill and asked Joel to preach. Joel refused, but finally relented. A week later, his father died. Despite Joel's shyness, he became widely popular, and the membership of his church grew immensely.

Joel is often described as "the smiling preacher," a description that is underscored by practically all photos available of him (Lee & Sinitiere, 2009, p. 26). He emphasizes the goodness of God, and seldom preaches about sin. Two of his slogans are "Discover the Champion in You" and "Be a Victor, not a Victim." Einstein claims that, with his presentation and narrative, Joel gives people the feeling that he is a personal friend (Einstein, 2008, p. 138). She argues that his televised sermons follow a solid pattern of elements that strengthen Joel as a brand, but that they also promote his products like events, books and DVDs. Einstein's critique of Joel Osteen is that he emphasizes positivity in all situations, but that his presentation of life is too simple. She stresses that his marketing follows the classical "problem-solution" marketing that promises things it cannot deliver. Just like using the right toothbrush does not provide success and good looks, the uplifting messages of Joel Osteen cannot solve life's problems. Moreover, she adds that Joel uses God as a middle man, "the means to a prosperous end instead of the end itself" (Einstein, 2008, p. 146).

---

[1] "About Joel Osteen," Joel Osteen Ministries, http://www.joelosteen.com/Pages/AboutJoel.aspx. Accessed May 30, 2015.

Rakow has studied why the messages of Joel Osteen are successful. She states, in line with Einstein, that his messages follow the same pattern as self-help books and workshops, adding God as the benevolent benefactor. Osteen makes use of the same rhetorical and narrative devices that are used in self-helps books and works of alternative spirituality (Rakow, 2015, p. 226). This could explain his popularity inside as well as outside his church.

3. *Marketing and Branding*

Marketing expert David Ogilvy defines branding as "the intangible sum of a product's attributes: its name, packaging, and price, its history, its reputation, and the way it is advertised" (Einstein, 2008, p. 70). Branding is related to marketing. Marketing is the idea of understanding the desires of customers and being able to reach them using the right channels. Marketers search for consumer needs and desires in order to create stories that resonate with what people want to identify with. Rakow states, "Brands do more than simply market and sell a product or service; they create a sense of affiliation and community and therefore can be conceptualized as a form of cultural production and as providers of contexts for interaction" (Rakow, 2015, p. 218).

In popular culture, brands have become part of identity creation. Brands like Coca Cola, Nike, Starbucks, Mercedes become part of people's lifestyle and identity. Brands employ a logo and a slogan, for example Nike with the swirl and the slogan "Just do it." Einstein develops the claim that religious organizations are marketing their message in the same way as consumer goods. Many religious organizations in the United States become faith brands, using their own logo, slogan and mythology. Religious leaders increasingly draw attention to themselves as personifications of the organizations and movements they represent. Joyce Meyer is known for the slogan "Sharing Christ – Loving People" and has connected her name to "Joyce Meyer Ministries."

Personal branding, the practice of people marketing themselves as brands, was popularized by the American management writer Tom Peters and has become one of the key concepts in the management literature. Peters argues that each person is in charge of his or her personal brand.[1] In her book *You are a Brand*, Catherine Kaputa defines a personal brand as "a special promise of value that sets you apart." Moreover, she claims:

---

[1] Tom Peters, "The Brand Called You," FastCompany, August 31, 1997. http://www.fastcompany.com/28905/brand-called-you. Accessed May 30, 2015.

> With branding, you learn how to look at yourself as a product in a competitive framework. Branding is the process of differentiating that product – you – from the competition and taking action steps to get where you want to go (Kaputa, 2012, p. 7).

Not surprisingly, Kaputa and many other writers on personal branding emphasize the importance of creating and sustaining a personal brand online. Websites and social media profiles become increasingly important for self-profiling, especially for jobseekers and entrepreneurs.

4. The Pastorpreneur

In 2003, John Jackson coined the word pastorpreneur to describe entrepreneurial pastors (Jackson, 2003). A pastorpreneur is someone who adapts strategies from business and combines them with elements of popular culture to package and distribute his message in order for his church to grow (Hope Cheong, 2016; Klaver, 2015; Rakow, 2015; Stevenson, 2013).

Televangelists have always been masters of marketing (Lee & Sinitiere, 2009; Moore, 1995). Their programs were used as promotions for live events and to create brand loyalty for the audience. In the past, television pastors preached fire and brimstone for those who would not believe. Nowadays, they promote fine living and abundance. The "new televangelists," as she calls them, exclude symbols of the cross, mentions of Jesus, contributions, or the suggestion that you could be going to hell (Einstein, 2008, p. 121).

Rakow suggests that Joel Osteen may be the perfect embodiment of a pastorpreneur. "He is at once a savvy businessman and a cultural broker; he combines business and marketing strategies with a message that resonates with the self-understanding of modern consumers shaped by contemporary discourses and practices of the self" (Rakow, 2015, p. 232).

Pastorpreneurs like Osteen have become personal brands. Personal branding is strongly related to the concept of authenticity. Spontaneity, self-expression, individualism, and creativity are highly valued in today's society, while traditional authority and "the system" are being perceived as restrictive and negative (Taylor, 2007, p. 76). This might be one reason why a personal narrative and personal style are so important for personal branding. They emphasize the unique characteristics of a person, not the doctrines and structures of organizations.

5. The Personal Narrative and Digital Storytelling

The personal narrative is highly valued in today's society. Giddens argues that:

> In the post-traditional order of modernity, and against the backdrop of new forms of mediated experience, self-identity becomes a reflexively organized endeavour. The reflexive project of the self, which consists in sustaining coherent, yet continuously revised, biographical narratives, takes place in the context of multiple choice as filtered through abstract systems. (Giddens, 1991, p. 5)

Not surprisingly, the personal narrative is a crucial part of personal branding. Stories are key to understanding the branding of Joel Osteen. Osteen was able to tell his stories long before the emergence of Twitter and Facebook, because of financial, cultural, and social capital. He was able to afford television productions that were broadcasted worldwide. How does this translate to social media? As Couldry states, "digital storytelling represents a novel distribution of a scarce resource – the ability to represent the world around us – using a shared infrastructure" (Couldry, 2008, p. 374) and in particular its potential to contribute to the strengthening of democracy. Through answering this question, it seeks to test out the relative strengths and weaknesses of two competing concepts for grasping the wider consequences of media for the social world: the concept of mediatization and the concept of mediation. It is argued that mediatization (developed, for example, by Stig Hjarvard and Winfried Schulz. This has many implications for the way organizations and people are able to communicate. Social networks like Facebook and Twitter allow any religious leader to create and build an online presence and construct a personal brand without needing the large financial investments that come with the publication of books or the production of television. However, televangelists like Joel Osteen have very successfully integrated social media channels with more "traditional" channels like television and books.

6. Mediation and Mediatization

The Internet is one of the most important platforms for communication in a network society. This has implications for the way religious leaders operate. Especially on social media, the boundaries between the public and private sphere have become fluid.

When we analyse the way religious leaders like Joel Osteen use social media, we position ourselves in a debate about the transformation of religious leadership. A core argument in this chapter is that religious leaders increasingly operate in a spiritual marketplace (Roof, 1999). Another important notion is the relationship between religious leaders and the transformation of the media landscape, especially the emergence of social media. Two contrasting concepts are important: mediation and mediatization. I will argue that both concepts are useful, depending on what we want to analyse.

HjaRvard (2008), Schulz (2004) and several others have developed the theory of mediatization. At the core of this theory is the thesis that media have reached such a position in society that all other institutions have become dependent on them. Mediatization is a transformation of society emanating from a single source, a transformation of society by "media logic." This media logic has organizational, technological and aesthetic functions. It prescribes how we should use symbolic resources and works through formal and informal rules. Applied to churches and religious leaders, this means that they should adapt the way they communicate to the rules of the media. Lundby has critiqued this theory because he states that, especially on the Internet, there is not one media logic (Lundby, 2009). Couldry (2008) argues that we cannot separate transformations of media from their cultural and social context.

If we apply the framework of mediatization to the analysis of Joel Osteen's use of social media, we might hypothesize that the emergence of social media will change the way he has to brand himself. Couldry mentions several features of digital storytelling that contrast with oral storytelling: a pressure to mix text with other audio-visual materials, limit the length of narratives, standardize and take into account the possibility that any narrative when posted online may have unintended and undesired audiences (Couldry, 2008, p. 382). However, this approach might not consider broader developments in society, such as globalization, the spiritualization of the self, the emphasis on personal development, mistrust in official institutions, etc.

Mediation, on the other hand, is defined by Silverstone as "the fundamentally, but unevenly, dialectical process in which institutionalized media of communication (…) are involved in the general circulation of symbols in social life" (Silverstone, 2002, p. 762). This definition implies that it is hard to isolate the media institutions. Couldry states that "media" do not merely function by transmitting textual units for moments of reception, they also function through a process of environmental transformation. This transforms the conditions under which any future media will be produced and understood. He states that mediatization implies a linear process, while mediation implies a more complex, non-linear process (Couldry, 2008, p. 280). This could also help in exploring the relationship between "traditional" and "new" media.

If we apply the framework of mediation to the personal branding of Joel Osteen on social media, this leads to very different questions: the process of production in relationship to the practices and styles of interpretation, the recirculation of storytelling and branding practices, and the long-term consequences of digital storytelling and personal branding for cultural transformations. Moreover, it could explain more easily how Osteen has translated his presence on television to his presence on the Internet.

The concept of mediation applies better to questions about the transformation of religious leadership in a changing media landscape. However, the concept of mediatization might help to clarify the way storytelling and branding on Facebook is different from the kind of storytelling in Osteen's heavily analysed television performances (Einstein, 2008; Rakow, 2015; Stevenson, 2013, pp. 163–227). For the exploration of what happens on the social media accounts of Joel Osteen, the perspective of mediatization helps us to focus on the very specific characteristics of social media posts. However, in a more in-depth analysis of the surrounding religious communities, actor-network analysis and the environmental social and cultural dimensions, the more fluid definition of mediation might be more helpful.

7. Methodology

We will analyse (1) the social media profiles of Joel Osteen and (2) his Tweets and Facebook posts. The enormous amount of data on several networks and social media platforms poses new challenges for researchers. It is clear that a systematic study of communication on the Internet requires new methods (Rogers, 2013). Over the last decade, several studies have been devoted to methodological issues of studying the relationship between religion and new media (Campbell, 2012; Helland, 2005). The methodology employed for studying the relationship between social media practices and religious leadership has been elaborated by Codone (2014). She has analysed the Twitter activity of the pastors Rick Warren and Andy Stanley. Her analysis and classification of their Tweets clearly show that most of the messages can be classified as encouragement, teaching, and ministry marketing. "Clearly, both pastors are not just sharing information for the sake of passing on titbits to their Twitter followers – they are sending messages of hope, encouragement and information about specific ministry opportunities" (Codone, 2014, p. 27). She claims that these pastors are building influence outside traditional church hierarchies through their use of social media platforms, which is evidenced by their higher follower counts. Because Facebook and Twitter posts are mostly text-oriented, I have applied this scheme to Facebook posts as well.

Because of the preliminary state of the research and the explorative perspective of this chapter, I found it very useful to use Codone's categorization of social media posts to describe what kind of content appears on the social media accounts of pastorpreneurs like Joel Osteen. This allows me to clarify what kind of content is widely posted. Some of the posts and the general information about the accounts (bios) will be analysed as media texts that are meaningful both as separate units and as part of the practice of digital storytelling by Joel Osteen Ministries. They show what visual and textual elements are used to create the brand of Joel Osteen.

The Tweets and Facebook posts of Joel Osteen in June 2015 will be analysed. Though this time span is limited, it is long enough to get a general impression of the content on these platforms and to classify it and gain insight into the way Joel Osteen uses social media on a regular basis to communicate with his audience.

This analysis is motivated by the fact that these two social media are widely used and by the number of followers Osteen has amassed on these platforms. YouTube videos have not been included because many of these videos, recorded church services, have been studied already. Because Instagram is image-based, and text is secondary, I will only touch on its content briefly.

The ensuing analysis pays attention to the statistics of the posts. For Facebook, these include likes, shares (people share the post on their personal timeline), and comments (reactions to the posts by users). For Twitter, these include retweets (people share the post on their own timeline) and favourites (comparable to likes on Facebook). Though these statistics should not be considered an objective measurement of the impact or influence of religious leaders like Joel Osteen on their audiences, it gives us some indication of the popularity of his posts as reflected by the amount of interaction with followers on these platforms.

The Tweet Classification Categories Scheme of Codone consists of the following elements (Codone, 2014, pp. 23–24):

- Encouragement/teaching (ET): Public encouragement or teaching.
- Personal statements (PS): Reference to personal activity, situation, or

issue facing the ministry leader.
- Marketing – self (MS): Promotion of the content the ministry leader has created as an individual, not within the context of a paid ministry position.
- Ministry marketing (MM): Promotion of churches, ministries, or other organizations with which the ministry leader is associated.
- Humour (HU): Jokes or silly comments.
- Random comments: Any posts whose meaning is not attributable to anything specific.
- Retweets or Modified Tweets (RT/MT): Any post from another user that is retweeted (shared) or in the case of a Modified Tweet (MT), annotated with a personal comment by the ministry leader.
- Endorsements (EN): Any tweet endorsing, supporting, or recommending another person.
- Information sharing (IS): Directing followers to information not directly related to ministry content from the ministry leader's church or personal content, usually including an URL.

8. Results

In the results, I will describe the profiles of Joel Osteen, followed by an analysis of his posts on Facebook and Twitter in June 2015.

The Facebook page of Joel Osteen has gathered 10 million likes.[1] It contains a large professional photo of Joel, his wife Victoria, and the logo of Joel Osteen Ministries in the background. Joel is wearing a simple blue polo shirt; Victoria is wearing a matching denim shirt. The background of the photo is vague, showing trees with leaves bathed in sunshine. Because the background is vague, attention is drawn to Joel and his wife. The profile picture shows a broadly smiling Joel Osteen.

On the "About" page of Facebook, we read a statement about the ministry of Joel Osteen, emphasizing victory and abundance. "When we believe, we can overcome any obstacle, achieve any goal and live the life of victory that God created us to live."[2]

The Twitter page of Joel Osteen is being followed by 3.48 million accounts and contains almost 13,000 tweets, including replies. This page shows the same background and profile image as the Facebook page. Twitter users are allowed to provide a bio of 140 characters, but the bio of Joel Osteen only refers followers to the website JoelOsteen.com.[3]

---

[1] Joel Osteen Ministries, Facebook, https://www.facebook.com/JoelOsteen/. Accessed July 3, 2015.

[2] "About Joel Osteen Ministries," Joel Osteen Ministries, Facebook, https://www.facebook.com/JoelOsteen/info/?tab=page_info. Accessed July 3, 2015.

[3] Joel Osteen Ministries (@JoelOsteen), Twitter, https://twitter.com/JoelOsteen. Accessed July 3, 2015.

Osteen's YouTube Channel has 75,000 subscribers.[1] The YouTube Channel shows the logo of Joel Osteen ministries and a panorama photo of Joel Osteen in a full stadium, showing Joel Osteen from the back and thousands of people sitting in the stadium. The description of the account is more focused on the person of Joel Osteen ("native Texan") and the success of his ministry in terms of attendees, viewers, and countries in which his broadcasts are seen.

In addition, the description includes hyperlinks to JoelOsteen.com, Twitter, VictoriaOsteen.com, Google+, Facebook, Instagram and LakewoodChurch.com

Joel Osteen has gained 216,000 followers on Instagram.[2] His profile picture shows him and his wife Victoria smiling into the camera. They wear clothes of the same colour: both in purple shirts. The background is vague, just like the Facebook picture, showing green leaves on the trees. The Instagram profile picture is very small and round, so it is hard to see more details. His Instagram account contains just 77 messages. This account seems to be the most personal: the pictures are mostly ones showing Joel Osteen with his wife, family and friends, but also with famous Americans like Larry King and Oprah Winfrey. Sometimes, his events and broadcasts are promoted.

Posts on Twitter and Facebook
In June 2015, Joel Osteen posted 30 messages on Facebook and 60 on Twitter.

On Facebook as well as on Twitter, the encouraging/teaching posts (E/T) are in the majority, respectively 70.7% on Facebook and 100%(!) on Twitter. An example of this category is:

"Live a life of excellence. Live in such a way that causes others to win." 2,400 likes, 3,200 favourites (Twitter, 3 June 2015).

The messages on Twitter cannot exceed 140 characters. Joel's Facebook messages are mostly short as well. The phrases are short and easy to understand and to quote. Another difference between Twitter and Facebook is that the Twitter messages contain no images or videos, though this is technically possible. Facebook posts contain an image in approximately 2/3 of the cases. These images show Joel Osteen on stage or are illustrated quotes, often containing the Joel Osteen Ministries

---

[1] Joel Osteen Ministries, YouTube, https://www.youtube.com/joelosteen. Accessed July 3, 2015.

[2] Joel Osteen (@joelosteen), Instagram, https://instagram.com/joelosteen/. Accessed June 30, 2015.

Logo. In this case I have also categorized the post as "Marketing Ministry" or "Marketing Self."

Promotions of self and promotions of ministry are hard to distinguish because Joel Osteen Ministries is so closely connected to the person. Added up, they form 23.9% of the posts on Facebook. These kinds of messages mostly contain a call to attend gatherings, or to watch or listen to broadcasts.

These promotional posts generate considerably fewer likes and shares than the encouraging posts. The categories Humour, Random Comments, Retweets or Information Sharing were non-existent this month; the category Personal Statement had 2 posts on Facebook, one thanking the audience at an event in the Twin Cities, the other one referring to Father's Day.

Note that in the results we have not counted responses to comments and replies. Joel Osteen does not react personally; his social media team takes care of that task. If people ask for a prayer, the team answers with a standard reply that contains a link to the prayer page and a telephone number.

9. Analysis

The messages of Joel Osteen on Twitter can be characterized as encouragement and self-help. They are not related to the news or actual events in the world. Facebook is used more broadly, also including announcements of performances, endorsements, etc. Clearly, in order to categorize the posts of Joel Osteen in the future, adaption is needed for the model of Codone. This is especially true for Twitter, because Osteen's Tweets can all be categorized as teaching/encouraging posts.

It is clear that Joel Osteen's social media accounts are very successful, considering the number of followers and amount of interaction. The profiles themselves depict a cheerful Joel Osteen with his wife, giving the impression that they are a happy family. Their casual clothes portray them as very "real" people, though the professionalism of the photo and the logo suggest otherwise. The descriptions are all written in the third person. They emphasize the brand message of Joel Osteen, focusing on victory, abundance, overcoming obstacles and "living a life of victory and abundance that God intended for you."[1] His bios on Facebook and YouTube emphasize the success of his ministries and the

---

[1] "About Joel Osteen Ministries," Facebook.

international scope of his messages. Apparently, Twitter and Facebook contribute mostly to enforcing the brand, connecting to the audiences online, but not to direct sales.

Joel Osteen never gets really personal on either Facebook or Twitter. The messages do not show us much about his private life, and his messages are most likely not posted by himself. All replies come from the Joel Osteen Ministries team, emphasizing the fact that professionals host this account. His profiles and activity on Twitter and Facebook are part of a very sophisticated, subtle way of maintaining the faith brand Joel Osteen.

The content of the social media accounts on Twitter and Facebook aligns with what Einstein and Rakow have concluded about his performances. Positive feelings and self-help positivism are emphasized. The message is: you could reach your goals, and God can help you to fulfil your dreams! Just like in his shows, the social media give the impression that he is a personal friend. His profile pictures show him as an ordinary man, wearing ordinary clothes (though on stage, he normally wears a suit and a tie). It is easy to understand why Einstein notes that many people do not perceive his teachings as particularly Christian. Though he surely prays, reads the Bible, and mentions Jesus in his shows, references to the Bible or biblical figures are very scarce on social media. Many of his encouraging tweets and teachings make no reference to Christianity at all.

Possibly the most interesting thing is what Joel Osteen is not tweeting or posting about. In the month of June 2015, some very significant events occurred in the United States. On June 26, the United States legalized same-sex marriage, a decision most evangelical Christians are opposed to. On June 17, nine Afro-American people were shot and killed in a Methodist Episcopal Church in Charleston, South Carolina. The suspect was a 21-year-old white male who had previously posed next to the Confederate flag. The shootings sparked national and international debates. Though Joel Osteen certainly paid attention to this drama, he hardly mentioned it on social media. Obviously, participation in religious or political debates is not a part of the social media strategy of Joel Osteen.

10. *Conclusion*

What is the relationship between the transformation of the media landscape and the way religious leaders can position themselves on social media?

Pastorpreneurs like Joel Osteen use social media for personal branding and personify the focus on personal wellbeing and a personal narrative. The pastorpreneurs of today preach fine living and abundance, things that resonate perfectly with the values of today's society.

Social media have opened new venues for interacting with existing and new audiences in virtual communities worldwide. Social media accounts enable individuals to act as brands, and promote valuable content that others may want to share. The nature of the internet and social media have, from the supplier side, created the need for valuable and shareable content that people want to share and spread to others. Joel Osteen and his organization are masters of using social media for personal branding. He has gained a worldwide audience, making him one of the most familiar faces of Christianity in the United States.

From a mediatization perspective, the short messages and the emphasis on encouragement are well adapted to the "logic" of Facebook and Twitter. They can be considered as very short stories that can be read as individual messages. These messages have to compete with the other messages on the timeline of the followers of Joel Osteen. Statistically, the posts perform very well, considering the thousands of shares and likes. However, just like Codone concluded in her analysis of Rick Warren and Andy Stanley, Joel Osteen seems to use social media more like a megaphone and not as a tool to interact directly with his followers. His messages do align with his brand image and might enhance his reputation as the one who emphasizes "to discover the champion in you." The number of followers could make personal interaction almost impossible, and moreover, it is clear that it is not Joel Osteen himself who is managing his social media accounts, but rather his social media team.

From a mediation perspective, we can conclude that this explorative research begs for more systematic research to study what happens when the messages of Joel Osteen are shared and commented on, how they relate to what happens on other media, such as television, and what the long-term consequences for pastors of mega-churches could be. The context of entrepreneurial pastors, advancing technologies, developments in personal spirituality and developing personal narratives is very complex. However, it is clear that the production of the brand Joel Osteen has been very carefully executed in order to build a coherent, positive brand that repeats and emphasizes the same meta-stories of positive thinking, encouragement and self-development. The "reputation management" that can be seen in the production of social media profiles and messages leaves no room for stories that do not align with brand stories and brand myths.

Applications for Leadership Theory
The issues raised in the research into the personal branding of Joel Osteen can enrich the debate about the transformation of leadership in a media society. Many leadership theories have a strong psychological focus, focusing on the person and personal motivations of the leaders (Furedi, 2013, p. 382; Saane, 2012). These theories often suppose a direct and personal contact with followers. For religious leaders, this applies to the setting of communication in a local community. The case of Joel Osteen shows how important the media dimension has become. The technological developments in our network society have enabled religious communities to become disembedded from the local context and religious leaders to gain global exposure. Personal branding happens in a context of the tough requirements of a religious marketplace, the importance of strong leaders as identity markers, and the entrepreneurial approach of many pastors (Rakow, 2015).

How can these findings contribute to leadership theory? What does it mean for religious leadership for the future? Religious leaders do not operate in a cultural vacuum. Therefore, it is impossible to define leadership separately from its cultural, religious and technological context. Clearly, the virtual dimensions become increasingly important in the analysis of leadership. As we stated in the introduction, the emergence of social media raises questions about the connection between online media and the construction of religious authority. Religious leaders who employ media to generate an audience beyond their local religious community rely heavily on the way their brand is constructed by media channels. The branding of pastors calls for a deconstruction of religious leadership in a media context. The perspectives of mediatization and media can contribute to the development of leadership theory.

The perspective of mediatization, with its focus on media institutions and the role of media logic, is very helpful in conceptualizing the relationship between the construction of religious leadership in very specific media conditions, for example, the rules that leaders need to apply to successfully brand themselves on Facebook and Twitter.

Religious leaders face many challenges, such as the context of consumer society, the entertainment industry, the many religious groups that offer their religious products in a global marketplace, the emphasis of authenticity and the distrust of authority. The case of Joel Osteen shows the importance of personal branding and the use of rhetorical and narrative devices that are used in the self-help literature. The perspective of mediation can be applied to the deconstruction of cultural symbols that circulate in the media around religious leaders.

The current transformations in media, religion and culture are strongly related to the transformation of leadership. The specific cultural, economic and religious context in which a religious leader operates requires specific abilities, people, organization and self-presentation (Klaver, 2015). Researching the relationship between leadership, media, religion and culture will lift the research on the future of religious leadership to a higher level.

Application for Religious Leaders Today
What is the role of religious leaders in a network society, in a world that is changing? The case of Joel Osteen is useful because it shows that pastors are able to communicate and present themselves far beyond the local and denominational boundaries of their religious communities. It is a very clear example of the way religious leadership is present in a network society.

The pastorpreneurial approach to self-promotion may turn off religious leaders who abhor such a commercial approach. The percentage of people using social media, especially in Western countries, makes the question of whether or not to be active on social media almost irrelevant, but the question of "how to" remains. Every religious leader has to face the fact that he or she is operating in a spiritual marketplace. This marketplace exceeds the boundaries of the local parish or community. Because people trust other people more than denominations or organizations, religious leaders are much more likely to function as an identity marker for a religious community. Being present on social media offers many opportunities to be visible and to reach the religious community and beyond.

Pastorpreneurs like Joel Osteen emphasize numbers. The size of the audience does matter. On social media, statistics of followers, likes and shares are completely transparent. However, having millions of followers also decreases the opportunity to have personal interactions on social media. The opportunities of social media are not limited to encouraging messages and marketing. Religious leaders with fewer followers on social media might be better able to build personal relationships with their followers.

Joel Osteen is a master at reaching out to very large groups of people in a very competitive spiritual marketplace. In his messages on social media, there is very little room for grief, sorrow, or confusion. In personal branding, these discordant events might not fit with the impression people want to manage, but it is exactly this which makes us human. Religious leaders who do not want to focus on a personal brand might want to focus on the breadth of human experience.

In an age where authenticity is one of the core values, it is hard to see personal branding as authentic behaviour. A brand is deliberately packaged, promoted and distributed. It consists of a clear promise of what a product can do. While authenticity might be a construction, especially on social media, religious leaders need to consider to what extent their personal presentation coincides with the religious message they seek to share.

Chapter Seven

Healthy Leadership: The Science of Clergy Work-Related Psychological Health

Leslie J. Francis

1. Introduction

According to a number of recent studies, religious leadership in the contemporary Western World carries emotional and psychological costs for those who serve in such positions. For example, Warren (2002) reports the impact of parish ministry on emotional, spiritual and physical health; Kaldor and Bullpitt (2001) speak of the impact on professional burnout; Burton and Burton (2009) look beyond the leaders to the stress in clergy families; and Peyton and Gatrell (2013) speak of the sacrificial costs of emotional labour. No overview of religious leadership would be complete, therefore, without serious reflection on the science of clergy work-related health.

This chapter, therefore, proposes to draw together and summarise the work of a research group, co-ordinated by Leslie J. Francis, that set out in the mid-1990s to undertake a systematic and scientific investigation into the work-related psychological health of clergy serving in a variety of denominations within the UK, and where possible to set this within a broader international and comparative context. The research group is situated at the interface between practical theology and the psychology of religion. Within practical theology, the perspective taken is that of empirical theology, whereby respected social science methods and theories are brought into the theological academy. Within the psychology of religion, the perspective taken is that of the individual differences approach, whereby constructs like personality are taken as fundamental. The research group is concerned with the conceptualisation and operationalisation of clergy work-related psychological health, with the development and testing of robust measures, and with testing theories and hypotheses through multi-variate models.

This review article begins by discussing and reviewing three standard measures that have been (and are) employed in the assessment of the work-related psychological health of clergy: the Maslach Burnout Inventory, the Maslach Burnout Inventory as modified especially for use among clergy, and the Francis Burnout Inventory. Next, we explore the empirical evidence published by Francis' research group on the power of four broad factors to predict individual differences in the work-related psychological health of clergy: personality (as defined by Eysenck's dimensional model of personality), psychological type (as operationalised by the measures proposed by the Myers-Briggs Type Indicator, the Keirsey Temperament Sorter and the Francis Psychological Type Scales), personal, professional and lifestyle factors (like engagement with supervision and prayer), and contextual factors (with special reference to the rural ministry).

2. Maslach Burnout Inventory (MBI)

When Francis' research group was established in the mid-1990s, the dominant model of work-related psychological health across a range of the caring professions was provided by the work of Maslach and Jackson (1986) through the development of the Maslach Burnout Inventory (MBI). Maslach's three-component model conceptualises burnout as beginning with emotional exhaustion. Then emotional exhaustion leads to depersonalisation, and depersonalisation in turn leads to a lack of personal accomplishment (see Maslach, 2003). According to this account, emotional exhaustion begins to debilitate the individual. As emotional resources are depleted, members of the caring professions feel that they are no longer able to give of themselves at a psychological level. With the depletion of emotional resources, members of the caring profession begin to adopt negative and cynical attitudes toward and feelings about their clients. As a consequence, the tendency toward depersonalisation grows, and members of the caring professions increasingly view their clients as somehow deserving their troubles. As a consequence of distancing their clients in this way and feeling diminished competence to help them, members of the caring professions increasingly lose their sense of achieving something worthwhile with their work. This leads to dissatisfaction with themselves and with their professional role.

The Maslach Burnout Inventory proposes three scales to assess these three distinct components of emotional exhaustion, depersonalisation and lack of personal accomplishment. In the original form of the Maslach Burnout Inventory, emotional exhaustion is assessed by a nine-item scale. The items describe feelings of being emotionally overextended and exhausted by one's work. An example item from this dimension is "I feel burned out from my work." Depersonalisation is assessed by a five-item scale. The items describe an unfeeling and impersonal response towards the individuals in one's care. An example item from this dimension is "I feel I treat some recipients as if they were impersonal objects." Personal accomplishment is assessed by an eight-item scale. The items describe feelings of competence and successful achievement in one's work with people. An example item from this dimension is "I feel I'm positively influencing other people's lives through my work." In contrast to the other two subscales, lower mean scores on the subscale of personal accomplishment correspond to higher degrees of experienced burnout. Maslach and Jackson (1986) score the Maslach Burnout Inventory by inviting respondents to evaluate each of the 22 items on a seven-point scale of frequency, from never, through a few times a year or less, once a month or less, a few times a month, once a week, a few times a week, to every day.

The scale properties of the Maslach Burnout Inventory were subjected to close and thorough scrutiny by a number of studies conducted during the 1980s and early 1990s. Reliability and validity have been supported by studies like Abu-Hilal and Salameh (1992), Corcoran (1985), Iwancki and Schwab (1981), Pierce and Molloy (1989), Powers and Gose (1986), and Schaufeli and van Dierendonck (1993). The factor structure has been tested and generally supported by studies like Belcastro, Gold and Hays (1983), Byrne (1991, 1993), Gold (1984), Gold, Bachelor and Michael (1989), Gold, Roth, Wright, Michael and Chen (1992), Green and Walkey (1988), Green, Walkey and Taylor (1991), and Walkey and Green (1992).

The original form of the Maslach Burnout Inventory has been and continues to be employed in a number of studies among clergy, including Warner and Carter (1984), Crea (1994), Strümpfer and Bands (1996), Rodgerson and Piedmont (1998), Stanton-Rich and Iso-Ahola (1998), Virginia (1998), Evers and Tomic (2003), Golden, Piedmont, Ciarrocchi, and Rodgerson (2004), Raj and Dean (2005), Miner (2007a, 2007b), Doolittle (2007), Buys and Rothman (2010), Joseph, Corveleyn, Luyten, and de Witte (2010), Parker and Martin (2011), Joseph, Luyten, Corveleyn, and de Witte (2011), Rossetti (2011), and Küçüksüleymanoğlu (2013).

3. Modifying the Maslach Burnout Inventory

Although a number of researchers have been content to apply the Maslach Burnout Inventory among clergy, Francis' research group suspected that some of the concepts and some of the language might not feel right to clergy. Some initial qualitative studies that interviewed clergy confirmed this suspicion and led to the development of a modified instrument, under license from the original copyright holders of the test. Further scrutiny of the original form of the Maslach Burnout Inventory led to a more extensive revision of the instrument than had been originally anticipated. The revision involved three steps. First, where necessary, the original Maslach items were redrafted to align the concepts and language with the ways in which clergy thought and spoke, recognising for example that clergy did not generally refer to those among whom they exercised ministry as "clients." Second, new items were constructed to bring each of the three scales up to the same length of ten items each, whereas in the original form emotional exhaustion was measured by nine items, personal accomplishment by eight items, and depersonalisation by five items. Third, the items were re-voiced to be assessed not on a scale of frequency, but on a scale of intensity employing the established five-point Likert scale: agree strongly, agree, not certain, disagree, and disagree strongly.

This modified form of the Maslach Burnout Inventory has been employed in a series of studies in the UK among Anglican clergy (Francis & Rutledge, 2000; Rutledge & Francis, 2004; Hills, Francis & Rutledge, 2004; Francis & Turton, 2004a, 2004b; Randall, 2004, 2007, 2013; Rutledge, 2006; Turton & Francis, 2007), Catholic priests (Francis, Louden & Rutledge, 2004; Francis, Turton & Louden, 2007, and Pentecostal pastors (Kay, 2000).

The basic application of the modified form of the Maslach Burnout Inventory can be illustrated by reference to the study reported by Francis, Louden and Rutledge (2004) conducted among 1,468 Catholic parochial clergy in England and Wales. Three primary findings emerge from this study that are of general interest and importance. First, the study confirms the satisfactory psychometric properties of the three scales among this specific group of clergy. The alpha coefficient (Cronbach, 1951) offers an established and recognised index of internal consistency reliability. On this index the scale of emotional exhaustion recorded an alpha of .88; the scale of depersonalisation recorded an alpha of .82; and the scale of personal accomplishment recorded an alpha of .79.

The second conclusion compared the mean scale scores of emotional exhaustion, depersonalisation, and personal accomplishment recorded by these 1,468 Catholic priests with the mean scale scores recorded by a comparable sample of Anglican clergymen in a study by Rutledge and Francis (2004). According to these data, Catholic priests experienced a higher level of emotional exhaustion and a higher level of depersonalisation than was the case among Anglican priests. At the same time, Catholic priests experienced a higher level of personal accomplishment than was the case among Anglican priests.

The third conclusion drew on the level of endorsement (agree strongly or agree) given to each of the thirty items of the modified instrument. This level of endorsement profiled a group of men who recorded quite high levels of emotional exhaustion, quite high levels of depersonalisation, and very high levels of personal accomplishment.

With regard to emotional exhaustion, over a third of the Catholic priests said that they felt used up at the end of the day in parish ministry (36%). Over a quarter of the Catholic priests found working with people all day was a real strain for them (27%) and felt that they were working too hard in their parish ministry (26%). Around one in five of the Catholic clergy felt frustrated by their parish ministry (22%) and emotionally drained from it (19%). Around one in six of the Catholic clergy felt fatigued when they got up in the morning and had to face another day in the parish (16%) and said that they felt burned out from their parish ministry (14%). Almost one in ten of the Catholic clergy said that they felt like they were at the end of their tether (10%), that working with people directly put too much strain on them (9%), and that they would feel a lot better if they could get out of parish ministry (8%).

With regard to depersonalisation, nearly a third of the Catholic clergy felt parishioners blamed them for some of their problems (31%). Over a quarter of the Catholic clergy recognized that they were less patient with parishioners than they used to be (27%) and that they found it difficult to listen to what some parishioners were really saying to them (26%). One in every six Catholic clergy worried that parish ministry was hardening them emotionally (17%), and almost as many felt they treated some parishioners as if they were impersonal objects (14%). One in every ten Catholic clergy recognized that they did not really care what happened to some parishioners (11%), that they had come to the conclusion that most people cannot really be helped with their problems (11%), and that they had become more callous toward people since working in parish ministry (9%). A significant minority of Catholic priests said that they could not be bothered to understand how some people feel about things (7%) and that they wished parishioners would leave them alone (7%).

With regard to personal accomplishment, nine out of every ten Catholic priests said that they gained a lot of personal satisfaction from working with people (90%). At least three-quarters of Catholic priests affirmed that, if they could have their time all over again, they would still go into parish ministry (81%), that they felt exhilarated after working closely with parishioners (76%), that they could easily create a relaxed atmosphere with their parishioners (75%), and that they had accomplished many worthwhile things in their parish ministry (75%). At least two-thirds of Catholic clergy felt that they were positively influencing other people's lives through their parish ministry (70%) and that they dealt with emotional problems very calmly in their parish ministry (69%). Three-fifths of Catholic clergy said that they could easily understand how their parishioners felt about things (59%). The proportions dropped, however, to less than one-third of Catholic clergy who felt that they dealt very effectively with the problems of their parishioners (32%) and who claimed to feel very energetic (31%).

4. The Francis Burnout Inventory

One of the key theoretical problems with the Maslach model of burnout concerns giving an account of the relationship between the three components (emotional exhaustion, depersonalisation, and lack of personal accomplishment). One account of this relationship is in terms of a sequential progression, according to which emotional exhaustion leads to depersonalisation and depersonalisation leads to loss of personal accomplishment.

Challenging the adequacy of the empirical foundations for this sequential model and recognising the apparent independence of personal accomplishment from the other two components (emotional exhaustion and depersonalisation), Francis, Kaldor, Robbins and Castle (2005) revisited the insights of Bradburn's (1969) classic notion of "balanced affect" in order to give a coherent account of the observed phenomena of poor work-related psychological health. They proposed a model of work-related psychological health according to which positive affect and negative affect are not opposite ends of a single continuum, but two separate continua. According to this model, it is reasonable for individuals to experience high levels of positive affect and high levels of negative affect at one and the same time. Warning signs of poor work-related psychological health then occur when high levels of negative affect coincide with low levels of positive affect.

Francis, Kaldor, Robbins and Castle (2005) tested this balanced affect approach to work-related psychological health in an international study conducted among clergy in Australia, New Zealand, and the United Kingdom. For research among clergy they translated the notion of negative affect into emotional exhaustion (measured by the Scale of Emotional Exhaustion in Ministry: SEEM) and the notion of positive affect into ministry satisfaction (measured by the Satisfaction in Ministry Scale: SIMS). Put together, these two 11-item scales form the Francis Burnout Inventory (FBI).

The Scale of Emotional Exhaustion in Ministry drew together items expressing a lack of enthusiasm for ministry, frustration, impatience, negativity, cynicism, inflexibility, profound sadness, the sense of being drained and exhausted by the job, and withdrawal from personal engagement with the people among whom ministry is exercised. The Satisfaction in Ministry Scale drew together items expressing personal accomplishment, personal satisfaction, the sense of dealing effectively with people, really understanding and influencing people positively, being appreciated by others, deriving purpose and meaning from ministry, and being glad that they entered ministry.

The internal consistency reliability and construct validity of the two component scales of the Francis Burnout Inventory have been recently tested and supported in a study by Francis, Village, Robbins and Wulff (2011). More importantly, this study tested and supported the balanced affect model of work-related psychological health by demonstrating how high levels of positive affect serve to offset high levels of negative affect in order to maintain a form of psychological equilibrium. Although a relatively new measure, the Francis Burnout Inventory has already been included in a number of studies concerning clergy work-related psychological health, including Francis, Wulff and Robbins (2008), Francis, Robbins, Kaldor and Castle (2009), Robbins and Francis (2010), Brewster, Francis and Robbins (2011), Francis, Gubb and Robbins (2012), Robbins, Francis and Powell (2012), Barnard and Curry (2012), Randall (2013), Francis, Robbins and Wulff (2013a; 2013b), and Francis, Payne and Robbins (2013).

5. Taking Personality into Account

A major concern of the early studies by Francis' research group concerned exploring the extent to which individual differences in clergy work-related psychological health or burnout could be attributed to personality. The practical relevance of this research question relates to the potential for personality screening to predict vulnerability to burnout and consequently to facilitate protective intervention strategies. From the range of available personality theories, including Cattell's Sixteen Personality Factor model (Cattell, Cattell, & Cattell, 1993) and the Big Five Factor model (Costa & McCrae, 1985), Francis' research group elected to work with the Three Major Dimensions model proposed by Eysenck and operationalised through the Eysenck Personality Questionnaire (Eysenck & Eysenck, 1975), the Eysenck Personality Questionnaire Revised (Eysenck, Eysenck, & Barrett, 1985), and the Eysenck Personality Scales (Eysenck & Eysenck, 1991).

Eysenck's classic dimensional model of personality has its roots in two main principles, one theoretical and one empirical. The theoretical principle is committed to the view that psychological disorders are continuous with normal personality rather than categorically distinct from it. For this reason it makes sense to employ language borrowed from abnormal psychology to define aspects of normal psychology. This view argues that individual differences in personality can be located on defined continua. One individual differs from another in respect of their locations on these defined continua. The empirical principle is committed to the view that the structure of human personality (in terms of the number and definition of the major personality constructs) can be determined by mathematical modelling of the wide range of individual differences in human behaviour. Higher-order factor analysis is employed to identify a small number of orthogonal personality dimensions, in which each dimension may embrace a number of lower-order personality traits (see Eysenck & Eysenck, 1985). In its present form, the Eysenckian dimensional model of personality embraces three major dimensions known by the high scoring poles as extraversion, neuroticism and psychoticism. The Eysenckian family of instruments also includes a lie scale. The definitions of these four scales (extraversion, neuroticism, psychoticism, and the lie scale) will be drawn from the Manual of Eysenck Personality Scales (Eysenck & Eysenck, 1991).

The extraversion scale assesses the continuum from introversion (low scores), through ambiversion, to extraversion (high scores). Eysenck and Eysenck (1991, p. 4) describe typical introverts as quiet, retiring, introspective, reserved and distant except to close friends. Introverts prefer books rather than people. They tend to plan ahead, to distrust impulse, and to be cautious. Introverts do not like excitement, prefer a well-ordered way of life, and approach matters of everyday life with proper seriousness. They tend to keep their feelings under control, avoid aggressive behaviour, and do not lose their temper easily. Introverts are reliable, somewhat pessimistic, and place great value on ethical standards. By way of contrast, typical extraverts are described as sociable and talkative, people who like parties, have many friends, and dislike reading or studying by themselves. Extraverts crave excitement, take chances, and are generally impulsive. They are fond of practical jokes, welcome change, and tend to be carefree and easy-going. Extraverts prefer to keep active, on the move and doing things. They tend not to keep their feelings under control, they are aggressive and lose their temper easily. Extraverts tend to be optimistic, but may not always prove to be reliable.

The neuroticism scale assesses the continuum from emotional stability (low scores), through emotional instability, to incipient neurotic disorders (high scores). Eysenck and Eysenck (1991, pp. 4–5) describe high scorers on the neuroticism scale as anxious, worrying, moody, and frequently depressed. They are likely to sleep badly and to suffer from various psychosomatic disorders. They are overly emotional, react strongly to things, and find it difficult to restore equilibrium after emotionally arousing experiences. Such strong emotional reactions interfere with their proper adjustment, making them react in irrational and sometimes rigid ways. There is a constant preoccupation with things that may go wrong, and a strong emotional reaction of anxiety to those thoughts. Low scorers on the neuroticism scale, by way of contrast, are usually calm, even-tempered, controlled and unworried. They tend to respond emotionally only slowly and generally weakly, and to regain equilibrium quickly.

The psychoticism scale assesses the continuum from tendermindedness (low scores), through toughmindedness, to incipient psychotic disorders (high scores). Eysenck and Eysenck (1991, pp. 5–6) describe high scorers on the psychoticism scale as being solitary, not caring for people, often troublesome, and not fitting in anywhere. They may be cruel and inhumane, lacking in feeling and empathy, and altogether insensitive. They may be hostile to others, and aggressive. They have a liking for odd and unusual things, and a disregard for danger. They like to make fools of other people, and to upset them. Low scorers on the psychoticism scale reflect the opposite of those characteristics.

The lie scale was originally incorporated into the Eysenckian family of personality measures to assess a tendency on the part of some people to "fake good" their responses. Eysenck and Eysenck (1991, pp.

13–14) affirm the continuing usefulness of the lie scale in this regard, but acknowledge that the lie scale also measures some "stable personality factors which may possibly denote some degree of social naivety or conformity" (p. 13).

A number of the early studies by Francis' research group reported on the association between burnout and the Eysenckian dimensional model of personality, including work reported among clergy by Francis and Rutledge (2000), Francis, Louden and Rutledge (2004), Rutledge and Francis (2004), Francis, Turton and Louden (2007), Turton and Francis (2007), and Francis, Hills and Rutledge (2008). These studies agree that the clergy most vulnerable to burnout are introverts who also score high on the neuroticism scale, while the clergy most resilient to burnout are extraverts who score low on the neuroticism scale.

6. Taking Psychological Type into Account

The strength of Eysenck's dimensional model of personality is precisely that it is based on a model of psychopathology intended to identify characteristic precursors of neurotic and psychotic disorder among the general population. Yet at the same time it is not astounding science to demonstrate the association between work-related psychological health and the precursors of neurotic disorder. What is somewhat more interesting is the routine finding that introverts fare less well in ministry than extraverts. According to the model introverts are not less healthy people than extraverts, but simply different people. The conclusion that may be drawn from the finding is that many aspects of the clerical profession may suit extraverts better than introverts.

There is a second model of personality that also includes a measure of introversion and extraversion, but which conceptualises those constructs on a somewhat different basis from the view taken by Eysenck. This is the model of personality known as psychological type theory. More recently, Francis' research group has paid particular attention to the power of psychological type theory to illuminate individual differences in clergy work-related attitudes, behaviours and experiences, including work-related psychological health. This psychological model has also given rise to serious reflection on the theology of individual differences as illustrated by Francis (2005) and Francis and Village (2008).

Psychological type theory has its roots in the pioneering work of Jung (1971) and has been developed and made more widely known through a series of type indicators, including the Myers-Briggs Type Indicator (Myers & McCaulley, 1985), the Keirsey Temperament Sorter (Keirsey & Bates, 1978), and the Francis Psychological Type Scales (Francis, 2005). At its core, psychological type theory identifies four key psychological characteristics and distinguishes between two expressions of each of these characteristics. The first characteristic is concerned with the source of psychological energy, and distinguishes between the two orientations of introversion and extraversion. The second characteristic is concerned with the way in which information is gathered, and distinguishes between the two perceiving functions of sensing and intuition. The third characteristic is concerned with the way in which information is evaluated and the way in which decisions are made, and distinguishes between the two judging functions of thinking and feeling. The fourth characteristic is concerned with the way in which the outside world is approached, and distinguishes between the two attitudes of judging and perceiving.

The orientations are concerned with identifying the sources of psychological energy. In this area, the two discrete types are defined as extraversion and introversion. For extravert types, the source of energy is located in the outer world of people and things. Extraverts are exhausted by large periods of solitude and silence; and they need to re-energize through the stimulation they receive from people and places. Extraverts are talkative people who feel at home in social contexts. For introvert types, the source of energy is located in the inner world of ideas and reflection. Introverts are exhausted by long periods of social engagements and sounds; and they need to re-energise through the stimulation they receive from their own company and tranquillity.

The perceiving processes are concerned with identifying ways in which individuals take in information. For Jung, the perceiving processes were described as irrational because they were not concerned with data evaluation, but simply with data gathering. In this area, the two discrete types are defined as sensing and intuition. For sensing types, the preferred way of perceiving is through the five senses. Sensers are motivated by facts, details and information. They build up to the big picture slowly by focusing first on the component parts. They are more comfortable in the present moment than in exploring future possibilities. They are realistic and practical people. For intuitive types, the preferred way of perceiving is through their imagination. Intuitives are motivated by theories, ideas and connections. They begin with the big picture and gradually turn their attention to the component parts.

They are more comfortable planning the future than making do with the present. They are inspirational and visionary people.

The judging processes are concerned with identifying ways in which individuals evaluate information. For Jung, the judging processes were described as the rational processes because they were concerned with data evaluation and with decision-making. In this area, the two discrete types are defined as thinking and feeling. For thinking types, the preferred way of judging is through objective analysis and dispassionate logic. They are concerned with the proper running of systems and organizations and put such strategic issues first. They are logical and fair-minded people who appeal to the God of justice. For feeling types, the preferred way of judging is through subjective evaluation and personal involvement. They are concerned with the good relationships between people and put such interpersonal issues first. They are humane and warm-hearted people who appeal to the God of mercy.

The attitudes (often more fully expressed as the "attitudes toward the outer world") are concerned with identifying which of the two processes (judging or perceiving) individuals prefer to use in the outer world. In this area, the two discrete types are defined by the name of the preferred process, either judging or perceiving. For judging types, their preferred judging function (either thinking or feeling) is employed in their outer world. Because their outer world is where the rational, evaluating, judging or decision-making process is deployed, judging types appear to others to be well-organized, decisive people. For perceiving types, their preferred perceiving function (either sensing or intuition) is employed in their outer world. Because their outer world is where the irrational, data-gathering process is deployed, perceiving types appear to others to be laid-back, flexible, even disorganized people.

Working within the context of practical theology, pastoral theology, and empirical theology, a series of studies published over the past twenty years has profiled the psychological type characteristics of men and women working in pastoral ministry within various churches in the United Kingdom, as illustrated by studies conducted among: clergy within the Church of Wales (Francis, Payne & Jones, 2001; Francis, Littler & Robbins, 2010), clergy within the Church of England (Francis, Craig, Whinney, Tilley & Slater, 2007; Francis, Robbins, Duncan & Whinney, 2010; Village, 2011; Francis, Robbins, & Whinney, 2011; Francis & Holmes, 2011; Francis, Robbins & Jones, 2012; Francis & Village, 2012; Village, 2013), ministers within the Methodist Church (Burton, Francis, & Robbins, 2010), ministers within the Free Churches (Francis,

Whinney, Burton & Robbins, 2011), priests within the Roman Catholic Church (Craig, Duncan & Francis, 2006), lead elders within the Newfrontiers network of churches (Francis, Gubb & Robbins, 2009), and leaders within the Apostolic Networks (Kay, Francis, & Robbins, 2011).

7. Work-Related Psychological Health and Psychological Type

Early research exploring the connection between work-related psychological health and psychological type was reviewed by Reid (1999), who drew together four unpublished doctoral dissertations and one published study which had assessed the relationship between psychological type and scores recorded on the Maslach Burnout Inventory. The consistent finding across four of these five studies was that individuals with a preference for introversion appeared to be more prone to burnout than individuals with a preference for extraversion. Later findings reported by Myers, McCaulley, Quenk and Hammer (1998, p. 238) confirmed that introverts recorded significantly higher scores than extraverts on the emotional exhaustion scale and on the depersonalisation scale.

Building on this earlier research, a series of seven recent studies have examined the connection between psychological type and work-related psychological health among different groups of clergy. All seven studies assessed work-related psychological health using the two measures of emotional exhaustion and satisfaction in ministry proposed by the Francis Burnout Inventory (Francis, Kaldor, Robbins & Castle, 2005). All seven studies assessed psychological type by means of the Francis Psychological Type Scales (Francis, 2005). These seven studies were conducted among 748 clergy serving in the Presbyterian Church (USA) by Francis, Wulff and Robbins (2008), among 3,715 clergy from Australia, England and New Zealand by Francis, Robbins, Kaldor and Castle (2009), among 521 clergy serving in rural ministry in the Church of England by Brewster, Francis, and Robbins (2011), among 874 clergywomen serving in the Church of England by Robbins and Francis (2010), among 134 lead elders within the Newfrontiers network of churches serving in the United Kingdom by Francis, Gubb and Robbins (2012), among 212 Australian clergywomen drawn from 14 denominations or streams of churches by Robbins, Francis and Powell (2012), and among 266 clergymen serving in the Church in Wales by Francis, Payne and Robbins (2013).

In terms of emotional exhaustion, all seven studies reported significantly higher scores recorded by introverts than by extraverts. Four of the seven studies also reported significantly higher scores recorded by thinking types than by feeling types. One of the seven studies reported significantly higher scores recorded by perceiving types than by judging types. In terms of satisfaction in ministry, six of the seven studies reported significantly higher scores recorded by extraverts than by introverts. Four of the seven studies also reported significantly higher scores recorded by feeling types than by thinking types. Three of the seven studies reported significantly higher scores recorded by intuitive types than by sensing types. The clearest message from these findings is that extraverted feeling types fare better than introverted thinking types.

8. *Taking Personal Factors into Account*

Studies undertaken by Francis' research group, employing either the modified form of the Maslach Burnout Inventory or the Francis Burnout Inventory, focussed on examining the effect of a range of personal, professional, or lifestyle factors as individual differences in levels of burnout. The following examples illustrate this.

Francis and Turton (2004a) tested the thesis that regular engagement with supervision designed to encourage reflective practice in ministry is related to better levels of work-related psychological health. Drawing on data provided by 1,276 Anglican clergymen and employing multiple regression to control for individual differences in age and personality, the study found that supervision was unrelated to levels of emotional exhaustion or depersonalisation, but associated with higher levels of satisfaction in ministry. This finding supports the beneficial effect of disciplined engagement with supervision.

Francis, Turton, and Louden (2007) tested the thesis that companion animals (specifically cats and dogs) may contribute to the work-related psychological health of Catholic parochial clergy and reduce levels of burnout. This thesis was based on the considerable literature that has identified social benefits, medical benefits and psychological benefits associated with companion animals across diverse populations. Using multiple regression models to control for individual differences in age and personality, the data indicated that, contrary to expectation, no psychological benefit accrued from owning a cat, while ownership of a dog was associated with statistically significant (but very small) increases in two aspects of professional burnout (emotional exhaustion and depersonalisation). These findings suggest that current pressures among Catholic parochial clergy in England and Wales are so great that having a dog within the presbytery adds to the burden rather than providing recreational relief.

Turton and Francis (2007) tested the thesis that confidence in prayer is fundamental to maintaining a good level of work-related psychological health among Anglican parochial clergy and that low confidence in prayer is associated with professional burnout. Data were provided by a sample of 1,278 male stipendiary parochial clergy working in the Church of England who completed the modified Maslach Burnout Inventory and the short-form Revised Eysenck Personality Questionnaire together with a scale assessing clergy attitude toward prayer. The results indicated that a positive attitude toward prayer was associated with lower levels of emotional exhaustion, lower levels of depersonalisation and higher levels of personal accomplishment. These findings were interpreted in light of a growing understanding of the psychological role of prayer in human functioning.

Francis, Robbins, and Wulff (2013a) tested the effectiveness of support strategies in reducing professional burnout among clergy serving in the Presbyterian Church (USA). Drawing on data provided by 744 clergy and employing multiple regression to control for individual differences in age and personality, they explored the impact of five support strategies (defined as spiritual director, mentor, peer group, study leave and sabbatical) on the two scales of the Francis Burnout Inventory (assessing satisfaction in ministry and emotional exhaustion in ministry). They found that none of the five strategies served as predictors of lower levels of emotional exhaustion in ministry, but two of them served as predictors of enhanced satisfaction in ministry, namely having a mentor and taking study leave.

9. Taking Contextual Factors into Account

Studies undertaken by Francis' research group, employing either the modified form of the Maslach Burnout Inventory or the Francis Burnout Inventory, examined the effect of a range of contextual factors on individual differences in levels of clergy burnout. One recurrent contextual theme concerns the distinctive experience of those engaged in rural ministry.

In an initial study, Francis and Rutledge (2000) drew on a survey of 1,071 full-time stipendiary clergymen serving in the Church of England to explore whether rural clergy were either more or less vulnerable to burnout than clergy serving in other contexts. This study, using the Maslach Burnout Inventory, employed multiple regression to control for age, marital status and personality. After these factors had been taken into account, the data indicated that rural clergy have a lower sense of personal accomplishment than comparable clergy working in other types of parishes, but that they suffer neither from higher levels of emotional exhaustion nor from higher levels of depersonalisation.

Research among rural clergy was then continued in a sequence of studies led by Christine Brewster. Drawing on data provided by 521 Anglican clergy serving in rural benefices of at least three churches, Brewster, Francis, and Robbins (2011) found that rural clergy reported both high levels of emotional exhaustion in ministry and high levels of satisfaction in ministry. For example, item endorsements for the Scale of Emotional Exhaustion in Ministry revealed that exactly half (50%) of the rural clergy in the survey felt drained by fulfilling their ministry roles, and just under half of these clergy (48%) found themselves frustrated in their attempts to accomplish tasks which are important to them. Item endorsements for the Satisfaction in Ministry Scale reported that almost four out of every five rural clergy in the survey (79%) gained a great deal of personal satisfaction from working with people in their current ministry, and that the same proportion (79%) felt that their pastoral ministry was exercising a positive influence on people's lives.

In a second study, Brewster (2012) conducted in-depth interviews with ten rural clergy in order to identify the aspects of ministry that they regarded as generating work-related stress. From these ten interviews, 84 distinctive statements emerged after removing duplicates. Brewster organized these 84 statements into 11 themes conceptually defined as: role conflict, logistics, administration, multi-tasking, anxiety, isolation, irritation, frustration, developmental issues, issues of commitment, and parish conflicts. These 84 statements were then incorporated into a questionnaire survey that was completed by 722 rural clergy. On the basis of the replies received to the questionnaire, Brewster was able to quantify the frequency with which each of these 84 sources of work-related stress was experienced.

In a third study, Francis and Brewster (2012) returned to the data provided by the questionnaire survey to test the specific thesis that the notion of time-related over-extension could draw together a number of the key sources of work-related stress specified by the clergy. The notion of time-related over-extension has its roots in a number of the broader studies examining clergy stress that consistently cite the difficulties generated by a profession that lacks clearly defined boundaries, that embraces multiple and often conflicting expectations, and that often blurs the distinction between work and family life (see, for example, Sanford 1982; Coate, 1989; Fletcher, 1990; Kirk & Leary, 1994; Davey, 1995; Warren, 2002; Burton & Burton, 2009). In short, there is too much to do and not enough time in which to do it. Francis and Brewster (2012) selected from the 84 sources of work-related stress included in the questionnaire survey those items that mapped conceptually into the notion of time-related over-extension. From this set of items identified on conceptual grounds, factor analyses and correlational analyses selected the 16 items that best cohered into a homogeneous unidimensional scale to produce the Brewster Index of Stress from Time-Related Over-Extension (BISTROX). The BISTROX generated an alpha coefficient of .90, a highly satisfactory indicator of internal consistency reliability.

Francis and Brewster (2012) then explored the extent to which individual differences in the experience of work-related stress from time-related over-extension were related to personal factors (sex and age), environmental factors (number of churches), psychological factors (extraversion and neuroticism), and theological factors (liberal or conservative, Catholic or evangelical, and charismatic or non-charismatic). The data demonstrated that personal and psychological factors were much more important than theological and environmental ones.

In a fourth study, Francis, Laycock, and Brewster (2015) employed factor analysis to clarify and distinguish between the main sources of stress experienced by rural Anglican clergy serving in multi-parish benefices. Data provided by 613 clergy (151 women and 462 men) who rated 84 potential sources of stress generated five distinct factors best characterised as the burden of administration, the burden of presence, the burden of isolation, the burden of distance, and the burden of visibility. Personality and age were stronger predictors of the levels of stress caused by these burdens than were sex, contextual factors or theological factors. Of these five burdens, the most damaging to the overall work-related psychological health of rural clergy was the burden of isolation and the least damaging was the burden of distance. The authors argued that clearer knowledge about the differential effects of different sources of stress on the work-related psychological health of rural clergy may lead to more targeted and more effective intervention.

Another core contextual factor explored by Francis' research group concerns the extent to which serving multiple churches may be detrimental to clergy work-related psychological health. Francis, Robbins, and Wulff (2013b) examined this issue by drawing on data provided by 735 clergy serving in the Presbyterian Church (USA) who completed the Francis Burnout Inventory. After controlling for individual differences in age and personality, the data demonstrate that clergy serving multiple churches in this context experienced no statistically significant differences in their susceptibility to burnout, either in terms of level of emotional exhaustion or in terms of level of satisfaction in ministry compared with colleagues serving just one church.

10. Conclusion and Application

After nearly thirty years of empirical research in the science of clergy work-related psychological health, two main conclusions can be drawn from the body of evidence that has emerged, which are of major importance for religious leadership.

The first conclusion concerns the conceptualisation and measurement of clergy work-related psychological health. Drawing on the notion of balanced affect, the Francis Burnout Inventory offers a model that is theoretically coherent, empirically robust, and practically useful. In essence, the notion of balanced affect suggests that positive affect is able to offset some of the effects of negative affect. While it may not be easy for clergy to reduce their exposure to those factors that generate negative affect (emotional exhaustion in ministry), it may be somewhat easier for them to increase their exposure to those factors that generate positive affect (satisfaction in ministry). At the same time, those responsible for the management, pastoral care and continuing professional development of clergy may be in a good position to help individual clergy to identify and maximise ways of enhancing positive affect.

The second conclusion concerns the relative weight given to psychological factors (like personality), personal factors (like age and sex), professional and lifestyle factors (like supervision and prayer), and contextual factors (like the location of the work). The consistent finding across the range of studies is that psychological factors provide the strongest prediction. This is important information for those responsible for the management, pastoral care and continuing professional development of clergy to take seriously, but not to misuse. If routine psychological assessment were applied at the time of selecting candidates for ministry, this information would not only identify the more vulnerable candidates but also facilitate the targeted intervention of appropriate protective strategies. Such psychological assessment would be no more sinister or threatening than health checks that in turn lead to reliable healthy lifestyle recommendations.

Recognition of the importance of psychological factors in predicting vulnerability to poor work-related psychological health leads to a further practical recommendation. Such recognition adds weight to the importance of education and formation programmes designed to enhance self-awareness concerning the ways in which individual differences in personality and psychological health may impact how clergy exercise and experience their ministry. How such education and formation programmes work in practice has been illustrated in a series of recent publications from Francis' research group (see Francis & Smith, 2012, 2013, 2015, 2016; Smith & Francis, 2015).

Chapter Eight

Lay Leadership in the Church of England: A Study in an Urban Diocese

David W. Lankshear

1. *Introduction*

Leadership of individual churches or small groups of churches within the Church of England is a shared responsibility between the priest(s) appointed to the church and the laity for whom it is their home church. The priests have been called to this ministry, undergone a selection and training process, and then been ordained into the role. They may be paid or volunteers. The laity are assumed to worship at the church because it is close to where they live and it exists in part to meet their spiritual and pastoral needs. From their number some are chosen to fill a range of leadership roles. There is significant research on the leadership provided by the priests but almost no research on the leadership provided by the laity. This chapter will argue that such a gap in the research should be addressed.

For the purposes of this paper a narrow definition of "lay leadership" will be used, confining it to specific identified roles in churches or parishes within the Church of England. The offices to which these roles are attached are considered sufficiently important for the names of the office holders to be published by the diocese each year in the annual listing of parish details in the diocesan directory or yearbook. A broader definition of lay leadership would encompass a wide range of roles and behaviours, including the moral and pastoral leadership or leadership exercised by their influence on events and decisions within the life of the church, despite the fact that they hold no formal office in the church at all.

Within the organization of each benefice in the Church of England, there is provision for a variety of formal roles that must or may be undertaken by lay people as part of their contribution to the "lay leadership" of the church. Some of these roles require those aspiring to them to undergo a process of selection and training. For some of the roles that must be undertaken by laity, the process required is one of election at an annual church meeting or of appointment by the Parochial Church Council (PCC).

Those who take on roles which require training usually undertake tasks associated with the leadership of worship, the nurture of church members in the faith (including the young in faith) or the pastoral care in the parish. For the purposes of this study, these people will be divided into "Readers" or "Pastoral Assistants," which are the two titles for such post holders used in the diocese where the study that forms the basis of this paper was undertaken. The elected roles included those of Church Warden, PCC Secretary and PCC Treasurer. People holding any of these posts are considered of sufficient importance to have their contact details listed in the parish details in the Annual Yearbook published by almost every Church of England Diocese (e.g. Diocese of Southwark, 2012).

Reader
Reader ministry is the only lay ministry in the Church of England that is authorized by the Canons (the laws) of the church. The role of "Reader" is well established nationally in the Church of England. As well as an established pattern of support in every diocese, there is also a national framework for the support of this ministry. The Church of England website describes the role of Readers as preaching, teaching and leading services. They may read the lessons, pray, administer the bread and wine, take communion to the sick and housebound, and publish the banns of marriage in the absence of a priest. They may conduct funerals, visit people in their homes, help with baptism, confirmation and marriage preparation, and offer such other assistance as the Bishop directs. There are 10,200 active Readers in the Church of England working alongside less than 10,000 paid ordained clergy (https://www.churchofengland.org/). For a full exploration of the role of the reader, see Rowling and Gooder (2011).

Pastoral Assistant
The identification of people for this role and their training are matters for each diocese, and for the reasons already indicated, it seems logical to use a description of this role taken from a Southwark Diocesan publication. The ministry is supported by the diocese, but there is no national structure in place to provide support and guidance. The emphasis of their role is on the caring side of the church's work, and there-

fore Pastoral Assistants may be involved in a wide variety of pastoral roles, for example, developing caring projects started by local churches, co-ordinating pastoral care teams, as members of chaplaincy teams or representing the Church in caring agencies in the wider community (The Bridge, 2001).

Church Warden
Church wardens are the principal lay officers of a parish and are officers of the bishop. Their duties include: representing the laity and co-operating with the incumbent; encouraging the parishioners in the practice of religion and promoting unity and peace among them; maintaining order and decency in the church and churchyard and ownership of the plate, ornaments and other moveable goods of the church. They are ex-officio members of the PCC. (For further explanation of the role of church wardens, see (Russell, 2000).) The role has a longer history than that of "reader" within the church's structures. There are normally two for each parish except that where a parish has more than one parish church, two wardens are appointed for each church, although all are wardens of the parish. Church wardens are elected by a parish meeting, at which any parishioner or electoral roll member may vote and which must be held on or before April 30th each year.

PCC Secretary
Every parish church or benefice must have a church council, usually referred to as the Parochial Church Council (PCC). The person appointed to be Secretary of the PCC has the task of keeping the records of the council's meetings and transactions, dealing with correspondence related to the council's work and working with the minister, the wardens and the treasurer to facilitate and enact the decisions and work of the council. Where a parish has a paid administrator, some or all of these tasks may be undertaken by the administrator.

The PCC's functions are to co-operate with the minister in the mission of the parish to the area that it serves, to make representations on behalf of the parish to the church as a whole, and to interpret policy and proposals from the wider church into parish practice in all areas except church doctrine (Parochial Church Councils (Powers) Measure, 1956).

PCC Treasurer
The Church of England website provides a resource for office holders on PCC accountability. In the introductory chapter it lays out the

PCC's financial responsibilities. The PCC Treasurer is the officer of the PCC responsible for ensuring that these are fulfilled on a day-to-day basis. As the PCC has a defined legal role as a charity for all its financial affairs, the Treasurer as its principal financial officer is responsible for ensuring that all the PCC's financial affairs are managed efficiently and for the purposes for which they have been accrued. A full statement of such responsibilities may be found on the Church of England website. The tasks of the PCC Treasurer can be onerous and time-consuming, but where a parish employs an administrator, some or all of the tasks may be shared with the administrator.

It will be apparent from the above brief descriptions that the roles and duties of these lay leaders are significant and have the potential to enhance or detract from the overall mission and ministry of the parish or benefice. Therefore, it is surprising that so little attention seems to be paid to these post holders in the research literature. Certain obvious questions arise. Is there evidence that supports the argument that these posts and the people holding them should be the subject of further research?

Within the Church of England, where most studies suggest that around 65% of attenders are female (e.g. Lankshear and Francis, 2009) and much attention has been paid to the introduction of women priests in 1992 and women bishops in 2014, it seems reasonable to explore the gender balance of those holding these lay offices in the church and whether this makes a difference to the effectiveness of the church's ministry. There is a further question about the meaning of "gender balance" in that it is generally assumed in the literature that men and women should be equally represented, but in a church where almost two-thirds of the congregation are women, would not an appropriate "gender balance" in leadership roles reflect this? Therefore, are there instances where the balance of post holders more accurately represents the balance of men and women in the pews?

The deployment of priests is a matter for the diocese, but Readers and Pastoral Assistants are directly recruited from the parish in which they will serve. Therefore, there is an issue about how far these trained lay people are being recruited and subsequently work in parishes where there are large congregations or where there are significant levels of deprivation or privilege.

Within the church more widely, much attention has been paid to factors that contribute to church growth. Does the presence of Readers or Pastoral Assistants in a church contribute to its growth? Does the gender of the post holders have an impact? Is there an impact on church growth from the Church Wardens, PCC Secretary or Treasurer?

In order to answer these questions fully, specific adaptations to some of the research tools and techniques currently in use would need to be made to ensure that the holders of these different posts were identified and their views, practices and contributions to church life compared to churchgoers more generally. However, before such work is undertaken, it is important to establish that there are issues in need of such detailed exploration and which might repay the effort involved. In reporting results from a project conducted in the Anglican diocese of Southwark, this chapter will suggest that the issues do exist and would repay further investigation.

2. *The Diocese of Southwark*

The Anglican diocese of Southwark covers most of London south of the River Thames and some of the towns and villages on the southern fringe of the Greater London area. It has a population of 2.7 million people served by 365 Anglican churches. In 2008 it initiated a research project working with the Religions and Education Research Unit of Warwick University, which had as its prime task exploring the reasons behind trends in church attendance and membership within the diocese. Initial reports on this project were made to each Episcopal Area as the work in that area was completed (Lankshear and Francis, 2009, 2011 and 2012).

The principle techniques employed by the project team were quantitative and made use of questionnaires and the re-analysis of data already held by the diocese, which had been collected for administrative purposes. This second source made it possible to focus on the identity of the office holders and their contribution to church growth. The office holders were identified through the entries in the Diocesan Year Books for 2009, 2010 and 2011.

Church growth was measured by taking the recorded figures collected for "Usual Sunday Attendance" at each church. "Usual Sunday Attendance" is established each year by requiring churches to submit a return showing the numbers of adults and children attending their church on each of the Sundays in October. The mean of these Sunday attendances is then used to establish the "Usual Sunday Attendance." The project collated these figures for the years 2000 to 2010 inclusive and took the mean of the first three years of this period and the mean for the last three years of this period. These two consolidated means were then compared. If the mean for 2008–2010 exceeded the mean for 2000–2002 by 10% or more, these churches were defined as "growing churches." If the mean for 2008–2010 was within 10% of the mean for 2000–2002, these churches were defined as "static." If the mean for 2008–2010 was 10% or more below that for 2000–2002, the churches were defined as "declining" churches.

3. Results

Of regular adult church attenders in this diocese, 66% are female and 34% male; this ratio will be used when seeking to understand whether the lay post holders reflect the adult membership of the church.

Readers

There were 362 readers licensed to work in parishes within the diocese, of whom 200 were male (55.2% of all readers) and 162 were female (44.8% of all readers). These figures show that the balance between the sexes amongst those serving as readers does not match the gender balance among those who attend church. With the data collected for this project, it is possible to explore three factors which might be influencing this imbalance. The first is the sex of the parish priest. Of the 352 parishes, 1% was vacant, 79% were led by a male priest and 20% were led by a female priest. While 36% of parishes led by a male priest had at least one male reader, 41% of parishes led by a female priest had at least one male reader. This does not represent a statistically significant difference. There is even less difference when it comes to parishes that have at least one female reader as there is only 0.4% difference between the figures for those parishes led by male and female priests. However, it seems that in this diocese, where a female priest leads the parish there is a greater likelihood of there also being a reader present. In parishes led by male priests, 54% have at least one reader, but in parishes led by a female priest, 67% have at least one reader (the difference is significant at the .05 level).

Given that pressure might arise from lack of choice in smaller parishes or the dynamics for new ministry in growing parishes and the reduction of motivation in declining parishes, these become the second and third factors. The second factor explores the differences between churches with congregations of under two hundred people (64.1% of all churches in the diocese) and churches with congregations of two hundred or more (35.1%). In those parishes with over two hundred in the congregation, 47% had at least one male reader present, while in smaller parishes 31% had at least one male reader (significant at the .01 level). Amongst those parishes with over two hundred in the congregation, 40% had at least one female reader, but in smaller congregations this proportion fell to 32%. While the difference among parishes with female readers was not statistically significant, it is logical to expect that larger congregations are more likely to have readers drawn from their number than smaller congregations.

Of the churches 41% were "growing parishes," 30% were "static parishes" and 29% were "declining parishes." When growing parishes were compared with those that were not growing and declining parishes were compared with those that were not declining, there were no statistically significant differences between the distribution of male or female readers.

The diocese works with deprivation statistics derived from the national census and calculated by the levels of deprivation or privilege found in each parish area. The diocese has 162 churches in parishes that are broadly defined as deprived, 110 churches within parishes broadly defined as privileged, and 85 which are so mixed as to be neither deprived nor privileged. When privileged parishes are compared with all other parishes, male readers are present in 46% of privileged parishes and 33% of other parishes (significant at the .05 level). The figures for female readers are 36% in privileged parishes and 35% in other parishes. When deprived parishes are compared with all other parishes, male readers are present in 26% of deprived parishes compared with being present in 46% of all others (significant at the .001 level). The figures for female readers are 32% in deprived parishes and 36% in all other parishes.

These figures suggest that amongst readers in the Southwark diocese, there is still an imbalance between the sexes, both in overall numbers and in their distribution among the parishes. Male readers seem to be more frequently found in larger parishes and in "privileged" parishes. There were no significant differences in the presence of readers within growing or declining parishes.

Pastoral Assistants
There were 220 pastoral assistants working in the churches in the diocese, of whom 32 (14.5%) were male and 188 (85.5%) were female. Pastoral assistants receive a shorter training than readers, and their ministry

is supported by the diocese, but not by the church nationally. There are so few male pastoral assistants that this section will focus mainly on the deployment of female pastoral assistants and only report on their male colleagues where the situation is different. Of parishes led by a female priest, 44% benefit from female pastoral assistants, whereas 33% of parishes with a male priest have female pastoral assistants (significant at the .05 level); for the presence of male pastoral assistants, the gender of the parish priest made no difference.

Female pastoral assistants are more likely to be found in churches with more than two hundred members of the congregation, where 48% have at least one, than in smaller congregations, where only 35% have one (significant at the .05 level). This difference is marked among female pastoral assistants but is not significant when it comes to male pastoral assistants. There is no significant difference in the deployment of pastoral assistants where the parishes are classified as growing, but there is a difference when those congregations that have declined are compared with ones that have not declined or are growing. In that case, 49% of declining churches have a pastoral assistant whereas only 36% of parishes that are not declining have a pastoral assistant (significant at the .05 level). This does not demonstrate a causal relationship, merely an association of two items of data. Indeed, it could be argued that in a declining congregation, there may be circumstances that would particularly benefit from the ministry of a pastoral assistant.

In terms of deprived or privileged parishes, there are no significant differences between the rates of deployment of pastoral assistants.

It is clear from these results that pastoral assistants in this diocese are overwhelmingly female and they are more likely to be found in the larger parishes that are showing some decline in numbers. Perhaps these are parishes where the dynamic is more about maintenance and sustaining the current congregation than in bringing new members into the fellowship.

The posts of reader and pastoral assistant both involve initial periods of training for members of the laity who volunteer for these roles. The roles of Secretary of the Parochial Church Council, Treasurer of the Parochial Church Council and Church Warden are taken on by people who volunteer or stand for election at the annual church meeting. There is no direct training before taking on the role, and while some may have life experience or training that prepares them for the post or may have served as a deputy prior to taking on the role, there are no requirements. The other major difference is that every parish must have these posts or at least their duties undertaken by someone. Occasionally, a reader or pastoral assistant may also hold one of these posts, but that is not standard practice. Therefore, this section will not compare the situation of churches with or without church wardens but will explore the balance in sex of the different post holders and whether the posts are held by four distinct people or whether individuals are holding more than one of these posts.

The Sex of Post Holders
Of all churches in the diocese of Southwark, 82% have a female secretary of the PCC, and 69% have a male treasurer. In 58% of churches, there are both male and female church wardens, in 24% all the wardens are male, and in 18% all the wardens are female. It is likely that in previous generations, only the secretary of the PCC would have been female, and so the current position in this diocese may represent considerable progress in the acknowledgement of the gifts and skills of women and the importance of according all people equal value; however, there is clearly still progress to be made, particularly if the gender balance within current congregations is to be reflected in those holding these formal posts. It might be argued that those congregations most likely to lack adequate resources amongst their male members would be the first to look for women to take on these roles. It might also be argued that the advent of women priests would encourage women to apply for election and for congregations to vote for female candidates. In order to explore these possibilities, each of the roles will be considered separately in terms of the sex of the parish priest, the size of the congregation, the level of deprivation in the parish, and the growth or decline in the number of members of the congregation.

Sex of the Parish Priest
Table 1 shows the percentage of churches with male or female post holders in these roles compared with the sex of the priest in charge of the parish. None of the differences shown are statistically significant.

Table 1. *Elected lay post holders and sex of the parish priest*

	Male priest	Female priest
Churches with a male secretary	20.2%	11.4%
Churches with a female secretary	79.8%	88.6%
Churches with a male treasurer	69.3%	70.0%
Churches with a female treasurer	30.7%	30.0%

Churches with all male church wardens	24.2%	25.7%
Churches with all female wardens	17.0%	21.4%
Churches with both male and female church wardens	58.8%	52.9%

From the data the sex of the priest in charge does not appear to have a direct influence on the sex of the lay post holders. It may be that other factors within the setup of the parish have more influence.

Congregation Size

Table 2 shows the percentage of churches with male or female post holders compared with the size of the congregation.

Table 2. *Elected lay post holders and size of the congregation*

	Churches with a congregation of under 200	Churches with a congregation of 200 or more
Churches with a male secretary	19.9%	16.4%
Churches with a female secretary	80.1%	83.6%
Churches with a male treasurer	66.4%	73.8%
Churches with a female treasurer	33.6%	26.2%
Churches with all male church wardens	25.2%	23.0%
Churches with all female wardens	20.4%	12.3%
Churches with both male and female church wardens	54.4%	64.8%

The differences in the percentages of congregations with all female church wardens and ones with wardens of both sexes are significant at the .05 level, suggesting that one of the factors that could be influencing these decisions is the size of the overall talent pool within congregations. A larger study involving a greater number of churches might enable this analysis to be sustained for churches with congregations significantly smaller than two hundred.

Deprived and Privileged Congregations

Table 3 shows the percentage of congregations that are serving deprived areas with male or female post holders.

The data in this table referring to PCC secretaries does meet the test for significance at the .05 level, suggesting that where a church is serving an area of deprivation, this may help people to see beyond tradition gender roles to those people within the congregation who have the talent and the time to fulfil the tasks needed in the service of the parish.

Table 3. *Elected lay post holders and deprived congregations*

	Churches serving a deprived area	Churches serving other areas
Churches with a male secretary	22.8%	14.9%
Churches with a female secretary	77.2%	85.1%
Churches with a male treasurer	64.8%	72.3%
Churches with a female treasurer	35.2%	27.7%
Churches with all male church wardens	21.5%	26.7%
Churches with all female wardens	21.0%	14.9%
Churches with both male and female church wardens	57.4%	58.5%

While the data applying to the role of Treasurer is suggestive of the same factor coming into play, it does not meet the test of significance for this size of data set.

Table 4 shows the percentage of congregations in privileged areas that have male or female post holders.

Table 4. *Elected lay post holders and privileged congregations*

	Churches serving a privileged area	Churches serving other areas
Churches with a male secretary	19.0%	17.3%
Churches with a female secretary	81.0%	82.7%
Churches with a male treasurer	65.2%	77.3%
Churches with a female treasurer	34.8%	22.7%
Churches with all male church wardens	22.7%	25.1%
Churches with all female wardens	10.0%	21.1%
Churches with both male and female church wardens	67.3%	53.8%

With respect to treasurers, the data in table 4 meets the test of significance at the .05 level. Perhaps in congregations serving privileged areas there are sufficient women with financial qualifications and experience to help congregations understand that it is the particular gifts of members of the congregation that are important and not the sex of the person when choosing someone to undertake this role. In respect of church wardens, the data suggest that churches in privileged areas are more likely to have church wardens of both sexes and least likely to have an all-female team. Taken with the data in table 2, this suggests that where there is a good pool of talent, there is the greatest likelihood of having both male and female wardens.

Declining and Growing Congregations

Table 5 shows the percentage of congregations where numbers are declining that have male or female post holders.

Table 5. *Elected lay post holders and declining congregations*

	Churches with a declining congregation	Churches with a congregation that is not declining
Churches with a male secretary	18.9%	18.2%
Churches with a female secretary	81.1%	81.8%
Churches with a male treasurer	68.4%	69.8%
Churches with a female treasurer	31.6%	30.2%
Churches with all male church wardens	21.7%	25.5%
Churches with all female wardens	23.6%	14.9%
Churches with both male and female church wardens	54.7%	59.3%

There are no statistically significant differences shown in this table except that the figures for all female teams of church wardens are different at the .05 level in the direction that supports the suggestion that where there is a sufficient pool of talent, the preference in most congregations is for a mixed team of wardens.

Table 6 shows the percentage of congregations that are growing that have male or female post holders.

Table 6. *Elected lay post holders and growing congregations*

	Churches with a growing congregation	Churches with a congregation that is not growing
Churches with a male Secretary	18.8%	18.2%
Churches with a female Secretary	81.2%	81.8%
Churches with a male Treasurer	69.2%	67.4%
Churches with a female Treasurer	30.8%	32.6%
Churches with all male Church Wardens	21.7%	25.5%
Churches with all female wardens	14.6%	19.7%
Churches with both male and female church wardens	61.1%	56.3%

The data in table 6 suggests differences that would support the proposal that given a sufficient pool of talent, a congregation will tend to elect a mixed group of church wardens, but this fails to meet the test for significance within the context of this data set.

There are two other issues that should be considered for the results from the Southwark diocese. First, in some parishes there are vacancies where no one has been found to take on these roles, and in others one person is taking on more than one of the roles. It might be assumed that these issues are associated with smaller, deprived or declining congregations. The failure to fill all these formal lay posts with different members of the congregation is associated with deprived parishes (significant at the .05 level), and the posts are most likely to be filled in privileged parishes (significant at the .05 level). But there is no significant difference when either congregation size or its growth or decline is considered.

Second, the balance between the sexes of the church wardens was examined because there are at least two wardens in every church. However, there may be differences when the posts of secretary and treasurer to the parochial church council are included. The only difference that emerges is that within privileged parishes, there is more likely to be a balance between the number of men and women holding these posts and less likely to be a majority of female posts holders (both significant at the .05 level).

4. Discussion

Two distinct groups of lay leaders were considered in these results. The first one consists of people who feel a call to serve their local church in one of two forms of ministry. They receive training for this service and are provided with a support network in their role.

Readers undergo more training, and their role is long established within the church. They undertake a longer period of training and benefit from a national support network as well as the one set up in the diocese. The majority of readers in the Southwark diocese are male and more likely to be working in the larger parishes. Male readers are more likely to be serving in parishes that are not deprived. A higher proportion of parishes led by a female priest will have a reader working with them.

Pastoral assistants are trained within the diocese, and the exact definition of their role and responsibility is a matter for the diocese. There is no national network to provide them with support. Within the Southwark diocese, the pastoral assistants are overwhelmingly female and are more common in parishes with a female priest than in parishes with a male priest. They are also more common in larger congregations than smaller ones and in declining congregations than growing ones.

It may be that the differences between the recruitment into these two lay ministries will be seen by some as an example of sexist stereotypes at work; males preach and lead services, females care for the congregation and for the parishioners. Others may point to the fact that pastoral assistants are present in a higher proportion of parishes led by female priests as an indication that female priests identify pastoral gifts in others more readily than male priests and then encourage these people to develop their gifts in the service of the church. Both these ideas are speculation suggested by the data, but given the growing shortage of priests in the Anglican Church, it may be important to ensure that laity capable of taking on leadership roles are encouraged and supported to find the right role for them and to play their full part in the leadership of the church. If there is still some gender stereotyping interfering with this process, then it may be the task of research to reveal this and for the church leadership to take steps to ensure that it does not continue in the future.

The second group of lay leaders are those who are elected to offices within the parish where they regularly worship. Each church should have at least four such office holders, two church wardens, a secretary and a treasurer to the church council. There will also be members of the church council and many other informal roles undertaken by laity that could be classified as leadership, but these four offices are identified by the diocese as the most significant ones as the holders of those offices are listed in the diocesan yearbooks. Most parishes are able to find people to undertake these roles. In the Southwark diocese, perhaps not surprisingly, those parishes serving deprived areas are most likely to struggle to fill the posts or to fill the posts without individuals having to take on more than one of the roles.

In terms of the sex of the post holders, 36% of all parishes in the diocese have the same number of women as men in the team of people holding these posts. This balance is most likely to occur in those parishes defined as privileged. The vast majority of secretaries of the PCC in the Southwark diocese are female, and only in deprived parishes are females slightly less common. Two-thirds of all treasurers are male, but this percentage is reduced in privileged parishes, where it might be assumed that there are a number of female members of the congregations with financial qualifications or experience that enables them to successfully challenge an entrenched tradition. It may be that because there is often a reluctance amongst worshippers to volunteer for this role, this apparent evidence of gender stereotyping is difficult to challenge. Because actual elections for these posts are rare, with the first, perhaps reluctant, volunteer being accepted with relief, the church may be missing out on talent from which it could benefit, because these posts are understood in very traditional terms.

If traditions are hard to change in the posts of secretary and treasurer, there does seem to be a greater flexibility when it comes to church wardens. The most common option is to have a mixed team. A core of parishes of all types opt for an all-male team, while an all-female team seems to be more likely in parishes where the pool of talent may be smaller because of deprivation or congregation size.

This study has focused on a single diocese within the Church of England, which is rather more urban than the majority of dioceses. The project which provides the basis for this study examined church growth and had a congregational survey at its core. It is unfortunate that this survey did not include a question about whether or not the respondent had held any of these posts, but to have included it might have raised issues about the anonymity of the respondents, which had been guaranteed.

5. Conclusions

The introduction to this study posed a number of questions, each of these will be considered in turn.

Is there evidence that supports the argument that these posts and the people holding them should be the subject of further research? Given the data contained in this study, the answer to this question must be yes. Where churches struggle to ensure sufficient professional leadership to meet their needs and therefore become more dependent on the leadership provided by volunteer laity, it may be increasingly important for the research community to study who is involved in the lay leadership of the church, the nature of their contribution, their attitudes, and how they understand their needs in the future.

Within the Church of England, where most studies suggest that around 65% of attenders are female and much attention has been paid to the introduction of women priests, what is the gender balance of those holding these lay offices in the church? The study has drawn attention to some significant gender imbalances among the various posts examined in this study. Evidence has not generally been found to suggest that the gender of the parish priest is having a significant impact in addressing these issues.

The deployment of priests is a matter for the diocese, but readers and pastoral assistants are directly recruited from the parish in which they will serve. Therefore, there is an issue about the extent to which these trained lay people are being recruited and subsequently work in parishes where there are large congregations or where there are significant levels of deprivation or privilege.

There is some evidence that male readers are more likely to be found in larger congregations and in privileged ones, but this is not true of female readers. Pastoral assistants are more likely to be found in large congregations and in declining ones. It may be that the church would benefit from actively seeking ways of encouraging people in smaller congregations to consider whether they have gifts that could be used in these ministries.

Within the church more widely, much attention has been paid to factors that contribute to church growth. Does the presence of readers or pastoral assistants in a church contribute to its growth? Does the gender of the post holders have an impact? Is there an impact on church growth from the church wardens, PCC secretary or treasurer? In this small scale study, the evidence is limited and insufficient to allow any conclusions to be drawn.

This study has significant limitations in terms of its size and its capacity to address the range of issues that might be relevant, but it could provide the stimulus for further research into lay leadership within churches that could be a source of data to enable churches to make realistic plans for a future in which professional ministerial resources may be at a premium.

Chapter Nine

Youth Leadership in Urban South-African Contexts

Shantelle Weber

1. Introduction

> "Leadership is one of the most vexing questions of our times. Societies will not always have great leaders. Good leaders will do for most of the time. However, given the daily reports of corruption, one begins to fear that we face the danger of lowering the bar of leadership even lower. We may now end up with individuals who are available to lead simply because they haven't done anything wrong. It would then take another generation to move from those leaders by default to good leaders to great leaders." (Mangcu, 2014, p. 118)

Xolela Mangcu is Professor of Sociology at the University of Cape Town. In his book, the *Arrogance of Power*, he reflects on the state of political leadership in South Africa and calls on youth in this country to take their leadership positions seriously. He cautions these youth in a context where authentic leadership is lacking. The reality of leadership positions being filled based on who is available is not a challenge exclusive to civil society. Practical theologian Mark DeVries (2008, pp. 28–29) cautions against churches choosing youth leaders as the next superstar in line. By superstar he refers to the next available person who will rescue the youth ministry and be all things to all people. He adds that "(m)ost young youth workers step into ministry ill-equipped to walk through the political minefields that are part of everyday church." Many times youth leaders are assigned to leadership without being equipped or even spiritually mature enough to accomplish the varied tasks they are called to. From a Catholic perspective, Arthur Canales (2014, p. 24) argues that "…authentic Christian leadership for youth ministry is much more than teaching young people about pastoral skills, but requires a lifestyle that empowers adolescents to become responsible and genuine leaders in their schools, churches, neighbourhoods, and communities." He adds that the term leadership is being misused and confused with learning the fundamentals and principles of youth ministry. This reflects that the challenge is not unique to any one denomination. I am of the opinion that one of the core reasons why youth leaders do not live up to the superstar expectations imposed on them is because churches have underinvested in their youth ministries (DeVries, 2008). Historical accounts of the church often refer to youth as excluded from faith discourses, only to be included at a later age (Ward, 1996, pp. 156–158; Nel, 1998, p. 59).

There is increasing pressure on the church and its leadership to develop strategies for youth ministry that would meet the depth of needs these youth encounter. Discipleship is mistaken for leadership; in reality, leadership is one of the many components of Christian discipleship (Canales, 2004, pp. 45–46). Among the many challenges facing South African churches is the decline in the number of youth attending. This challenge is also not unique to the South African church, but this chapter highlights it in light of the theme being discussed here. This decline in youth attendance is connected to the decline in youth leadership and in active congregational youth ministries (Weber, 2014, p. 9). Part of the challenge, however, is that academic resources of leadership within youth ministry contexts are limited. Most resources describe the "how to" of youth ministry with an emphasis on the need for leadership, but do not give an in-depth description of what this leadership requires. The literature on leadership often fails to address what leadership means to young people and whether this differs from generic models. This chapter discusses what Christian leadership could look like to youth in specific urban South African contexts. The primary research question posed is: What is required of youth leadership within evangelical Christian youth ministries ministering in cities in South Africa? This question is explored by giving a brief and broad description of the challenges faced by young people in South Africa; reflecting on a recent case study (Weber, 2014) to highlight this; and engaging with various leadership theories with the aim of finding one best suited to youth ministry in urban contexts. As a practical theologian, I lean quite heavily on the works of scholars within this particular theological discipline to guide me.

2.1 Youth Ministry in South Africa

Youth in South Africa

According to the National Youth Act of 1996, youth in South Africa are defined as persons in the age group 14 to 35 years old, with early youth between 14–24 years old and later youth or early adulthood as 25–34 years old (National Youth Policy, 2009). Youth in South Africa account for more than two-thirds of the population. The challenge of writing a generalised paper about all young people in all Christian faith communities in South Africa lies in the rich diversity of youth and churches in this country. That is not the intention of this chapter; rather, it hopes to share a bird's eye view into one evangelical youth ministry context.

As noted earlier, this paper focuses on urban contexts in South Africa. In an article entitled "Doing urban public theology in South Africa: Introducing a new agenda," Swart and de Beer (2014) address the lack of theological discourse on urban challenges within South Africa. Theology needs to engage very seriously with what is produced by actors from the state, civil society and the corporate or private sector in shaping the urban environment. The term urban itself is complex and diverse because it has developed into "… a socio-economic and political priority in public, intellectual and civil society discourses" (De Beer & Swart, 2014). To highlight this complexity, South Africa has several institutions focussed on urban thought such as the African Centre for Cities, Isandla Institute, the Social Justice Coalition, Institute for Urban Ministry (De Beer & Swart, 2014, p. 4). This chapter will connect the term urban to the city and refer to it as such. According to Roebben (2009, p. 18), "…the city is the root metaphor for a postmodern society on the move. (It symbolizes) the complexity and plurality of organizational principles of contemporaries to live a meaningful life." In this complex society, youth are bombarded with the many voices that are assumed to be meaningful. These voices sometimes contradict each other to the extent that they stand in the way of each other morally and spiritually (Roebben, 2009, p. 18). Part of the challenge in addressing or describing youth in South Africa lies in the fact that "(c)ities in the global South experience unprecedented in-migration…South African cities and towns experience the reality of such massive migrations and its accompanying vulnerabilities on a daily basis" (De Beer & Swart, 2014, p. 2). Understanding the faith formation of youth within such a dynamic and diverse context becomes one of the biggest challenges faced by youth leaders within urban congregations. This faith formation process contends with the many paradoxes of being a young person in this country.

Youth within urban South Africa are both heterosexual and homosexual, in secondary and tertiary institutions, school aged and out of school youth. They are unemployed youth and youth in the workplace.

They come from poor households and different racial groups. They are teenage parents, orphaned, heading households, have disabilities, live with HIV and Aids and other communicable diseases. These youth are in conflict with the law and are abusing addictive substances. They are homeless youth living on the street, in rural areas, in townships, in cities and in informal settlements. These youth are young migrants and refugees (National Planning Commission, 2011). This a rather broad reflection of youth in this country. The recent protests (#Fees Must Fall movement) by university students have reflected a dissatisfaction with the above-mentioned contextual issues.

I have connected the broader South African youth context to my discussion of youth ministry in South Africa because it is these very youth who are also present in our faith communities. Many youth leaders in this country could testify to these complex realities of the youth they minister to. It is important to note that these realities cannot be separated from the discussion at hand as they are frequently key to why youth leaders feel ill-equipped, unsupported and burnt out. According to Nell and Nell (2014, p. 32), "African leadership is a complex and multi-layered concept which encompasses different perspectives and is located in various leadership theories. At its deepest core African leadership is situated within the wider community and African context." Even leaders with academic training are sometimes vexed by feeling ill-prepared for the above-mentioned realities faced by the youth they minister to. In an article discussing the complexities of theological training on leadership within South African theology faculties, Nell (2014, p. 1) notes that "(we) see challenges to deeply-held convictions on the traditional understanding of the offices and ministry of the church…we see the development of alternative forms of leadership." He adds that leadership is always contextual because it is deeply shaped by a culture of symbols, heritage, relationships, and arrangements of authority created over generations (Nell, 2014, p. 7).

This chapter calls for youth leadership approaches that will be able to address these complexities. In doing so, we reflect on a recent study conducted within one particular urban context within South Africa.

2.2. *A Case Study from an Evangelical Context*

American youth have been described as having an instrumental view of religion which is evident through a moralistic approach to life where personal potentials are realised, other people like them, and they feel good about themselves. This became known as a Moralistic Therapeutic Deism (Smith & Lundquist, 2005, pp. 26–29; Dean, 2010, pp. 201–205). Walt Mueller (2006, p. 107) describes young people within postmodern urban societies as deeply spiritual yet not adhering to one particular faith group. More than a decade ago, South African youth were described as highly religious, with most youth reporting that church was something they attended regularly (Swartz, 2002).

During my involvement with youth and their leadership from different faith communities, I discovered that many young people are leaving these youth ministries soon after they have completed secondary school. I also discovered that many youth leaders are burnt out by July or August of the year. This stimulated me to conduct an empirical study to explore why this was this case (Weber, 2014). My study focussed on the faith formation of youth between the ages of 14 and 17 years old in one of the evangelical faith communities in South Africa. An empirical and theoretical investigation was conducted into the ecclesial, familial and societal influences on the faith formation of this age group within a predominantly coloured, evangelical and relatively poor faith community in South Africa. Empirical research was conducted by interviewing the youth and their immediate leadership, which consisted of the youth leaders and the pastor (who in some cases served as the youth leader as well). After 42 interviews were conducted and transcribed, the data was examined by thematic analysis. Thematic analysis is a method for identifying and reporting patterns (themes) within data in an attempt to interpret various aspects of the research question. It is used for reporting the experiences, meanings and realities of participants and also for acknowledging the ways in which meaning is created within the participants' social contexts (Braun & Clark, 2006, p. 79; Ezzy, 2002, p. 88).

As with most churches in South Africa, this faith community was founded by a mission organisation which impacted the local denominational structure, governance and theological framework. It was founded in 1952 during the time Hendrik Verwoerd served as prime minister of South Africa. The missionaries responsible for the church were mainly white males, which suited the social context of the country at the time. By the 1950s almost 100 apartheid laws had been adopted, one of which was the Population Registration Act, in which people were defined according to the colour of their skin. Another was the Group Areas Act, in which race groups were separated according to the geographical areas they were restricted to (Weber, 2014, pp. 41–45). This climate affected the manner and place where these faith communities were established. Missionaries, by offering education, served as the key leaders of this faith community and brought with them their American evangelical doctrine and ecclesial praxis. This impact had a ripple effect on the youth ministry, which was evidenced by the way in which youth ministry structures and leadership were neglected through a lack of youth ministry foci in the mission organization's ministerial succession plan for this faith community.

The discussion that follows interchangeably focuses on the youth involved in this particular case and the youth leadership these youth are entrusted to. This reflects the importance of considering the youth being ministered to when selecting its leadership. The research findings of this study reflected a comparison of what older leadership (pastors) considered valuable for a youth leader in the past to what the younger youth and its leadership deemed important for the present realities they face. I discovered that in the past, the youth were self-motivated, involved within the life of the faith community and considered leadership positions as something prized and worth attaining. Youth ministry in the past was characterised by the church (members and leaders) being involved in the lives of the young people. The pastoral leadership of this faith community described past youth as "the feeding body to the church"[1] and the youth "became leaders in the church," resulting in the youth ministry being "always pleasant" and "always good and fun because the leaders went out of their way." The findings of this study also reflected that one of the reasons for this faith community's youth ministry crisis is the type of young people it now needs to minister to: The youth at present have "(b)ecome materialistic through giving into worldly standards" just like the adults of this faith community. They have "no relationship with Christ" and have "(c)ompromised by moving away from foundational beliefs" of the church. The youth of today are "(u)nruly" and are "(o)nly interested in games and fun." This can also be evidenced in the "(t)ypes of dance" they are bringing into the church. Someone even added that "some have learning disabilities," broadening the scope and challenges of what the youth ministry should be addressing (Weber, 2014, pp. 157–158). The following quotations are extracts from the interviews conducted with the youth leaders described above which reflect the challenges they are experiencing (Weber, 2014, pp. 163–165):

---

[1] All references in parenthesis are quotations taken directly from the data extracts. This usage of participants' verbatim phrases and quotations is intended to create a narrative approach to writing of the research findings.

> I think it gets harder each year. The more you learn about what the teens go through, who they are – I don't think it becomes more complicated, but it becomes more in-depth, more involved, more commitment becomes necessary. (Int. 4, Cong. 2, YL 1)
> There is really no set form of structure …The youth leaders also don't work together or want to work together. They are not really connecting… they choose youth leaders because they need somebody for that role. And then that person is not equipped. The (name of church missing) should have a structure where they really give a year or two years training for a youth leader. They should have something in place like that… the pastor just takes somebody to fill that position… young people, they need somebody that they can respect, who knows what they are talking about. (Int. 5, Cong. 1, YL 1)
> As far as leadership is concerned on youth level quite early they are asked to presume a leadership role in the youth. They are in charge of programmes and stuff like that and I give them readings and I want them to be able to share from the Bible even if it is their own devotion but share it with a group of 10 to 15 people and to be able to be confident in sharing that. (Int. 5, Cong. 2, P 1)
> The problem with (this church) is they (are) what you call it.. programme orientated. Everyone is trying to get the best programme on the market to entertain the youngsters and I believe that is the wrong way to go. If we do not teach our young people, that listen, the word of God is the first and foremost thing for doing youth ministry, then we have lost the battle. (Int. 4, Cong .4, P 1)
> There is no national structure, no national structure. There is no regional structures in the sense of regional youth; you know, co-ordination, co-operation. And so, each individual, each youth group is actually operating in isolation… no co-ordination between the various bodies or groups with the result that our young people are isolated. In fact, our young people don't really know the youth of the other churches…they themselves (youth leaders) are battling and the youth are looking to them for leadership. And if they see that this person doesn't really know where he is going, how can they follow, you now? And I would say, from that perspective, if the leader knows where he is going, the leader knows exactly, this is where I intend, where my youth are, and this is where I want them to be… the fact of us not electing leaders as they ought to be elected. (Int. 1, Cong. 6, P 1)

Present-day youth are less interested in church life and its leadership positions because there is a "lack of co-operation" amongst the youth leaders and also "inconsistency" of the ministry, resulting in many youth groups closing. Youth ministry resources in this context were limited. Many local congregations (within this particular denomination) do not have youth clubs or a formal youth ministry because of insufficient leadership. People are afraid of volunteering themselves because the local congregation does not have the finances and administrative support to sustain these ministries, resulting in past leadership being burnt out. A second reason for this faith community's youth ministry crisis has been the lack of prioritizing of its youth leadership. "(T)here's no national structure" in which the youth ministry operates despite this (faith community) being governed by a national council. This council does not include a youth ministry portfolio. "(Y)outh leaders are not being included in planning." Some participants said that there is "no development of youth leaders" whilst others have noted the opposite. Many of the youth leaders interviewed were quite young (between 22–30 years old) with relatively no training and experience of youth ministry. Some complaints against the youth leaders were that the "Word of God is not first"; there are no "relationships with youth" as was the case in earlier years; and also the "youth leaders are not working together." Most of the youth leaders interviewed in this case were categorized as part of the younger generation of church leadership (Weber, 2014, p. 159). This means that many of the youth leadership were considered youth themselves (according to the South African definition given earlier in this chapter).

As reflected by the opening comments on DeVries' research, the faith community has neglected the hard work of teaching, shepherding and mentoring these youth through discipleship. The research findings also reflect that a strong focus on biblical truth has helped maintain a solid foundation for faith but has also led to inappropriate rationalism and false denigration of spiritual practices (Weber, 2014, p. 159). Youth leaders were taught at church but did not understand the biblical relevance for their lifestyles. This poses the challenge of whether these leaders are able to teach youth truth from a biblical text which they personally do not exemplify or understand. These discouraging descriptions do, however, caution faith communities to not continue doing youth ministry without considering the context in which they minister. Most of this ministry was, and still is, the burden of the youth leader rather than the church, resulting in the cessation of many of these youth activities.

Experience in youth ministry within various denominations in South Africa has shown a lot of similarity in the types of youth leadership challenges these faith communities face. Some faith communities do have national structures and policies for their youth ministry but fail to implement them. This, too, reflects a lack of investment in a faith community's youth leadership. Spiritual and scriptural ignorance is increasing among young people in Africa because of the ignorance of its youth leaders (Maiko, 2007, p. 60). Youth leaders have not been equipped for the position they hold, and they need to be trained to guide young people in their faith formation. Better care needs to be taken when selecting youth ministry leadership (Maiko, 2007, p. 10). Youth leaders are respected greatly by the youth (Powell et al., 2013, p. 140). They also have the responsibility of helping youth wrestle through their faith formation process by helping them align their faith with their daily lifestyles. Many youth come to a youth group because they want to see their youth leader and not necessarily their peers. Having a youth leader or adult in one's life who is grounded in his or her own faith helps the young person grow spiritually (Maiko, 2007, p. 31).

The discussion thus far has focussed on the challenges faced by youth leaders within evangelical faith communities in South Africa and has used a case study example to explain how these challenges have impacted one such community which has not prioritized its youth leadership. I now shift to answering the question of what is required of youth leadership within evangelical Christian youth ministries ministering in cities in South Africa by engaging with various leadership theories which could be adopted, with the aim of proposing one that is best suited to this discussion.

3. Leadership Theories

In an article describing "The Changing Landscape in Religious Leadership: Reflections from Rural African Faith Communities," Nell & Nell (2014, pp. 29–41) discuss four categories of leadership theories to help clarify some of the conceptual contestation on religious leadership. Essentialist theories focus on identifying leadership traits and behaviours. Leadership is thus considered to be situated within the person and identity of the leader. In critical theories, leadership is used to maintain power and status, rather than empower followers. Relational theories view leadership as a group quality that resides within the relationship between leaders and followers and emphasizes the distribution of influence and expertise amongst them. Constructionist theories evaluate how leadership constructs meaning and helps people to make sense of situations. Here, leadership is exercised in narratives used by the leader to help communities to reframe their understanding of social problems and to solve them. This same article reflected that leadership in Africa is understood as being chosen, as relational, for the service of the community, and as pedagogical (Nell & Nell, 2014, p. 40). Nell &

Nell also found that leadership within an African context has shifted towards the inclusion of the faith community. In a later article entitled "The end of leadership?: The shift of power in local congregations," Nell (2015, p. 7) confirms that a shift in perception concerning leadership is evident in the direction of democratic and egalitarian approaches where the priesthood of all believers and the importance of relationships and networks are significant in South African faith communities. My earlier contention in this chapter has been that leadership theories have not taken cognisance of the youth ministry contexts discussed above. The theories highlighted by Nell helped me to name academically and theoretically the phenomenon that has been so evident within youth ministries across faith communities in this country. It is against this background that I propose that faith communities are more intentional in exploring what this would look like within their urban evangelical contexts.

4. A Call for Intentional Youth Leadership

Practical theology is at the heart of youth ministry (Dean & Root, 2011, p. 17). It gives youth ministry the language and direction to describe how the youth construct their faith. It releases youth leaders from the challenge of knowing it all. It reminds them that ministry outside of this framework of understanding lends itself to hindering the faith formation of these youth more than helping them. As with practical theology, youth ministry requires relationships and Christian education, not only one at the expense of the other. Understood as a theological discipline, youth ministry takes the faith formation of youth seriously because these youth are called to participate in every practice of the Christian ministry (Dean & Root, 2011, pp. 20–21). Youth ministry then is the call of the church to relationally pass on the gospel to the youth (Dean et al., 2001, pp. 19, 42). This means that the church needs to take its young people (who are not excluded from the youth described above) and its investment in its youth leadership seriously by being more intentional about who they appoint as leaders alongside these youth and how.

Leaders should not be confused with managers. "Managers value stability, predictability, efficiency and rational control over organisational processes. They are infatuated with strategy...leadership arises out of the ability to mobilise people around what may initially seem to be hopeless causes" (Mangcu, 2014, p. 43). Leaders influence change and empower through giftedness and effective relationships (Maxwell,

1993, pp. 1–19). Leaders take risks, experiment and are creative whilst managers are loyal, focus on survival and keeping the peace (Mangcu, 2014, p. 45). At this point, I shall briefly discuss a few leadership theories in an effort to recommend one suitable for the evangelical context and youth described thus far. Autocratic leadership is the assumption that leaders have absolute power over their workers or team (Nash & Whitehead, 2014, p. 249). The weakness with this type of leadership is that it leads to high levels of absenteeism and staff turnover. This can also be called task-oriented leadership in that it focuses only on getting the job done while not paying much attention to the well-being of the team. Democratic leadership or participative leadership invites other members of the team to contribute to the decision-making process, increases job satisfaction by involving team members, and helps to develop people's skills (Nash & Whitehead, 2014, p. 249). It is also known as people-oriented leadership or relations-oriented leadership because it aims at developing the people in their teams. Transformational leadership inspires the team constantly with a shared vision of the future and an enthusiasm that is often passed to the team. Some would refer to it as charismatic leadership, but if they tend to believe more in themselves than in their teams, this creates a risk that a project, or even an entire organization, might collapse if the leader leaves. This type of leadership is most often seen in the youth ministry leadership described at the beginning of this chapter (DeVries, 2008) because here success is directly connected to the presence of the charismatic leader.

This empirical case also highlights that youth and its leadership should be developed through a mentorship program. The "training of young people" should be prioritised by giving them "information that will develop them spiritually to practice their faith every day." This training should include the "mentoring of youth leaders" because they too are young and also a "focus on identity formation" of the youth themselves. The present intake of youth leaders seems younger than in the past. Some of these leaders are dealing with the same issues that the youth are and find it difficult to lead. This means that the age and qualifications of the youth leader need to be reconsidered in the above-mentioned policy (Weber, 2014, p. 209). In a recent (2014) study conducted on leadership mentoring and succession in the charismatic churches in Bushbuckridge, South Africa, Ngomane and Mahlangu investigated what leadership mentoring programmes or succession plans these congregations (in urban and rural contexts) had in place. This study was theologically motivated by the biblical examples of Moses and Joshua (Exodus 18:17–27), Eli and Samuel, Elijah and Elisha, Jesus and his disciples (Acts 6:1–7; Luke 6:12–16; 9:1-6; Mark 3:13–19) and Barnabas and Paul (Ephesians 4:11–18), who all considered leadership mentorship crucial to their ministerial succession (Ngomane & Mahlangu, 2014, p. 1). The above-mentioned study was conducted with leaders younger than 50 years old, including one 16-year-old, many of whom were women (Ngomane & Mahlangu, 2014, p. 3). This implies that many of these leaders have been in these positions for more than 15 years and have not made the necessary transitions to younger leaders as biblically portrayed. Despite many of these leaders reporting that they were indeed mentoring someone, the study found that there were no intentional leadership mentoring programmes in place (Ngomane & Mahlangu, 2014, p. 3). This study confirmed that leadership succession programmes require long-term planning. "By the nature of their one-man-founder-leader, charismatic churches are likely to experience the same leadership succession problems that are prevalent in family business structures" (Ngomane & Mahlangu, 2014, p. 7). One of the reasons for this is that these leaders prefer leadership succession within their own families. This study also found that the leaders' educational background (primary and secondary schooling) impacted whether they valued leadership succession or not (Ngomane & Mahlangu, 2014, p. 9). This depiction of leadership in the charismatic church is similar to that of the evangelical church described above. In the same way as mentioned in the evangelical study, many youth do not value the importance of leadership succession because they do not think beyond their immediate contextual challenges. "The study also revealed that location has no significant statistical effect in explaining leadership mentoring – meaning that as far as leadership mentoring is concerned, urban churches have no advantage over rural churches" (Ngomane & Mahlangu, 2014, p. 10).

The opening quotation by Mangcu (2014) challenged South Africa's lack of presidential histories. He argues that many of the presidents (and leaders) of this country have not passed on the traits important to lead a country to their successors, resulting in each one reinventing the wheel of trial and error. This has resulted in what he terms self-reliant leadership development (Mangcu, 2014, p. 12). He also states that this has added to the dependency syndrome that has plagued black people in this country. "At the heart of our leadership malaise is the absence of a common national purpose, and a collective failure of imagination" (Mangcu, 2014, p. 13). According to Mangcu, the decline in electoral support for the African National Congress (ANC), for example, has not happened imminently. The crisis of poor leadership in this political party, and any leadership context I may add, is the result of qualitative decline over time (Mangcu, 2014, p. 14). One of the leadership challenges Mangcu (Mangcu, 2014, p. 41) addresses lies in the fact that research on policies and political scholarship in South Africa never seems to reach discussion forums of the general public (lay people) of this country. He argues that this disparity of not engaging and equipping the people of the country accounts for one of the major influences behind the unrest and distrust in government. Again, I would connect this argument to the church as well. As shown in the two cases presented (evangelical and charismatic) in this chapter, many times churches do not pass on their traditional heritage to the next generation. Youth leaders are chosen on the basis of availability, age and energy rather than on theological compatibility and a passion or calling to ministry (DeVries, 2008; Nash & Whitehead, 2014). They are expected to lead without understanding the policies, doctrines, confessions and traditional praxis of their church. This in turn creates a gap in the corporate identity of the church because the youth do not understand how they fit into this identity. When the leader is unable to understand the weaknesses and strengths of those in front of him/her, they tend to internalise the social stress around them and isolate themselves as victims (Mangcu, 2014, p. 74). Leadership cannot happen in isolation and must recognise the context within which he/she ministers. "The succession debate must not be just about the replacement of individuals by others. It must also be about making the transition from one generation of leaders to another" (Mangcu, 2014, p. 138).

Many debates around leadership have been around the priority of scripture, ecclesial traditions and contextual issues faced. Frank (2006, p. 130) describes "reflective practice" as a useful, practical, theological approach in this regard. "This may still be the most constructive way to address both scripture and ecclesial traditions in one direction and contemporary situations and cultural changes in another. That is, leadership is best developed conceptually through a continuous conversation between practice and reflection, between situations and concepts, between depth understanding of current circumstances and sophisticated perception of situations that faith communities have faced in the past." It is against this background that I would like at this point to propose the relational youth leadership model as the one best suited to the complex and diverse youth ministry context in South Africa. The practical theologian Andrew Root (2007, p. 10) notes that relationships in such contexts are not only significant for youth ministry but for transformation within these contexts to take place. He adds that this model is specifically relevant to evangelical contexts because relational youth ministry was birthed within the context of evangelicalism itself (Root, 2007, p. 18). This understanding of youth leadership correlates with the discipline of practical theology. "Practical theology may be reflection on human action within the church and society, but it is also, in the same breath, theological reflection on God's distinct and unique act of revelation within history and for humanity. Practical theology then is essentially reflection on both divine and human action, discerning and articulating ways that they find association and ways that human communities should respond to God's action in the world" (Root, 2007, p. 19). This call for relational youth leadership implies that these leaders are intentional about enhancing the quality of the relationships they have with the young people and the faith communities they serve.

Intentional youth leadership in urban contexts has to plan for ministry to a diversity of young people. A large part of the complexity of doing youth ministry in cities lies in the complexity of where these youth come from. Youth ministry in urban contexts includes youth who have migrated to South Africa from other cities. "Migration is often the result of deep vulnerabilities – cross-border migration as a result of war, hunger, natural disasters, or political unrest; or rural-urban migration as a result of perceived economic opportunities that do not exist in similar ways in rural areas. It seems to be the minority of urban migrants that benefit from access to urban resources such as educational or employment opportunities. And although migration often results from vulnerability, it also seems to exasperate the vulnerability of many by intensifying the realities of homelessness, ethnic conflicts and violence, unemployment, and contests over meagre resources" (De Beer & Swart, 2014, p. 3). "Urban theologian Ray Bakke (1997) speaks of God's incarnation as a refugee child in a foreign land, which places Jesus in a similar situation to millions of urban migrants around the globe today. Could our theologies find, affirm and embrace the gift of Jesus in the faces of nameless migrants in urban neighbourhoods across the globe, but also in the cities of South Africa, articulating new knowledge from 'strange' places?" (De Beer & Swart, 2014).

Intentional youth leadership in urban contexts addresses youth marginalisation. The varying social issues mentioned earlier in this chapter lead to many youth facing these issues being marginalised. Faith communities that do not prioritise authentic youth leadership are in essence marginalising the youth they serve. In an article entitled "Discerning the role of faith communities in responding to urban youth marginalisation," Nel (2014, pp. 1–8) highlights a shift in the focus on young people involved in apartheid activism to young people now being the object of social inquiry and welfare. Many of South Africa's prominent political leaders arose as young people who stood up to the injustices of the apartheid era (Mangcu, 2014). Nel (2014, pp. 1–2) argues that these leaders should not be separated from the contextual (economic, institutional and demographic) influences of their time. We could argue that many of the youth in this country still suffer the political and economic injustices of the apartheid era, but these youth have now developed an international youth culture in which access to information from globalised youth has been made possible (Nel, 2014, p. 5). This then impacts how these youth follow their ecclesial leaders. Nel (2014, p. 6) further argues that "…a deeper and broader framework for understanding the newer expressions of youth" is still lacking today. Young people should be engaged as agents within their faith formation processes. They are the ones experiencing the societal challenges and benefits of an urbanised South Africa. They would be able to assist the church in understanding what and how these challenges impact their views on church. Nel (2014, p. 6) refers to these challenges as a struggle for identity within a globalised notion of self as opposed to the struggle against apartheid which was previously the case. "The rules of accountability or lack thereof that pertained in the liberation movement are suddenly unacceptable in a context that emphasises codes of government" (Mangcu, 2014, p. 119).

Religious diversity is also ascribed to the youth in South Africa. Postmodern youth are deeply spiritual (Mueller, 2006, p. 107; Powell et al., 2011, p. 60). The problem is that these youth do not adhere to any one particular faith group. They want to be able to choose from a variety of faith systems and make up their own. Many youth have become disillusioned by orthodox Christianity in which rules are seen as the final authority. In fact, these youth do not call themselves religious, yet at the root of their pluralism and relativism, postmodern youth have a deep hunger for God. It is for this reason that congregations need to do everything possible to engage these youth, helping them understand the meaning of the delinquent behaviours they are involved in and pointing them to the redemptive and transformative message of the cross (Mueller, 2006, pp. 107–108). In a postmodern, urban context, intentional youth leaders need to instil hope within the youth they are ministering to. This includes a willingness to walk alongside them while they discern their changing identity in Christ. In order to fulfil such challenging and vulnerable roles, youth leaders need to reflect the moral and spiritual life they are calling youth to live. They "...wrestle with the complexity of modern existence...let (their) own values, norms and meanings be challenged by everyday life..." (Roebben, 2009, p. 13). Roebben (2009, p. 14) reflects on Proverbs 29:18 in saying that "(w)henever a society as a whole decides not to see and articulate the vision of hope expressed in their children, the youth starts to run wild." Dean and others (2001, pp. 246–253) add grace to this hope. They believe that youth leaders need to minister from the perspective of grace towards youth who are so bombarded by differing messages, values, belief systems and challenges today. Grace allows the youth leader to love unconditionally and yet discern when and how to act on behalf of and alongside these youth.

Intentional youth leadership prioritizes the biblical text as relevant to the lives and challenges of the youth they serve. Referring to Thomas Ruster, Roebben (2009, p. 175) warns "...that modern individualized religion and Christianity are so tightly interwoven that the latter has merged with the former...Our modern, autonomous religious experience has become completely incompatible with the heteronymous language and religious reality of the Bible." As noted earlier, this becomes challenging for youth leaders who are older and fixed on their traditional readings and exposition of Scripture and also for younger leaders who have not been discipled to contextualize Scripture appropriately. The personal life stories of youth leaders are integral to building a relationship with the youth they serve, but the reading and exposition of Scripture should not be limited to their personal contexts exclusively. Youth should be directed toward an omnipresent, omniscient and omnipotent God. "The church seems to give answers to irrelevant questions and, at the same time, remain silent on what people find to be authentic personal and societal issues" (Roebben, 2009, p. 220).

Intentional youth leadership to youth in urban contexts calls for a reframing of the youth leader's theology. This requires that the leader critically reflect on his/her knowledge, wisdom and engagement with a living God. This reflection enters into hopeful dialogues with the emerging issues and initiates this theological reflection (Roebben, 2009, p. 19). "Youth ministry is an expectant ministry where any well-trained pastor should be in a position to communicate coherently, compellingly and consistently the Word of God" (Maiko, 2007, p. 123). "Youth people want action, rather than reflection. They do not ask for the meaning of things, they use the meaning … There is a need for a real life and semantically explicit religious leadership that is food for thought, which can be disrupted, questioned and tested … the future wellbeing of the youth in a globalizing society should be the centre of interpretation for these origins (what and how to tell youth)" (Roebben, 2009, pp. 23, 81, 87). Rather than comparing present day youth to youth in the past, youth leadership needs to advocate for safe spaces in which youth are able to question, experiment with and fail at their faith. It is through these safe spaces that young people return to a deeper and firmly grounded faith (Weber, 2014). "Nowadays being young means that one has to learn to deal with the fact that as a future (young) adult one will have to live continually in a situation of transition" (Roebben, 2009, p. 17). Youth in an urban South Africa require the life skills that will empower them to make wiser choices today that will impact their future. This calls for leadership that is relevant, biblically equipped and relational. It calls for authentic leaders who live their lives reflecting the youth they envisage.

5. Conclusion

The socio-cultural context in which young people grow up influences their faith formation greatly because faith formation happens through these daily societal interactions (Groome, 1980, p. 107). The social community plays a big role in helping young people achieve identity and personality as well as develop faith (Maiko, 2007, p. 166). Faith as a lived reality has to interact with the society by which the faith of these young people is formed. This chapter has evidenced the complex realities faced by many youth in urban evangelical faith communities in South Africa. It has also highlighted the important role youth leaders play in the lives of these youth (be it from a Christian perspective). Faith formation is part of everyday life and should not be isolated to one context of life but take place in daily lifestyle events of the youth (Wilhoit, 2008, p. 38). According to Maiko (2007, p. 168), faith is a contextual experience which includes believing, understanding, acting and relating to others. It is this relational component of faith that allows the formation of communities of people who share common priorities, and these priorities keep them connected. This is very important for youth as they are searching for spaces of belonging and where they can connect. Youth in evangelical contexts in South Africa are not growing in their faith because of the ignorance of their youth leaders (Maiko, 2007, p. 60). Right action, right belief, and right heart relate to one another in shaping the life of these youth (Maiko, 2007, p. 11). The youth are also shaped by their peers, neighbourhoods, schools, religious communities, and wider political and social contexts (Bunge, 2008, p. 350). Each of these contexts transfers worldviews different to their familial or spiritual ones, and each speaks to the lives of these youth (Groome, 1980, pp. 123 -124). Youth leadership should not be taken lightly in terms of qualification and training but also the network of support this leader requires.

Chapter Ten

The Common Priesthood and Swedish Church Politics: An Analysis

Thomas Girmalm

1. Introduction

Previous research has argued that hardly any other church has so consistently tried to unite the episcopal (church office) and synodal (a democratic organisation) in the church's organisation than the Church of Sweden. The combination of the two is related to questions of democracy and authority in the church and how secular power structures can be transferred into the field of the church (Ahrén, 2000, p. 72). These concerns regarding democracy and authority are also closely linked to understanding the church's organisation and church management and leadership.

In ecclesiological research, it has been stated that "democracy" in the latter part of the twentieth century became an "ecclesiological category" in the Church of Sweden, especially in the way the church has come to define itself as a Folk Church (Lundstedt, 2006, pp. 177–178).[1] It has been argued that the understanding of democracy affirmed by the Church of Sweden does not differ significantly from the field of state governance as expressed in the Swedish Constitution and in the principle of popular sovereignty (Lundstedt, 2006, p. 177).[2] The similarities can be interpreted as a heritage from the earlier longstanding relationship between the state and the church.

Since the turn of the millennium, the Church of Sweden is no longer a formal state church. However, state regulation of the church still exists in the form of a framework law. This law stipulates that the church, in addition to being an Evangelical-Lutheran faith community, shall be an open Folk Church, have nationwide coverage, and have a demo-

---

[1] See also Brodd, 2012, p. 46.
[2] The Swedish Constitution states: "All public power in Sweden proceeds from the people" (*Kungörelse*, 1974).

cratic organisation. The law also says that the Church Assembly (*Kyrkomötet*) is the Church of Sweden's highest decision-making body (Lag 1998). The members of the Church Assembly are directly elected by the church members according to the principle of popular sovereignty. At the same time, an important theological justification for the democratisation of the church has been "the common priesthood," a theological concept associated with Martin Luther (1483–1546) and with Reformed and Lutheran pietism.

This essay's problem definition is how the concept of "the common priesthood" has been understood and used in contemporary Swedish church politics and its ecclesiastical consequences. This includes a historical background and analysis of possible shifts and parallels in the understanding of the concept of "the common priesthood" over time. The purpose of this is to challenge popular ideas about the concept of "the common priesthood" and to offer starting points for further critical discussion concerning contemporary church organisational structures.

In this essay, the relevance of leadership is linked to the organisational structures of the church and not specifically to leadership on an individual level. Interest is therefore focused on implicit theological interpretations behind the organisational structures and approaches to leadership.

2. Background

To offer a broad perspective of the topic, the change in the composition between the clergy and the laity in the Church Assembly over time is described first. In this way, it can be shown how the church followed the democratisation process in society at large and how that process influenced the church's organisational structures and leadership. Until 1865, the Church of Sweden was represented by the "Diet of Four Estates" (*fyrståndsriksdagen*), with the clergy included as one of the four estates (Berntson et al., 2012, pp. 249–250). In the first order of the Church Assembly (*Allmänna kyrkomötet*), which represented the Church of Sweden after the reform of representation, it was stated that it would be composed of 60 members. This was almost as many as in the previous Diet. The distribution of seats was equally divided between clergy and laity (Bexell, 1990, p. 129). The Church Assembly, according to Bexell (1990, p. 133), was constructed as a politically neutral meeting place made up of two parts. These included representatives of the clergy and of the laity, and the numerical balance between these two parts was perceived as something essential to the Church Assembly at this time.

With regard to the extensive social changes in Sweden during the first half of the twentieth century, with the modernisation of society and the emergence of democracy, public opinion of the division of the Church Assembly into two parts came to be questioned. Instead, opinions shifted to a Church Assembly that could represent the members of the church in a more accurate way. However, a change in the numerical distribution between the clergy and laity did not take place until 1951 when the Church Assembly met for the first time in a new composition. The number of members was increased to 100, of which 43 were clergy and 57 were lay members (Bexell, 1990, pp. 142–154). The year 1951 was also the year when full freedom of religion was introduced in Sweden with new legislation (Religionsfrihetslag, 1951). Sweden was now a modern, democratic, and industrial society, and several religions and beliefs besides the Lutheran could now be represented among the population.

A further major reform of the composition of the Church Assembly was decided upon in 1982 (Bexell, 1990, p. 162). The previous system with given members (i.e. the bishops) was now considered to be in contradiction to democratic ideas. A state committee – *1979 års kyrkomöteskommitté* – was set up by the government in 1979 to investigate the status, powers, and composition of the Church Assembly. It considered the distinction between clergy and laity as outdated, undemocratic, and a relic from a pre-modern society. The committee suggested that the Church Assembly should consist of 251 freely elected members and that the archbishop would no longer be the chairman. However, specific concerns about church teachings and doctrine would, according to the proposal, be addressed by the establishment of a "Doctrinal Commission" (*Läronämnden*) where the bishops would be in the majority (Bexell, 1990, pp. 159–160).

The proposal came to be adopted by a decision of the Church Assembly, and the bishops lost their representation. They were instead expected to take an active part in the Church Assembly's work without voting rights. The consequence was that the bishops no longer participated in the Church Assembly's final decisions. In questions about doctrine, however, the bishops maintained a powerful influence through the Doctrinal Commission. However, the Doctrinal Commission could only delay matters, not go against the Church Assembly's final decision. This meant that the Church Assembly's members ultimately determined the church's belief and its order of worship (Girmalm and Rosenius, 2013, p. 54).

When the new Church Assembly met for the first time in 1983, the Church of Sweden had a decision-making structure that on all organisational levels was taken directly from the ideals of democracy in secular society. This also meant that secular political parties in Swedish society were involved in the power structure because they formed the basis of the democratic system in the society. When the Church of Sweden was officially separated from the state in 2000, the political parties maintained their influence. The reason for this was that secular parties were allowed to participate as "nominating groups" (nomineringsgrupper) in the church's elections. The church politicians in the local parishes, and also on the diocesan and national level in the Church Assembly, thus also represented common secular parties, even if there were also non-party political nomination groups (Girmalm and Rosenius, 2013, pp. 54–55).

In the 2013 Church Assembly elections, twelve "nomination groups" received enough votes for representation in the Church Assembly. Of these, three parties ran under the same party label as in the general elections. These were the "Social Democratic Party" (*Arbetarpartiet – Socialdemokraterna*), the social conservative and nationalist "Sweden Democrats" (*Sverigedemokraterna*), and the social liberal and green "Centre Party" (*Centerpartiet*), and these secular parties had specific church political programmes for the Church of Sweden. These nomination groups gained almost half of the 251 seats in the Assembly, and the Social Democratic Party had the largest proportion of seats.

There were also nomination groups that were spin-offs from the secular parties in society, such as the "Conservative alternative" (*Borgerligt alternativ*), the "Christian Democrats in the Church of Sweden" (*Kristdemokrater i Svenska kyrkan*), the "Free Liberals in the Church of Sweden" (*Fria liberaler i Svenska kyrkan*), the "Green Party members in the Church of Sweden" (*Miljöpartister i Svenska kyrkan*), and the "Left-wing in the Church of Sweden" (*Vänstern i Svenska kyrkan*). Finally, there were groups with no party political connections such as "Courageous Church" (*Frimodig kyrka*), "Open Church – a church for everyone" (Öppen kyrka – En kyrka för alla), and "Party-politically independent in the Church of Sweden" (*Partipolitiskt obundna i Svenska kyrkan*).

Of the 5,453,234 members with voting rights, 695,834 voted in the elections in 2013, which was a turnout of around 12.8% (Svenska kyrkan, 2013). This shows that only a small minority of members determined who was elected to the decision-making bodies of the church. Another aspect of the election system, with its direct election of members, is the high cost. The 2013 church election amounted to a total of SEK 145 million (Sveriges radio), which was equivalent at that time to about EUR 16.9 million.

3. The Common Priesthood as Justification for Secular Orders

The current forms of distribution of power between democratically elected members and the church office in the Church of Sweden have, on the whole, been taken from the secular orders within the state and municipality, with regard to the election system. Some of the system's proponents, though, believe they have found a theological justification for this system in Lutheran theology. Through a particular way of interpreting the Reformation concept of "the common priesthood," they have come up with a theological foundation for the process of democratisation and popular sovereignty applied to the church. This interpretation is clearly represented in the Social Democratic church platform *Öppna kyrkan* (Open the church) in 2000, which was approved by the party's executive committee (*partistyrelsen*) close to the time when church and state were formally separated. The platform was sanctioned with a preface by the former Social Democratic Party leader Göran Persson, who was Sweden's Prime Minister at that time (*Öppna kyrkan*, 2000, p. 3).

The reason for providing an analysis of the Social Democratic church political platform is its use of the concept of "the common priesthood."[1] In the party's platform, the view is expressed that Martin Luther's thesis of the "common priesthood" can be seen as support for Social Democratic values. Thus, under the headline "Freedom, equality and solidarity" (*Frihet, jämlikhet och solidaritet*), there is stated:

> The Church of Sweden is Evangelical-Lutheran. In his critique of the medieval notion, where priests were considered to have a special spiritual status, the reformer Martin Luther formulated the thesis of the common priesthood. All people have the same value before God and all the baptised are therefore seen as priests. We see this as constituting support for Social Democratic values.[2]

---

[1] The approach of the Platform as a theological document is evident by its use of theological concepts and with the engagement of a "theological expert" in the working group that prepared it (*Öppna kyrkan*, 2000, p. 2)

[2] "Svenska kyrkan är evangelisk-luthersk. I sin kritik av den medeltida uppfattningen, där prästerna ansågs ha en särskild andlig status, formulerade reformatorn Martin Luther tesen om det allmänna prästadömet. Alla människor har samma värde inför Gud, och alla döpta ses därför som präster. Vi ser det som ett stöd för socialdemokratiska värderingar" (*Öppna kyrkan*, 2000, p. 11).

The statement that Martin Luther's thesis of "the common priesthood" and the theological content of the Reformation movement indirectly justify the party-political democratic system, with a focus on lay influence in the church, was also described in official state reports concerning the church's office during the second half of the twentieth century. Lundstedt has demonstrated that the idea of "the common priesthood" served as an important theological justification for democratisation and had an influence on the design of the bishop elections in the church. This was shown in a state committee – *Biskopsvalskommittén* (The committee of bishop's election) – that was established in 1957 and was concerned with the election of bishops. When it delivered its final report, democratisation was partly seen as a restoration of the Evangelical church constitution from the Reformation period (Lundstedt, 2006, pp. 51–52). The committee wrote:

> A reform in order to prepare the laity for empowerment in the election of bishops would thus be in harmony with the principle of the common priesthood of Christians. The reform should be seen as a restoration of the church constitution in the Evangelical spirit rather than an introduction of a fundamental novelty in it.[1]

However, Lundstedt is of the opinion that the concept of "the common priesthood" was given new content. It was no longer linked to the church's teaching on baptism and justification but to the field of church legislation where the laity's rights and influence came into focus. The theological discussion about the church office was instead brief, and there was no further discussion of the common priesthood. Lundstedt (2006, p. 55) argues that the new interpretation of the concept would lay the foundations for further developments and become important for the theological justification of the democratisation of the church.

A reference to "the common priesthood" was also given in the official state report *Församlingar i samverkan* (Congregations in cooperation) in 1985 that investigated ecclesiastic structural issues at the local level. Here it was claimed that the rules of democracy should be applied everywhere and that this development could be given theological justification from the Lutheran reformation views on "the common priesthood." The report suggested that the Lutheran idea of reformation meant that the office, the preaching of the Gospel, and the admin-

---

[1] "En reform i syfte att bereda lekmän ökat inflytande vid biskopsval skulle sålunda stå i samklang med principen om de kristnas allmänna prästadöme. Reformen torde snarare böra fattas såsom en restauration av kyrkoförfattningen i evangelisk anda än som införande av en principiell nyhet i densamma." Biskopsvalkommittén, 1957, p. 56.

istration of the sacraments are functions carried out by all Christians. The local parish would then assign these functions to specific persons, while the responsibility that it commissioned, in agreement with the church's faith and confession, remained in the parish (p. 121). The perceptions of "the common priesthood" mentioned here are all justified by a reading of Luther's theology.

4. *Martin Luther and the Common Priesthood*

To provide more perspectives on how the common priesthood has come to be linked to questions about power and rights in the church, a historical overview of the development of the meaning of the concept is useful. Martin Luther's use of the priesthood as applied to all Christians is one area where there is a risk that he might be misunderstood. It is therefore important to put Luther's statements in the larger context of his thoughts and to investigate how his thinking about the common priesthood has been interpreted in different historical contexts.[1] In such an analysis, it soon becomes clear that the phrase "the common priesthood" has different meanings depending on whether the common priesthood is referring to "the baptised," "the believers," or "to all" in a more open understanding. The most common combination in use today is certainly "the common priesthood of all believers." If we start by trying to find Luther's own interpretation of the concept, the first thing we notice is that the specific phrase is hardly used by Luther himself. Timothy J. Wengert (2008, p. 1), using the critical Weimar edition (WA) in digital form, has tried to find the phrase "Das allgemeine Priestertum aller Gläubigen" (The common priesthood of all believers), or its Latin replacement, in Luther's texts. He argues that the phrase is nowhere to be found in Luther's writings.[2] Although Luther explicitly claims that all baptised are priests, it is problematic in Wengert's perspective to assert that "the common priesthood of all believers" is Luther's own phrase.

An early writing by Luther often associated with "the common priesthood" is *An den christlichen Adel deutscher Nation von des christlichen*

---

[1] Regarding misunderstandings of Luther's view of the concept 'the common priesthood', Jorgenson (2009, p. 249) states, "[Luther's] treatment of the priesthood as applied to all believers is especially misunderstood," and that his insights of the concept "are only properly understood in concert with broader themes of his thought and the history of tradition."

[2] According to Wengert (2008, p. 111 n. 1) the closest is "das eynige gemeyne priesterthum" (*the one common priesthood*) (WA 8, 254).

Standes Besserung (To the Christian Nobility of the German Nation Concerning the Reform of the Christian Estate) from 1520. Here Luther describes the three walls that he believes "Romanists" (advocates of papal supremacy) had set up around their church to protect themselves from reformation. First, when pressed by the temporal power, they (the Romanists) declared that the temporal power had no jurisdiction over them because the spiritual power is above the temporal. Second, when attempts were made to reprove them with the Scriptures, they objected that the Pope alone had the right to interpret the scriptures. Third, if threatened with a church council, they said that only the Pope had the right to summon a council (Luther, 1888, p. 406; Luther, 1968, p. 126).

Wengert (2008, p. 5) argues that even the title of the writing, "Concerning the Reform of the Christian Estate," shows that Luther did something remarkable, namely that he spoke of a single Christian estate. The three walls that Luther described were based on the presumption that there was both a spiritual and a worldly estate, where the worldly estate had no influence on the spiritual in ecclesiastical matters. In contrast, Luther declared that all Christians belong to the spiritual estate. Luther described and based this reasoning on biblical texts such as 1 Corinthians 12 [:12–31], stating that we are all one body, yet every member has their own work by which they serve others, and referring to 1 Peter 2 [:9], stating that everyone becomes ordained priests through baptism where they are called to a royal priesthood (*kuniglich priesterthum*) and a priestly kingdom (*priesterlich kunigreych*) (Luther 1888, p. 407; Luther, 1968, p. 127). By arguing that all Christians are priests, Luther includes a breakdown of the wall that defended the opinion that the spiritual estate was considered to be more holy than the worldly estate. Baptism became the crucial concept, not the ordination of priests. Baptism, in a sense, could therefore also be understood as an ordination. But it did not mean that Luther did not distinguish between the baptised and those who had been ordained for the task of ministering to congregations. In *An den christlichen Adel*, he writes:

> For whoever comes out of the water of baptism can boast that he is already a consecrated priest, bishop and pope, although of course it is not seemly that just anybody should exercise such office. Because we are all priests of equal standing, no one must push himself forward and take it upon himself, without our consent and election, to do that for which we all have equal authority. For no one dare take upon himself what is common to all without the authority and consent of the community. (Luther 1968, p. 129)

While Luther emphasised equality by arguing that all are priests, he believed that there must be something more to exercising this priesthood. We can understand that not everyone is meant to exercise their priesthood, as Wengert (2006, pp. 11–12) also points out, through the fact that he lumped priest, bishop, and pope together, and because of that no one even talks about a "common bishopric" or a "common papacy." In *An den christlichen Adel*, there is also a story about what a group of Christian lay people would do if they were captured and placed in a desert. Because they had no ordained priest among them, they would elect one of their own to baptise, say mass, pronounce absolution, and preach the gospel (Luther, 1888, pp. 407–408; Luther, 1968, p. 128). This is seen as possible because all Christians are priests, but from Luther's point of view, this would only be practised in emergency situations.

In a later text *Der 82. Psalm Ausgelegt* (Commentary on Psalm 82) from 1530, Luther writes about the difference between the common priesthood and the ministerial office: "It is true that all Christians are priests, but not all are pastors. For to be a pastor one must be not only a Christian and a priest but must have an office and a field of work committed to him. This call and command make pastors and preachers" (Luther 1956, p. 65). This text, written 10 years after *An den christlichen Adel*, claims that all are priests but insists at the same time that there is a special vocation to be a pastor, that is, a priest who ministers to a congregation, the person we normally associate with the word priest or pastor. There is also a clear signal that this calling is not something the individual can decide; it is based on an external calling to conduct these tasks. And, in *Von den Konziliis und Kirchen* (On the Councils and the Church) in 1539, Luther specifies the ministerial office as one of the marks of the church (*notae ecclesiae*). He writes that the church is recognised externally by the fact that it ordains or calls ministers. He states that there must be bishops (*Bisschove*), pastors (*Pfarrher*), and preachers (*Prediger*) who give or administer sermons, baptise, distribute communion, etc. in the church's name, or rather by their institution by Christ (Luther 1914, pp. 632–633; Luther 1966, p. 154). It is possible to discern a shift in emphasis with respect to changes in the surrounding context. In 1520, when Luther wrote *An den christlichen Adel*, the Reformation movement was in its infancy. Nineteen years later, an Evangelical church body had arisen in need of ordained leadership.

In previous research, Brodd has argued that "the common priesthood" as a model for the church is not supposed to be interpreted on the basis of primary institutional connotations. The common priesthood then becomes a question of regulations and power and is a response to questions about who should do what and, if so, why. From this point of view "the common priesthood" does not use power as a reference, but instead it refers to sacrifice (Brodd, 1990, p. 57). Such an understanding can be based on New Testament texts that suggest that Christians sacrifice themselves for the sake of the Kingdom of Heaven. The common priesthood's task is to sacrifice itself by carrying out spiritual sacrifices. An expression of this is that "the common priesthood" in the worship service brings bread and wine before God as an expression of everything that has been created. Similarly, we can talk about the collection and praise in the worship service as a sacrifice to God (Brodd, 1990, pp. 62–63). With such an understanding of "the common priesthood," according to Brodd's interpretation, it becomes clear that its centre is about sacrifice and an expression of the church as *communio* (Brodd, 1990, p. 67). In contrast, it will be discussed below how the concept of the common priesthood came to be "politicised" in its further development in Protestant Pietism in a later step after Luther and the period of Reformation.

5. The Church Divided into Clergy and Laity

The division in the church between the clergy and the laity, where the laity is sometimes understood as being synonymous with the common priesthood, has deep historical roots. This division has been associated with the movements of Pietism from the latter part of the seventeenth century and onwards. About 150 years after Luther's *An den christlichen Adel*, Philip Jacob Spener (1635–1705) wanted to implement a new reformation through a programme of church renewal. The Orthodox Lutheran church tradition was at the time perceived by the Pietists as being spiritually parched. Luther's principles for the church would now become a reality again. Spener, at the time pastor in Frankfurt am Main, published *Pia Desideria* (Pious Desires) in 1675, a pietistic manifesto for church reform in the spirit of the Reformation (Gritsch, 2010, pp. 142–144). Alongside a revival of "the common priesthood," Spener wanted to implement a more intensive use of the Bible, with an emphasis on Christian praxis based on loving one's neighbour, the limiting of unnecessary dogmatic quarrels, a theological teaching reform where everything is directed to the practice of faith, and simpler and more edifying sermons (Gritsch, 2010, pp. 145–146). Spener, who saw himself as working in the spirit of Luther, claims in his manifesto *Pia Desideria* that Luther had advocated the common priesthood very strongly and that all Christians are dedicated to performing spiritual-priestly acts. Spener's term, however, was "the spiritual priesthood" (*das Geistlische Priesterthum*) (Spener, 1964a, p. 58).

Wengert (2008, p. 38) argues that what Luther intended to overcome in Roman clericalism with *An den christlichen Adel* resulted instead in Spener in separation between clergy and the laity. He writes, "The only difference between late-medieval clericalism and Lutheran Pietism was that under Pietism the laity finally gained ascendency over the clergy rather than the other way around. Either way, Luther's point is lost to church politics."

A reading of Spener's *Pia Desidera* shows that he wanted to return to what he understood as Luther's point of view. Spener mentions, with clear reference to Luther, whom he calls "the sainted man" (*der selige Mann*) (Spener, 1964a, p. 58), that all Christians have been made into priests and thus dedicated to performing spiritual-priestly acts. Spener also thought that the public exercise of spiritual functions requires appointment by a congregation aside from emergency situations. Spener was a pastor himself and did not want to abolish the ministerial office. But according to Spener, all Christians are obliged to perform spiritual acts and to occupy themselves with the Word of God, prayer, study, and teaching and to admonish, comfort, chastise, etc. In this work he sees the "spiritual priesthood" as a support for the ministerial office. All Christians can therefore exhort the ministry in a fraternal manner when necessary and be a support to the pastor. Spener (1964a, pp. 58–60) claims that it would not harm the ministerial office if "the spiritual priesthood" were carried out in such a way.

However, the division between clergy and laity that Wengert describes as a consequence of the pietistic programme becomes clearer if another aspect of "the common priesthood" in its pietistic setting is considered. In the Pietist understanding, it is the "reborn Christians" who belong to the spiritual priesthood. This means that there is a split right through the territorial parishes based on which people are considered reborn and faithful Christians. With this perspective, Wengert's comparison with late-medieval clericalism becomes evident. In the understanding and developments of Pietism, the spiritual priesthood becomes a secluded "Believers' Assembly" in the larger church (*ecclesiola in ecclesia*), but both the laity and the ordained ministry could be part of this group. It includes, therefore, not only the laity. Consequently, it also opened up a division among the ordained ministry because some of them were seen as belonging to the Believers' Assembly and some of them were seen as non-believers.

As demonstrated above, the concept of "common priesthood" has been reinforced during different epochs and used to highlight specific church-political beliefs. Legitimacy has been taken directly from Luther, although this is problematic from a theological and historical point of view. In the context of the Church of Sweden, "the common priesthood" has not only been used to support reforms in the organisational structure of the church, but has also had consequences for the liturgy.

6. The Common Priesthood and the Liturgy

In the 1960s, church statistics began to indicate a downward trend in church attendance in the Church of Sweden. The decrease became an indication that something was wrong with the liturgy. In this situation, the lay influence of the worship was emphasised (Brodd, 2012, p. 46). It was first and foremost the Social Democratic Party that made use of "the common priesthood." This was presented as a theological justification for the democratisation of the church organisation and worship. In ecclesiological research about the Social Democratic understanding of worship in Sweden, it was argued by Ahlbäck that a consistent theme in Social Democratic church policy documents has been to express the openness of the church. This means that the church services should not be designed to be solely a matter of concern for the people who are already active church attenders. The Social Democratic interpretation is, according to Ahlbäck, that active church attenders as a group are considered to be too narrow to express an "open Folk Church," and the church is therefore in danger of moving in an exclusive direction if it is formed only from the requests of the active church attenders. It is believed that an open Folk Church should endeavour to have church services that constitute a meeting place between people (Ahlbäck, 2003, p. 157). In the same context, the opposite of what is desired is called "Priest's worship" (prästens gudstjänst). The "Priest's worship" functions here as an expression of a hierarchical church structure that would be phased out through democratisation. Different forms of worship (varierat gudstjänstutbud) with lay participation was something that also was understood as being in accordance with Lutheran tradition (Ahlbäck, 2003, p. 162).

In the Social Democratic church platform *Öppna kyrkan* (Open the church), we find an argumentation with a direct reference to "the common priesthood." Regarding worship issues, the common responsibility shared by the Parish Council and the vicar is highlighted. The Parish Council with elected church politicians is understood as being responsible for the overall direction and development of worship life, while the vicar is seen as being responsible for the individual services. The worship service is described here in a way that could be interpreted as an "immanent" understanding of worship: "the occasion at which both problems and subjects for rejoicing may be expressed and put into a larger perspective."[1] The employed (clergy) are supposed to be in need of support in this work from what are referred to as the "common" priests (de "*allmänna*" prästerna) (*Öppna kyrkan*, 2000, p. 16). The common priests are related to the parishioners and implicitly to the church politicians as well. Here, perhaps surprisingly, a similarity to the Pietist pastor Spener is found, who argued that the clergy would receive support from the laity, whom he called the "spiritual priesthood." However, while the "spiritual priesthood" of Spener corresponded to the reborn group in the church (*ecclesiola in ecclesia*), the comprehension of the laity is broader here and refers to all people living in the parish (*församlingsborna*). In comparison with the understandings of Luther and Spener described above, it is possible to find a shift in the meaning of "the common priesthood." In Luther's view it is the baptised, in Spener's view it is the believers, and finally, in the Social Democratic platform, the common priesthood refers to all of the people living in the parish.

One specific example where democracy and the notion of "the common priesthood" have affected the liturgy of the Church of Sweden is in the ordination of bishops, a topic that has been analysed by Lundstedt. A new manual for the ordination of bishops was introduced in 1987. In addition to international ecumenical influence, the order that was introduced would reflect more clearly the lay people's new and more democratic role in the church. One important change from the earlier ordination manual from 1942 was the fact that the ordination was integrated into the common Sunday service. Changes in the liturgy were also made. The word "deliver" (*antvarda*) in the wording of ordination was removed because it was seen as expressing something hierarchical and feudal and related to enfeoffment, where the office was handed over from one bishop to another like a fiefdom (Lundstedt, 2006, p. 126).

Similar influences on the liturgy are apparent in the proposals made for changes in the worship service when drawing up a new Church

---

[1] "det tillfälle då problem och glädjeämnen får komma till uttryck och sättas in i ett större perspektiv" (*Öppna kyrkan*, 2000, p. 16).

Manual in the Church of Sweden in 2006. Rosenius (2002, p. 84) demonstrated that the proposals indicated a shift in ecclesiology where the focus moved from God to the people, in the sense that the church no longer appears to be a "church for the people" but instead "a people's church," where the people are the centre of the church and its subject. This becomes evident in the turning away from hierarchical structures in the liturgy. With respect to the church service and its aspects of leadership, we can therefore note a corresponding development between organisational aspects of the church and liturgy in a broader sense.

7. The Common Priesthood and Church Politics

The most evident theological motif of the democratisation of the Church of Sweden during the latter part of the twentieth century was "the common priesthood" (Lundstedt, 2006, p. 178). Lundstedt mentions that the problems and tensions that arose when popular sovereignty was transferred to the church were not primarily linked to the fact that the church was democratised, but because such sovereignty was transferred without profound theological reflection or anchoring (2006, p. 164).

The Swedish example of church democracy, where the church has adopted secular society's model of democracy, can in fact be seen as being less democratic regarding the actual distribution of power among church members. The legitimacy of the principle of popular sovereignty is based on the idea that the majority of the people will also vote in elections. It is in these elections that the church members hand over their powers and responsibilities to the elected members at different levels of the church. When the turnout is as low as it was for the church elections in 2013, it is in fact not the majority of the members who decides. If the turnout had been this low in a general election, it would certainly have been perceived as a democratic problem because only a small minority would have influenced who was elected. There is also a common risk for election coups when the great majority is silent and passively allows a small minority to appoint candidates to decide church issues. With a turnout as low as in the church election in 2013, it would be enough for 6.5% of the total number of members with voting rights (i.e. everyone who is 16 years and older on the day of the elections) to win the majority in the Church Assembly, a majority that in principle has the power to decide about the church's belief, confession, and order of worship (Kyrkoordning, 2016).[1]

---

[1] As previously described in this essay, in questions about doctrine the bishops have a powerful influence through the Doctrinal Commission, which can delay decisions.

Aside from the risk of election coups, a low turnout can of course be considered a democratic problem. We might suppose that only those who are interested actually vote and that the others are happy with the situation, and therefore that the democratic system is working. But a high turnout is usually associated with a strong legitimacy for an electoral system and a more equal distribution of power as well as improved representativeness.[1] A low turnout should then logically be associated with the opposite.

The election system that makes it possible for secular parties to participate as "nomination groups" in the church's elections is a heritage from the previous state church system. The fact that secular parties in the Swedish Parliament (*Riksdagen*) continue to work with church politics in one (and only one) of the country's religious denominations could certainly be criticised for confusing the borders between church and state according to the secular principle of the religious neutrality of the state. The implicit influence of secular ideologies on the church body could turn it into an arena for different secular ideologies such as "Social democracy," "Social conservatism and nationalism," or "Social liberalism and green politics." The fact that active participation in church work and worship services on a local parish level is not required for the candidates could easily allow candidates with weak church anchoring to run for the Church Assembly or for other levels of the church's decision-making bodies.

Consequently, the current system could fortify a division in the church between those who are elected to govern the church and those who are church workers, worshippers, and communicants, although these two groups to some extent naturally overlap. The current situation could be interpreted as a new variant or form of the divided church. Historically, this can be associated with the division of the baptised into a spiritual and worldly estate in the late-medieval church and with the divided churches of Pietism with its division between believers and non-believers.

But because of the leading principle of popular sovereignty, it is the Church Assembly that must take the final decisions in questions about doctrine and worship. If the Doctrinal Commission wants to stop a decision, there must be a new Church election, and the decision must achieve a qualified majority with ¾ of the votes of the Assembly (Kyrkoordning, 2016).

[1] Regarding the democratic value of election participation, see for example Martinsson, 2007.

8. Concluding Discussion and Remarks

It is now possible to discern some themes of understanding in the various interpretations and applications of "the common priesthood." The sharp criticism that Martin Luther expresses against the late-medieval church in *An den christlichen Adel* (To the Christian Nobility) in 1520 was revived in the Social Democratic platform *Öppna kyrkan* (Open the church) in 2000. In the Social Democratic platform, Luther's criticism is mentioned in connection with what is described as "the medieval notion," where priests were considered to have a special spiritual status (*Öppna kyrkan*, 2000, p. 11). "The medieval notion" functions as a contrast to the democratic view of the church that is understood here as corresponding to Luther's vision. The sixteenth-century struggle between Luther and the papacy can be seen as being moved into the contemporary Swedish church debate in order to legitimise an election system sourced from secular society and to provide this system with a harmonising ecclesiology. The theme of "the medieval notion" in the Social Democratic church platform can be found already in Spener's *Pia Desideria*, where he writes, "The papacy could suffer no greater injury than having Luther point out that all Christians have been called to exercise spiritual functions."[1] Spener also regrets the ecclesiastical conditions within the papacy when the spiritual acts were only assigned to the ordained priesthood (Spener, 1964a, pp. 58–59), namely "the medieval notion."

The politicisation of the common priesthood that Wengert associates with the movement of Pietism in the seventeenth century obviously has continued into the Swedish modern church context with the debate of democracy in the church. In the same way as with Spener's pietism, different groups of the church are set up against each other with regard to the question of power in the church; the difference is that today secular parties participate in these battles. Both examples are at the same time based on an argumentation derived from Luther, although the interpretation of what "the Lutheran" would mean is essentially quite different. Luther himself emphasised the opposite in *An den christlichen Adel*, by stressing the single Christian Estate (*des Christlichen Standes*) and his reference to the biblical notion of the body of Christ (1 Corinthians 12:12–31). These are notions that take the church into account as one varied but cohesive body. The church as a cohesive body has strong ecclesiological implications and could work as a corrective in

---

[1] Translation in English from the edition by Tappert, Spener 1964b, pp. 93–94.

further reform and development of a democratic church organisation and church leadership.

Finally, when considering the organisational system of the Lutheran Church of Sweden today, with the power structures it implies, it seems that the robust criticism of the power structures of papal supremacy that Martin Luther expressed in *An den christlichen Adel* in 1520 could likewise be directed at systems and power structures in place today.[1]

---

[1] This essay was submitted in 2016, a new Church election took place on September 17, 2017.

Chapter Eleven

Pre-Military Academies and and the "Making" of Religious-Zionist *Communal Leadership Capital*

Udi Lebel

1. *Introduction*

In 2013, the Minister of Defence and former Israel Defence Forces (IDF) Chief of Staff, Moshe Ya'alon, spoke at the Eli settlement in Samaria, at a ceremony commemorating the 25th anniversary of the establishment of the "Bnei David" (Sons of David) pre-military academy, where he said, "Here is a revolutionary educational establishment that has changed the face of higher education in Israel: the Bnei David pre-military academy… after which many others have been established as well… I have come here, residents of Eli, to congratulate you on behalf of the government of Israel. May you continue to grow and prosper, and to spread the special Torah being taught here at this place of study: the Torah of the Land of Israel among all the avenues of its people, and for the benefit of us all" (Ya'alon, 2013). The Minister of Defence, a secular kibbutz member, came to congratulate the emergence of pre-military academies, most of which are located in Judea and Samaria, outside of Israel's sovereign land. He aligned the institution with a Zionist, nationalist value, emphasizing its place as a role model for the entire Israeli society.

This chapter presents the establishment of pre-military academies as institutions that have accelerated the transition of the image of the religious Zionist movement in Israel, and especially institutions that have provided this social movement with Communal Leadership Capital that is based on militaristic symbolic capital (excellence in military service). This follows years during which the religious-Zionist leadership was sectoral. The transition is considered revolutionary, as the religious Zionist movement has acquired a new positioning in Israel society: it is identified with heroism and self-sacrifice – a positioning that grants it a new-found legitimacy that has enabled it to join the ranks of national leadership.

2. Structure and Methods

This chapter will discuss the concept of *Communal Leadership Capital*, explaining Israel's "Leadership Capital Regime" and the fact that it is formed by cultural militarism that grants Leadership Capital to army veterans. We shall then discuss the leadership generations of the country's religious-Zionist community up to Israeli society's so-called "motivation crisis": avoidance by the secular elites to enlist in combat units in the army and command positions. The pre-military academies will be examined as institutions which create a reserve for combat and command military service roles, a process that for the first time in the history of the State of Israel has led to the acquisition of *Communal Leadership Capital* for the religious-Zionist community. The paper relies on a communal discourse analysis (Nickels et al., 2012) of the religious and settler population, based on transcribed religious lectures, op-eds, media interviews, and halakhic (Jewish legal) literature on current affairs. The religious-Zionist movement and the settler community are perceived as a discourse community which positions itself within the broader discursive, cultural and political arenas (Wesley, 2005).

3. Leadership Capital

Since the first attempts at the study of leadership, it has become clear that leadership is strongly related to public perceptions and social reception processes more than to actual skills. This can be noted in Webber's discussion on the legitimacy of leaders (Riesebrodt, 1999), as well as in Pareto's findings on elites and the importance of balancing between leaders perceived by the public as "lions" and those perceived as "foxes" (Ashin, 1996).

According to the Capital Leadership approach, the leader is perceived as such by the individual not only thanks to his skills and performance, but also to the social constructs that have led to his perception, framing and reception as a leader (Gunter, 2010). Thus, among one community a person may be perceived as a leader, while in another community, comprised of different cultural dispositions, he will not be perceived as such. The Leadership Capital approach relies on Bourdieu's Field Theory, by which leadership should be researched as a field in which agents are positioned and perceived as leaders because they have exchanged a certain capital (social, familial, intellectual) for Leadership Capital and thus achieved positions of immense influence and accumulation of capital (Bourdieu, 1986). According to this approach, image and reputation are responsible for the fact that some people are perceived as potential leaders in society.

Leadership Capital is a meaningful resource which forms the Political Opportunity Structure available to the individual. Clearly, anyone holding such capital has more opportunities for accumulating power and for social leadership (Helms, 2015). The concept of Leadership Capital does not ignore the fact that the people who possess it may have leadership skills, but this does not explain their social reception as leaders, since the source of the capital is not in skills but in the social discourse that marked them as born leaders rather than others who may also possess identical skills and experience. This preference grants those who possess Leadership Capital preferred chances of filling leadership positions, both formal and informal, and so of accumulating the experience, knowledge, social capital and other relevant resources needed for developing leadership skills. This process will lead to a future public view that perceives such a person's leadership as "natural," because he would already have a history of leadership (Helms, 2015, p. 3).

4. Institutions and the Creation of Leadership Capital

The Sociology of Leadership has always identified that certain institutions use leadership "Launch Pads" in a range of areas, be it in the social, commercial or political arenas (Sagawa & Schramm, 2008). Each society has what Eichler refers to as "Bases of leadership" – organizations that are the main producers of leaders (Eichler, 1977). McCarthy and Zald (2002, p. 543), senior social movements researchers, have also stated that behind "spontaneous" organizations of pressure groups, protests movements, etc., we will always find institutions that have created or initiated the formal or informal leadership of these organizations, and that it is thanks to their existence that collective actions have been transformed from spontaneous to rational and controlled. Similar findings were described by Banaszak (1996) and Morris (1984).

But although it is commonly stipulated that leadership development institutions are making what Letender and his colleagues refer to as "the evolution of elite pathways," traditionally the study of those institutions was mostly qualitative, consisting of an examination of the skills that they provide to their participants. These studies were mostly directed by the sociological and organizational psychology disciplines (Letender et al., 2006). But following the emergence of the concept of

Leadership Capital, researchers realized that these institutions need to be examined as issuers of symbolic capital and the framing of their graduates as leaders. This realization has led Tomlinson et al. (2013) to define the concept of "Developing Leaders as Symbolic Violence." It's a study that demands a methodology from the world of discourse and culture analysis to follow the ability of those institutions to form a legitimacy for society's "leadership regime" (Kerr & Robinson, 2011, p. 155).

The Grandes Ecoles in France, Cambridge and Oxford in Britain, and the Ivy League in the USA are examples of institutions that provide its members with "Leadership Capital" and which have been studied as institutions whose graduates have enjoyed a symbolic rather than a material advantage (Baker, 2014).

Graduates of these institutions are able to convert ascription status into achievement status (Kalmijn, 1991). Potential leaders will always be around, but the symbolic power of a certain leadership development institution will lead to its graduates achieving Leadership Capital and not others, thereby granting a higher legitimacy to their inclusion in leadership positions (Kerr & Robinson, 2011; Malhota & Margalit, 2014). Hence, they will be called to realize their leadership potential (Helms, 2005), thereby breaking into the field of political opportunities (Goldstone, 2001). The "naturalness" of a leader is the product of social construction, which reproduces itself as if in a magic circle: because of the Leadership Capital held by some people, i.e., graduates of certain institutions, they will be found suitable to man leadership positions and roles, where they will actively experience all aspects of leadership: decision-making, motivating people, etc., and will become individuals who also possess proven leadership experience.

A further component of converting ascription status into achievement status is manifested thanks to the epistemic expectations instilled by these institutions in their members. Bourdieu himself researched the French *Grandes Ecoles*, whose graduates exclusively become part of the political and bureaucratic elite (Bourdieu, 1989). According to Bourdieu, these institutions teach an *Esprit de Corps* along with skills – an awareness of "natural" partnership and belongingness to an elite community, with informal codes and habits – that not only assist graduates of these institutions to be perceived by the public as natural leaders, but also assimilate this sense among themselves, making them believe that they represent a purposeful community. These findings were also identified by Kenway and Koh (2013) in their study of the elitist schools, which they defined as "cognitive machines" producing the ethos of those destined to become a leadership authority who must therefore excel and live up to these expectations. Similar conclusions were drawn by Leithwood and Mascall (2008) in their study on the relationship between public capital and the performance of individuals in leadership development institutions.

5. *Communal Leadership Capital*

Johnson (2010, p. 7) argues that the main challenge in terms of leadership development is to create a community of leaders. This, he believes, is the difference between leadership development and what he refers to as the development of strategic leadership. He too discusses the social construction processes that grant a community such a status, stating that this challenge would be achieved via social acknowledgement of the leadership skills among those belonging to a certain community, naturally in parallel to the establishment of a social and intellectual network to be used by these leaders.

Based on the concept of Leadership Capital – a community would be perceived as a "community of natural leaders" thanks to the fact that its members would exclusively obtain Leadership Capital and control society's leadership positions. This would lead to the community possessing what Helms refers to as "performative capital." This is a process of visibility: when society sees leaders, they will generally belong to the same community (Helms, 2016, p. 3), thereby attaching a leadership myth to that community. Naturally, this would also instil social expectations of the community, which in turn would urge its members to choose institutions and paths that would lead them to leadership positions (Leithwood & Mascall, 2008), thus creating a leadership community ethos (Kane, 2009). This is a significant resource in favour of mobility processes and social and political efficacy, as a community lacking the ability to provide the relevant capital that can be converted into a leadership image shall be forced to experience exclusion and inferiority in its efficacy for tracking its members in the social stratification (Brown, 1995).

6. *Cultural Militarism in Israel and the Leadership Capital Regime*

Since the establishment of the State of Israel, Israeli society has been characterized by cultural militarism, having adopted a "national security religion" as an Israeli version of the civil religion coined by Bellah (1967). This situation developed as a result of a number of factors, the main one being the need to survive in an almost constant state of military conflict, alongside the fact that the Zionist idea included many aspects of rebellion against the religious Jew of the diaspora, who were dedicated to learning the "Tora," as well as against any sign of femininity among its men, lack of self-respect and passiveness. This has led to a situation in which the formative experience of the diaspora in Israeli society is one of pogroms and the holocaust – situations in which the Jew was unable to protect himself. In Israel the warrior soldier – and especially the commander – was constructed as the ideal type of the new Jew: a Jew who is also masculine, in possession of self-respect, national awareness, and secular (Almog, 2000). Religious Jews were left out of this image, due in part to political arrangements that allowed them not to enlist in the army, or to opt for marginal positions. In addition, agricultural settlements in the early State of Israel – which alongside the military also characterized the new, muscular Jew – consisted almost entirely of secular groups, most of them socialist in nature.

The settlers, the farmers, and most of all the army commanders and warriors became the new symbols of Israel. They gained political capital, erotic capital, and Leadership Capital. In fact, from the establishment of the State of Israel until today, any political party, social movement, Business Corporation and other civil organization that does not include a senior reserve commander at its helm pushes itself to a marginal position (Lebel & Hatuka, 2016). Even in the "Post-Heroic Condition" (Lebel, 2016, 228) "military capital" remains a resource that is converted to Leadership Capital: retired officers are marked as "natural" leaders, even granting legitimacy to an anti-establishment social movement calling for Israel's withdrawal from the occupied settlements or from Lebanon, as well as to initiatives that are unrelated to the security agenda but wish to put purely civil issues in welfare, health or public administration on the general agenda. A range of studies have found that these retired army commanders are perceived as natural leaders and therefore as ideal candidates for handling crisis situations. Thus, for instance, governments have appointed retired generals as mayors of failing peripheral cities and as principals of schools and educational institutions (Lebel & Kaleb, 2005). Boards of Directors of business corporations in crisis have chosen to appoint a retired general as their top official, as have colleges and other higher education institutions. A similar trend can be seen in sports, education and culture. Finally, political parties are constantly courting retired generals, offering them leading positions, as it has been proven that without them, the parties would be perceived as lacking in Leadership Capital and sufficient legitimacy to form the nation's leadership (Lebel & Hatuka, 2016). In studies of retired generals from the establishment of the State until present times, it was found that the vast majority have transitioned from the army to leadership positions – in politics, public administration, foreign services, the legal system, academics, business or civil society (Barak & Tsur, 2012). In contrast to the situation in other countries where retired officers often face anonymity and the absence of purpose or occupation in civil life, the Israeli army equips its senior officers with Leadership Capital.

7. Zionist Religious Communal Leadership

Absence from the National Leadership and National Ethos

Israel's national leaders, from both the left and the right wings of the political map, were completely secular, viewing the establishment of the State as a rebellion against religious life (Conforti, 2011). Alongside the *haredi* (ultra-Orthodox) religious parties, who refused to recognize the Zionist endeavour, a small number of Religious-Zionist parties were established, led by lobbyists or rabbis. However, the vast majority of the Religious-Zionist population did not vote for these parties, whose activities were limited to minor efforts to exert influence in the religious realm, on matters such as kosher food, observance of the Sabbath, conversion to Judaism, the marking of holidays, and they were not perceived as major contributors to the national effort. When these parties were included in government, their leaders were awarded minor ministries such as Health, Internal Affairs, and Welfare (Goldshlag, 2007), as opposed to the top-tier ministries that spearheaded the national Zionistic vision, such as Foreign Affairs, Defence, Industry, or Finance. For the most part, leaders of the Religious-Zionist parties and institutions were political activists with rabbinical and academic training, mostly originating from Central or Eastern Europe (Don-Yehiya, 1981). In the eyes of the general Israeli public as well as the religious-Zionist population itself, Religious-Zionist leaders occupied the "last coach of the Zionist train" with no special accomplishments or contribution to their name and were devoid of any Leadership Capital (Leon, 2015).

The Rabbinical-Settler Leadership

In 1967, in the wake of the Six-Day War, Israel occupied Judea, Samaria and the Gaza Strip (in addition to Sinai and the Golan Heights). While the position of most of Israel's leadership was that these territories would not become part of the sovereign State, an alternative political approach began to emerge among Religious-Zionist groups, advanced by the students and followers of Rabbi Zvi Yehuda Kook, expressing the Religious-Zionist aspiration to settle these territories and annex them to the State, in fulfilment of the biblical command of settling the Land of Israel (Don-Yehiya, 2014a). This line of thought, enveloped in messianic-religious rhetoric, was first institutionalized in 1974 with the establishment of *Gush Emunim*, a social movement whose leaders initiated the replacement of leadership of the Religious-Zionist Party (*Mafdal*) (Leon, 2009). While prior to the establishment of *Gush Emunim* the rare individual attempts to settle in "the territories" had generally been regarded as an esoteric and marginal phenomenon, from this point onwards settlement became an institutionalized sub-culture within religious-Nationalism. Its leaders began expressing themselves for the first time on external and security matters, setting aside other agendas and focusing on settling Judea and Samaria and opposing any territorial compromise.

Gush Emunim had a tremendous impact on Religious-Zionist society. Many in the Religious-Zionist sector felt that this was their opportunity to "get into Zionism" and to replicate in Judea and Samaria what the Socialist-Zionist leaders had done during the establishment of the State: settling the land and "blooming the desert" (Harnoy, 1994). Over a short period of time, increasing numbers of official and non-official Religious-Zionist leaders became part of the settler community. Most of them had pursued advanced religious studies, generally at the *Merkaz Harav Yeshiva* or one of its affiliates (where Rabbi Kook's doctrine was taught). In parallel, Judea and Samaria quickly became an inseparable part of the lives of most Religious-Zionists in Israel, because of their visits to the many sacred Jewish sites situated in these areas and because their sons and daughters built their homes in new settlements established as religious communities. Most importantly, the vast majority of the educational institutions orientated to this sector of the population – elementary schools as well as yeshiva high schools and religious high schools for girls – were established in Judea and Samaria, thereby transforming this region into an inseparable part of the childhood landscape of the younger generation (Leon, 2015). At the same time, the dominant Religious-Zionist political worldview became increasingly hawkish, with support for annexation of these territories and opposition to any territorial concessions as the top item on its ideological agenda, consolidating the *Mafdal* party as a manifestly right-wing party (Pedahzur, 2012). A slew of surveys and studies indicate that the Religious-Zionist sector is the only sector in Israel for whom the "Green Line" does not exist, and that the vast majority of this population votes for right-wing parties (Mozes, 2009).

The embedding of Religious-Zionism in Judea and Samaria was counterproductive in terms of its position within Israeli society. The Leadership Capital of its leaders was internal and sectorial, relevant only within the settlers' society, and those who used it were perceived by the general Israeli society as having deviated from the democratic game. This perception was reinforced by such statements as that of Rabbi Zvi Yehuda Kook, for example, asserting that there would be no legal validity to a decision by the Israeli government to withdraw from the territories or to prevent their settlement because "These areas have belonged to us [the Jews] since the times of Abraham, Isaac and Jacob, and they are also the inheritance of millions of our brethren around the world" (Don-Yehiya, 1998, p. 445).

Despite their aspirations, the settlers were not ratified by the Israeli elites as successors of the Zionist movement. When asked whether the settlements were the continuation of Zionist settlement in Israel, Israeli writer Amos Oz responded, "No. I don't see them as a continuation of Zionist settlement. I opposed them from the very first settlement to the very last" (Hadari-Ramage, 1994, p. 3). Former Prime Minister Yitzhak Rabin, who was the IDF Chief of Staff during the Six-Day War when the territories were occupied, wrote in his book, "I see *Gush Emunim* as a very grave problem – a cancer in the body of Israeli democracy" (Rabin, 1979, p. 551).

The Israeli left-wing perceived the settlers as having "savagely raped the State […] tricking their way to building their settlements" , in the words of former Minister and MP Yossi Sarid, who opposed the settlers' socio-political aspirations to join the national leadership on the basis of their settlement enterprise. "The settlers have always pretended to have inherited the Labor movement, its values and symbols, to continue its path and to inherit its honor […] This is their staged production about the history of Israeli settlement," he wrote (Sarid, 1991). A 2004 study found the Israeli left to be more antagonistic towards the settlers than it was towards the Palestinians; and the settlers, more than the Palestinians, were perceived as obstructing the peace process (Moore & Aweiss, 2002; 2004). Academically, most studies on the Religious-Zionist movement during the settlement period were based on theoretical models borrowed from the academic realms of criminology, fundamentalism and colonialism (Lebel & Orkibi, in preparation).

Such perceptions were not limited to the Israeli left. A number of studies showed evidence of alienation and apprehension towards the settlers even amongst secular right-wing population, and even those sympathizing with their cause asserted their willingness to evacuate settlements as part of a peace process (Bilig & Lebel, 2013). This situation caused much frustration among Religious-Zionists, as expressed, for example, by Meir Harnoy, a founder of *Gush Emunim*, "How is it possible that those same settlers, pioneers of the national movement, who – despite all the political disputes – were regarded as admirable pioneers, were transformed overnight into enemies of peace, […] money-grabbers, and a drain on the State's resources?" (Harnoy, 1994, p. 219).

The Religious-Zionists themselves contributed to the growing sense of alienation towards them through the development of a separatist lifestyle, both in Judea and Samaria and in religious neighbourhoods within cities, setting themselves apart from general Israeli society (Leon, 2015).

8. *The Promotion of National Elite Exchange*

Towards the end of the millennium, and following the implementation of the Disengagement Plan (2005) with the support of a majority of the Israeli public, a third generation of Religious-Zionist leadership began to evolve among those whose formative years where marked by the Oslo Accords (1993), the assassination of Prime Minister Yitzhak Rabin (1995), and the Disengagement Plan (2005) – three events that increased the sense of isolation among the Religious-Zionist sector and the sense that the Israeli public did not perceive it as a legitimate partner for leadership of the country. In view of this situation, two parallel and seemingly opposing trends began to emerge from the Religious-Zionist leadership.

A Growing Hatred towards Israeli Neo-Liberal Founding Elites
This approach marks the "liberal elites" as bearing responsibility for Israel's transformation into a weak, defeated country that has lost its national conscience and adopted global neo-liberal values that will lead to its destruction. This attitude was expressed especially against the legal system, the media, academia, and Israeli culture – arenas of power controlled mainly by the secular upper-middle class, which exists in a state of post-modernism and even post-nationalism. Religious-Zionist opposition perceived this mind-set as preferring territorial concessions

for peace over maintaining the will and resilience necessary to pursue the nation's historic vision.

Thus, for instance, Rabbi Yosef Weitzen, of the Beit El Yeshiva, in an article entitled "Perceptions towards the State of Israel," explained that Rabbi Zvi Yehuda Kook, the spiritual guide venerated by rabbis in Judea and Samaria, anticipated that "The secular national movement will not persist for long... it will soon become a movement opposed to the national idea," because the secular Zionist "has been influenced by the ideas of the gentiles and the left... [and may be compared to] an 'infant taken captive'[1]...by the religion of democracy's values of false freedom." Weitzen also wrote, "Not only can the State not be trusted in matters of religion, it also cannot be trusted in matters of nationality," explaining that "this is a cultural war. A war for life and death [...] a war against confused people who are dragging the nation towards terrible deeds. Acts of self-destruction" (Lebel & Lubish-Omer, 2012, pp. 182–183).

Integrating into the Secular Arenas of Power
In parallel, and sometimes among the same speakers, there developed a discourse which called upon the younger generation of Religious-Zionists, especially settlers, to integrate into those same institutions and arenas of power controlled by the elite against which the "culture war" was supposed to be fought. Thus, for instance, in a widely distributed leaflet addressed to Religious-Zionist youths by Rabbi Eli Sadan, today the head of the pre-military academy at the settlement of Eli in Samaria, there is repeated emphasis on the concept of "taking responsibility," and the religious public is repeatedly asked the same question: "Where were we?" "Where were we when they established *Hashomer* [the pre-State Jewish defence organization], the work battalions, the *Palmach* and the *Haganah*? Where were we when pioneering settlements were established, when the underground organizations and then the IDF were established? Where have we been when the national institutions were founded and the leadership was established? Taking responsibility for the establishment of the Jewish State, which to our regret has become a Jewish-secular state? [...] It is much easier to blame others, but we should look in the mirror and ask ourselves some hard questions" (Sadan, 2007, pp. 7–9).

Sadan explained to the younger generation that their sense of disappointment and anger towards the State, especially in view of the evac-

---

[1] Talmudic term referring to a Jewish individual who sins inadvertently as a result of having been raised outside of a Jewish community and hence without an appreciation for the principles and practices of Judaism.

uation of settlements as part of the Disengagement Plan, would lose all its relevance if they would now act via institutionalized (Religious-Zionist) channels against the army and the government, dismissing them as belonging to a secular world in which the religious public has no place. Instead, Sadan proposed a "Great and sacred ideal to leave the religious study-hall and 'assume responsibility'" (Sadan, 2007, p. 31).

These two voices seem to be contradictory. While the first points to a loathing and fear of any contact with the Israeli secular world, which had led most Religious-Zionist youths to study in separate schools, consume sectorial media, and live in homogenous neighbourhoods or settlements, the other aspires to lead the younger Religious-Zionist generation into the very same secular arenas which disseminate the ideas that Religious-Zionist leaders regard as a threat (neo-liberalism, feminism, postcolonialism, anti-militarism, globalization, and more).

Towards a New Communnal Leadership Development
I argue that there is no contradiction, but rather attributes that have been implemented in the pre-military academies. The purpose of these institutions was to send the young generation to the army – and hence, to the general society. But this process must gain legitimacy within the community, and this can only be achieved if it is made clear that during this process the religious soldier will not become secular, but rather that during his studies at the pre-military academy he would experience ideological processes which would enable him to maintain his religious identity even when serving alongside secular soldiers. Thus, the pre-military academy is presented as an "immunizing" institution that enables its graduates to remain loyal agents of the religious Zionist movement even while integrating into Israeli society.

Rabbi Elli Horowitz is one of many to express this theme, which bridges between these two voices. According to Horowitz and his colleagues, a negation of secular Israeli culture alongside a desire to join its ranks "with immunity" requires that a special status be awarded to a rabbinical leadership that could offer the appropriate "immunization" to religious youths before they enter secular arenas, as well as during their stay (Horowitz, 2007, pp. 90–92). He believed that what is needed are special processes to prepare the Religious-Zionist youths prior to entering Israel's public arenas. "We are at war […], we are soldiers […] soldiers in the war of beliefs and opinions. Therefore, before heading out into battle, we too must be trained. One cannot go into battle without having the foundations of fighting embedded in the depths of one's soul [...] so that in the heat of battle [...] he can react automatically [...]. So it is in the culture war" (Horowitz, 2007, pp. 68–70). As shall be illustrated below, this line of thought underlies the logic behind the pre-military academies established in order to prepare Religious-Zionist youths for their military service.

9. The Establishment of the Pre-Military Academies

Since the end of the millennium, Israeli elite groups – mostly secular, middle class and upwards, in cities and kibbutzim – have become increasingly more cosmopolitical, postmodern and even postnationalist. These Israeli elites have come to be characterized by what has been referred to as a "civil-military gap" (Lebel, 2010), which in Israel has led to moral panic or "the motivation crisis": a dramatic decline in the willingness to enlist in the army in general and in combat and command positions in particular (Levy, 2009). Among these groups it became legitimate not to rely on military capital to achieve promotion in individualistic careers. This left a vacuum in the community's identification with Israeli Leadership Capital as the kibbutz movement, which has undergone a postmodernistic privatization process, stopped being the reserve of military leadership. Thus, for instance, towards the end of the millennium, the commander in chief of the IDF, in a meeting of the Knesset's foreign affairs and security committee, complained about the many youths evading the army, saying that "the kibbutz movement has lost the battle in its rates of volunteering to combat units and willingness to serve as officers" (Haaretz, August 22, 1996). The State began searching for a solution among new groups.

The process of the establishment of the pre-military academies began in 1987, when two IDF Major-Generals (Amram Mitzna, then head of the IDF Central Command, and Yossi Ben Hanan, then the IDF's Armoured Corps Commander) summoned Rabbi Yigal Levinstein, then Deputy Commander of a reserve armoured battalion, to try and convince him to return to the army as a career officer. During the meeting, the men discussed the army's difficulty in continued reliance on the recruitment of secular Israeli populations, which until then had comprised most of the army's combat soldiers. The two Major-Generals complained to Rabbi Levinstein that "the religious youths do not continue to officers' training courses and do not assume responsibility." Major-General Mitzna said that "Israeli society today is undergoing a crisis of values that keeps growing [...] The religious public has deep motivational values [...] we believe that this public should make a greater contribution to the army" (Huberman, 2004).

Following the meeting, Rabbi Levinstein and his teacher, Rabbi Eli Sadan, embarked upon the establishment of "Bnei David" – the first pre-military academy, which opened a year later in the settlement of Eli in Samaria.

This religious institution was the first of its kind. While secular youths enlisted in the army immediately after finishing high school, the purpose of this institution was to prepare religious youths, after completing high school, for their integration in the army, by means of a one- or two-year program that would equip them with spiritual and religious resources, along with physical training, and a special group consciousness and cohesion aimed at minimizing the risk of losing their religious identity during their service in the IDF or a lessening of their motivation to contribute to the army. The program also sought to gain legitimacy among the rabbinical leadership for army service outside of the special *"yeshivat Hesder"* units, while still ensuring "immunity."

In the Israeli context this was a pioneering initiative in terms of military service amongst the religious public. Until then, 18-year-old religious men belonged to one of three groups:

- The alienated group: the *haredi* [Ultra-Orthodox] population, essentially absent from the Israeli draft (Bick, 2010)
- The integrated group: Religious-Zionist youths who enlisted after completing high school. Few served in combat units, and of those who did, many ended up assimilating into the secular environment.
- The "gated" group: Religious-Zionist youths who, after completing their high school studies, joined *hesder* ("arrangement") yeshivas – so-called because of the arrangement between the Religious-Zionist heads of these institutions and the Ministry of Defence, which enables these students to engage in religious studies for five years, during which they serve in the army for a period of 16 months. During their army service these students serve within homogenous units, where they are able to conduct a fully religious life (Cohen, 1993). In this respect, the *hesder* yeshivas are actually a sort of "gated community" within the army, preventing its members from being exposed to the Israeli army's melting pot (Thurau-Gray, 2002). This reality necessarily relegates *hesder* yeshiva students to a rather marginal status in the army, mostly owing to the fact that the shortened service does not allow for commander training courses or a commitment to serve an extra year.

The pre-military academy established in Eli was innovative in that its purpose was seemingly the exact opposite to that of the *hesder* yeshivas: not to enclose the religious soldier within the confines of a religious unit, but rather to encourage him to enlist in regular army units, alongside secular soldiers. At the same time, he remains conscious of his affiliation to a community which was part of his identity before, during and even after his military service; a community whose leadership of military personnel and rabbis represented his "significant other" throughout his military service, providing encouragement, advice, problem-solving, and – where necessary – advocacy within the army. Rabbi Eli Sadan explained that he had consciously chosen the name *mechina* (preparatory program) for the institution and not yeshiva because he believed that the range of experiences gained at the *mechina*, including in the intellectual and religious realms, are intended to offer students "spiritual preparation [...] for coping with the spiritual and mental challenges of military service" (Huberman, 2004).

The Israeli pre-military academy is similar to the American military academy, although its graduates are recruited together with the general population and not in separate military units. The curriculum – as developed in Eli and replicated in other religious pre-military academies – includes sports, navigation training, and drilling of combat methods, along with an in-depth study of military history and issues of national security, and lectures by current and former senior army commanders. Religious studies are mandatory, as in the yeshivas. The all-round environment frames the importance of the military service as a religious commandment, and maintains a fully religious life. The academy itself is a sort of cross between a yeshiva and an army base, as the students' daily lives – from cleaning through guard duty, community work, and regular religious studies – are managed by the students themselves. They leave the academy premises only occasionally, visiting their families on alternate weekends.

During their army service, the pre-military academy remains a "second home" for its soldiers – a supportive institution, a place for meetings and consultation, ceremonies and holidays; a place they visit during furlough. A contact person is appointed for each class, and his role is to maintain contact with the students while they are soldiers. Representatives of the academy attend their graduates' military ceremonies, and the soldiers themselves participate in ceremonies held at their academy, with the approval of their army commanders. Newsletters from the academy are sent to its graduates by post or by e-mail. Academy heads visit their graduates in the mobilization areas for the battalions in which they serve, to wish them well. The knowledge that academy representatives are to be found throughout the army is a source of pride among students and academy heads alike. In 2006 Rabbi Sadan reported that, at any given time, 450–500 graduates of his pre-military academy are serving in the army (Rossman-Stollman, 2006, p. 169). Moreover, this has led to the creation of a new class identity in the army, referred to as the *mechinistim* – the name given to pre-military academy graduates in the army (Evenshpanger, 2011, p. 57).

10. A Culture Shift in Religious-Zionist Society

The pre-military academy revolution has led to the establishment of a heroic militaristic subculture, characterized by a new lifestyle that has not been part of Jewish religious society since biblical times, it seems. Historically, religious Jews tended to avoid military service, whether via formal financial arrangements with their host nations in the Diaspora, or via collective avoidance and desertion (Cohen, 1997). However, while in the past the rabbinical leadership attempted to keep the young generations away from military service, both in the Diaspora and in Israel, since the establishment of the pre-military academies, Religious-Zionist rabbis – especially in Judea and Samaria – have been encouraging youths to embark upon meaningful military service, which has begun to be framed as a religious commandment. Rabbi Horowitz wrote, "Following years in which young religious men were encouraged to become learned scholars, they are now urged to become brave soldiers […] when war is upon us we shall not turn our backs or cry over our bitter fate. War is not like a bothersome fly that we can wish was not there. War is a challenge that we need; it deepens our self-knowledge and requires us to find and expose among ourselves and our people the powers and spiritual insights that were unknown to us until now" (Horowitz, 2007, p. 262).

Amongst Religious-Zionist society, this seems to be a granting of legitimacy to an existing disposition among the youth, which has been routinely suppressed since the establishment of the State. Israeli Religious-Zionist youths have grown up in a country characterized by cultural militarism, where military service is considered the ultimate masculine experience, where the cultural heroes are brave commanders and battle stories and legends abound. However, this sector of youths, despite their passion to be part of this "true Israeli-ness," was instructed by its religious leadership not to serve in the army. Gideon Aran, who studied the *Gush Emunim* movement, wrote that *Merkaz Harav* Yeshiva students always idolized the warrior and military officer, and that even Rabbi Zvi Yehuda Kook himself, "despite the fact that he set many restrictions on military service, worshipped militarism," with the result that "the yeshiva adhered to a sort of militaristic cult" (Aran, 2013, pp. 193–194). It is therefore no wonder that suddenly, when it became possible for religious youths to become part of this military physical self-fulfilment, after years in which this dimension had been closed off to them, they responded with alacrity and enthusiasm.

The message has spread, and since the establishment of the pre-military academy at the settlement of Eli, 36 additional pre-military academies have been established throughout the country, most of them religious. The academy at Eli is known today as "the mother of all pre-military academies" and is a role model for all others. Forty-two percent of these academies are located beyond the 1967 border, and even the first secular pre-military academy was established beyond the Green Line.

11. *National Recognition in the Zionist-Religious Communal Leadership Capital*

Gradually, the Ministry of Defence and the army began to encourage religious enlisters to undertake a period of study at the pre-military academy prior to their enlistment, and began to show a preference for pre-military academy graduates for placement in prestigious positions. It was found that the proportion of combat soldiers among pre-military academies graduates is twice as high as their proportion among general intake recruits; the number of commanders among their graduates is proportionately 3.5 times higher; and there are proportionately three times as many officers among them. In June 2012, a quarter of those completing infantry officers courses were graduates of pre-military academies, and 18% of graduates of officers courses in combat support corps (artillery, armoured corps and others). Notably, at the time, graduates of pre-military academies counted for only 4% of the total enlistment figures (Harel, 2013, p. 54).

The Judea and Samaria region – home to a large portion of the Religious-Zionist population – has attained a unique status in terms of rates of enlistment for combat and command positions. In 2010, investigators from the IDF Manpower Division analysed the data for enlistment among the regional councils. Mount Hebron regional council achieved first place in overall enlistment with a rate of 96.4%. Of these recruits, 83.3% were serving as combatants (Rubin, 2010). In the same year, 61% of those who enlisted in the army from Samaria choose to serve in combat units, compared with 36% from Tel Aviv (Heller, 2011).

In 2011 the proportion of young men from Samaria enlisting in the army was on the rise, reaching 81.2% compared with a national average of 74.8%. In addition, the proportion of combat soldiers among all recruits from Samaria was 67.1% (meaning that 2 out of every 3 recruits are combat soldiers), compared with a national average of 39.5%. The Samaria region also leads in its proportion of officers: 15.9% (meaning that 1 out of every 6 soldiers from Samaria becomes an officer) compared with a national average of 9.3%. Finally, 88% of all army enlisters from Samaria (9 out of 10) opt for a "meaningful army service" (combat units).

According to an article published in the IDF's *Bamahane* weekly magazine, 13% of the IDF's company commanders come from settlements (Hendel, 2012, 295). The same figures were repeated in 2013, when proportionally the greatest number of soldiers enlisting in combat units came from Judea and Samaria (Harel, 2013, pp. 87–89). Of the five leading municipalities in the number of combat soldiers, three are in Judea and Samaria. Settlements in Judea and Samaria also provided the highest number of officers.

12. Conclusions

Religious-Zionist Community Empowerment
In 2002, on the occasion of 100 years of existence of the Religious-Zionist movement, researcher and writer Assaf Inbari wrote a mass entitled *One Hundred Years of Solitude*. He described how "Religious-Zionism has defeated itself by becoming a settlement movement," transforming it into an "unloved, misunderstood, and barely legitimate movement" (Inbari, 2002). A decade later, Anat Roth wrote about the effect of the pre-military academies revolution on the Religious-Zionist sector, describing the process as transitioning "from Decline to Political Recovery" (Roth, 2015, p. 209). In the political context, she shows that the process has created a transition from a sense of defeat and lack of political efficacy to unprecedented empowerment: for the first time the sectorial party affiliated with the Religious-Zionist movement attracted voters who are not part of the religious sector, and the party started perceiving itself as suitable for voicing its opinions on all public issues in Israel, not just religious-educational ones, and most importantly, for the first time in its history, the party and its voters began to perceive themselves as a group whose goal is to one day lead the entire country. Naftali Bennett (reserved major), chosen to lead the party in the 2013 national elections, stated that at this point the goal of the Religious-Zionist movement is to "take com-

mand…finish with the 'sectorial' business… our public knows how to lead wherever it is: in IDF command, in the education system…." He emphasized that change should be brought on also in the political arena and that also in this area religious people will become "the commanders" (Roth, 2015, p. 223). Naftali Bennett is an example of a person in possession of Leadership Capital: he served as an officer in a special IDF combat unit. After his retirement from the army, he entered the hi-tech sector and even became a millionaire. He then managed the Prime Minister's office and headed a prominent civil society movement, positions that for years were traditionally carried out by secular officials (Roth, 2015). Clearly, the unprecedented integration of religious Zionists in army command and in the political arena has led to a de-segregation of religion in Israel, following years in which the public was only exposed to religious Israelis in religious arenas (Cohen, 1999).

Assimilating the Logic behind the Secular Power Elite
The leadership of Rabbi Eli Sadan, founder of the pre-military academies, may be perceived on the one hand as manipulative, as being a leader of a sect working to overpower the State. Roy Sharon, a Religious-Zionist and reporter for Channel 10, wrote about Rabbi Eli Sadan in an article entitled, "The most influential Religious-Zionist of our generation." "He doesn't speak on stage or write public articles. Hundreds of his students are spread all over Israel's most influential places […] mostly in the security establishment, the IDF, Israel Security Agency, and the Mossad. Chiefs of Staff and army commanders of all ranks have consulted with him for years, as do government ministers and other senior political figures. Everyone recognizes the power of this man; he is the mentor of Religious-Zionism" (Sharon, 2014).

On the other hand, the work of Sadan and other rabbis and former army personnel leading the pre-army academies may be viewed as proof that the Religious-Zionist community has internalized the secular logic of creating leadership for political efficacy, and has begun to act in a way that corresponds with the conventional concepts of political science such as the development of a power elite and social networks, as has been described from the time of C. Wright Mills' pioneering paper to today (Barratt, 2014): a realization of the fact that presence in the public arena is the key to forming its policy. Following in Sadan's footsteps, many other rabbis realized this and called on their students to enlist in the army – not so as to "take over the country," but to maximize the impact of their community. As Rabbi Shlomo Aviner wrote about the army, "If you are not inside – you don't make an impact. You only cause harm to yourself and others will fill your place – as had happened to the leftist refusers" (Aviner, 2005).

The accelerated participation in military leadership roles gave rise to a sense of capability and a passion to lead parallel revolutions in other public arenas as well. In 2002, Rabbi Aryeh Stern, now Chief Rabbi of Jerusalem, wrote an article entitled "Towards a Jewish Leadership" in which he, too, expressed a desire for Religious-Zionists to take positions in Israel's arenas of power, thereby strengthening the community's Leadership Capital and its social mobility. "It's time to dare to take action that would result in the integration of Religious-Zionist leaders in senior positions within the country's central leadership […] Extensive efforts must be invested in the struggle against the ideological secularism which has gained a place for itself in the urban setting and among the elites controlling the main systems that affect our lives. There is no doubt that the only power that can counter this situation is the power of Religious-Zionism, which – with the right organization and good leadership – would be able to provide talented people for any position and offer an alternative in governance to the secular movements […] The people of Israel are yearning for a fresh leadership by people of faith, and such leadership can and must arise from within Religious-Zionism. May it be God's will that the following would be true for us: 'Open for me a slot like the eye of a needle and I will open for you a space like a hall'" (Stern, 2002).

On the tenth anniversary of Israel's disengagement from the Gaza Strip, Rabbi Abraham Wasserman wrote, "During the past twenty years extra-parliamentary forces have gained power and the nation is being led also – perhaps mainly – from outside the Knesset […]. Despite their small numbers, the members of these groups work consistently, powerfully and systematically, recruiting many Parliament members and gaining much power […]. The weight of the individual or the small group has become central in political, military, social, cultural and economic decision-making." Wasserman further claimed that "Over the past 35 years, a majority has voted – almost consistently – for parties whose platforms support settling the land, but small and persistent groups that are highly influential in the media, the legal system, the cultural sphere, and academia, lead the elected [decision-makers] to implement a completely opposite agenda." His conclusion is clear. "We will not consolidate our path solely by settling in our sacred land […] From now on the aim is to settle within the centres of power" (Wasserman, 2015).

Religionization of the Military or Militarization of Religion?

It appears that the main question to be asked is which side will co-opt the other. The focus of our discussion is a group that enjoys ongoing communal immunity, knowing that they are in the midst of a culture war against secular Zionism, that they must not be influenced by it, and that their job is to inherit its place. Similar "immunizing" institutions are already working to build a religious/settler leadership in academia, culture, and civil administration (Lebel & Lubish-Omer, 2012, p. 186). But is it really possible to integrate into secular fields without being affected by the rules of the game, by the organizing culture, and by its world of values? It seems that only the future will tell. On the one hand, some neo-liberal secular voices have expressed concern over the increasing numbers of Religious-Zionists holding senior positions in state institutions in general, and in the army in particular. They perceive the openly stated aim of this development – not integration but rather immunization and repair – as a danger, threatening the imposition of a religious, conservative, militaristic agenda. On the other hand, is it truly possible to enter into the secular arena without being affected by it, by the organizing culture and its values?

A range of studies on armies in general and on the Israeli army in particular have shown that homogenous groups, with a communal agenda and sectorial awareness, that have entered the army have eventually experienced assimilation and co-optation. In an attempt to predict the future – the Israeli army, although perceived by the Religious-Zionist movement as a launch pad for their revolution – is in practice a regulating place, which will expose Religious-Zionist youths to the secular world and enable them to adopt the national-secular rationale. In this context, the "cultural war" discourse is in fact meant to grant legitimacy to integrating within general society, more than it is intended to form concrete behaviour in daily life.

Leadership Capital for Israel's Religious-Zionist Community

Following years in which the military establishment perceived the community of settlers as "a problem," especially because they included groups that engaged in direct confrontation with the army in an attempt to defend illegal settlements in the occupied territories, they are now perceived by the military establishment as a "solution." This precedential realization that the settlers can be a positive role model for Israel's secular community can be expressed in the words of the spokeswoman of the "Yesha" Council (council of settlements in Judea and Samaria): "Our fallen soldiers fill the military cemeteries and through their deaths give the Israeli public a short lesson in loving their country" (Amarusi, 2007).

Israeli society has absorbed this message. Year after year, in a survey examining positions towards settlers and settlements among Israelis living west of the Green Line, when asked "Who best represents the settlers?," most respondents answer, "Religious-Zionists serving in combat roles in the army" (Bilig & Lebel, 2013).

Even Reuven Rivlin, current President of the State of Israel, visited the pre-military academy at Eli settlement, where he told students that he believes they are worthy of being a part of the country's national leadership: "Over time this place of Torah study has become a place that is producing a generation of leaders [...]. You can be company and platoon commanders, battalion and brigade commanders – and yes, also Major-Generals, Chiefs of Staff and Prime Ministers. We cannot demand the blood and sacrifice of different parts of society and not allow them to lead the people and steer the ship [...]. The principle must be clear: sharing the burden means equality in leadership" (Rivlin, 2014).

Israel's Military and the Communal Leadership Capital Regime

For nearly three decades the pre-military academies have acted as Institutional Launch Pads of security leadership and providers of *Communal Leadership Capital* for Israel's Religious-Zionist community. This case study has shown that in Israeli culture the Military and other security institutions continue to be the main institutions that brand *Communal Leadership Capital*.

Epilogue

Back to the Roots: Paradoxes in the Development of Leadership Theories

Joke van Saane

1. Introduction

In the previous chapters several divergent research studies on leadership in a religious context are presented. Obviously, the discussion on religious leadership reflects the discussion on leadership in general. However, this volume shows a remarkable theoretical paradox. On the one hand, the discussion in the religious domain follows the development in leadership theories from a focus on the personal traits of effective leaders to a focus on socially constructive ideas about leadership. On the other hand, within the religious context, the discussion about leadership does not abandon the focus on the traits and skills of the leader at all, due to specific developments within institutional religion. In this chapter this paradoxical theoretical development will be explained by referring to some of the previous chapters, illustrating this theoretical tension.

2. Leadership and Personality

Leadership is in the spotlight, not only in society but also in diverse disciplines such as psychology, social sciences, economics and theology. However, leadership is certainly not a new scientific concept; theories in modern psychology and business administration still refer to authors who published a century ago, while the sources of theology are of course much older. It is striking that in traditional theories of leadership, much attention has been paid to the person of the leader. The classic work of Stogdill (1948, 1974) presents the characteristics and skills of the leader as predicting the effectiveness of leadership. In a review of multiple studies, Stogdill presents common traits associated with effective leadership. Characteristics are mentioned like intelligence, initiative and self-confidence. Dominance, assertiveness, ambition, decisiveness and stress tolerance traits also turn out to be characteristic of effective leaders. This type of knowledge seems to be useful in selection procedures for leaders. The *Center for Creative Leadership* nuances the significance of these properties, however, while effective leadership is also related to the extent to which these properties match the characteristics of the followers. That does not prevent the CCL presenting another list of relevant characteristics for successful leadership in its *Handbook for Creative Leadership* (Van Velsor et al., 2010). This list includes the following traits: emotional stability, self-defence, interpersonal focus, and technical or cognitive skills. According to CCL, these traits are predictors of effective and successful leadership in different domains, in both the profit and the non-profit sector. Training programmes on leadership should focus on strengthening these traits and skills.

Isolating personality traits and skills to provide predictors of successful leadership has a long history in leadership theories. In some cases, these theories are very detailed. The work of Nauss can be seen as an example. Skills for successful predecessors and leaders of interest are identified by Nauss (1996) as having no fewer than 65 variables in 56 dimensions. The most important ones seem to be: persuasion, relationship orientation, task orientation, teamwork ability, and stress tolerance. In other words, successful leadership has to do with communication skills, social skills and the appropriate cognitive skills. In addition, skills can be taught, learned and developed – in contrast to personality traits.

This classic paradigm in the leadership discourse with its strong focus on personality traits and skills has been very influential in theories about religious leadership for a long time. Within this frame, successful and effective leadership within religious groups is related to the characteristics of the leader or the pastor. Obviously, this frame is constructive because of its clarity. Within this frame, the effectiveness of leadership can easily be increased: if we know which traits and skills are good predictors of effective leadership, training programs and selection procedures can become far more efficient. Indeed, these insights about predictive traits not only play a role in selection processes, they also provide a basis for training programs for religious leaders or pastors. In many programs, in addition to the classic curriculum with a focus on sources, exegesis and systematic theology, attention is paid to the development of self-confidence, assertiveness and social skills, for example.

The focus on training leadership traits and skills is obviously intended to increase the effectiveness of religious leadership. In addition, however, these training programs are important for the sake of protecting the psychological health of religious leaders. Within the domain of religion, the leadership discourse on traits and skills is very often related to the discussion about psychological tensions as a result of ministry. Several extensive research studies on the well-being and risk of burnout of predecessors have led to this strong focus on psychological health in relation to leadership.

The contribution of Leslie Francis in this volume demonstrates that this research has resulted in an extraordinary number of good instruments to monitor the mental health of religious leaders. The Francis Burnout Inventory shows that psychological factors weigh heavily in the development of tension in mental health experiences. Personality, personal factors such as age and gender, and professional style factors like participating in supervision appear to be strong predictors of burnout, alongside more contextual factors such as the location of the work. This implies that the personality traits which are so important for effective leadership can turn into their opposite, forming a strong factor in causing stress and decreased mental health.

In short, the classic research on leadership, including leadership in religious organizations such as churches, is characterized by a strong emphasis on personality traits and skills as predictors for effective and successful leadership, addressing the same properties as potential drivers of stress.

3. A Shift in the Leadership Paradigm

From the beginning of the 21st century, this influential paradigm relating personality traits to effective leadership has turned out to be quite problematic. An increasing number of authors stress the importance of the interaction between the leader and follower as being greater than the importance of the properties and personality traits of the leader. This leads to different concepts of leadership. The work of Yukl (2010) is prototypical for this change. Yukl, a much quoted author in the secular literature on leadership, defines leadership as follows:

> Leadership is the process of influencing others to understand and agree about what needs to be done and how to do it, and the process of facilitating individual and collective efforts to accomplish shared objectives. (Yukl, 2010, p. 26)

This widely used definition focuses on leadership as a process. It is about the dynamics of leadership: leader and followers influencing each other.

It is not about the leader convincing others based upon a certain set of characteristics or skills; in this definition, leadership shows up as a reciprocal interaction process. In this view on leadership, three dimensions interact: (1) the person of the leader, (2) the individual followers, and (3) the structure of the group or organization as a whole. Variables in each of these dimensions have an impact on the effectiveness of leadership. This means that a particular set of properties of the leader is no longer decisive for effective leadership. A particular leader can be successful in one group, but fail in a different context. This not only happens in secular domains. In the religious field we also see ministers being successful in one church, but facing all kinds of problems in another community. Within this new frame on leadership, these differences can be explained by focusing not only on the leader, but also on the individual followers and the group in general.

Indeed, individual followers not only have their own needs and interests, they also possess diverse skills that have an impact on the process of leadership. As a result, individual followers differ a lot from each other in their expectations of the leader.

In the literature on leadership in religious groups, much attention has been paid to this complexity of the process of leadership (Brouwer et al., 2007). The reasons for successful religious communities are not only attributed to charismatic leaders with the right set of features. Features of the followers also appear to play an important role: age, context, education and available skills as variables of the followers and the group may be more important predictors of the effectiveness and success of leadership than the personality traits of the leader.

The conceptualization of leadership as a dynamic process fits into the scientific paradigm of social construction. In this paradigm, meaning is not only an attribute of an object, but also something that is created in the perception by the subject. Meaning is subjective and occurs in the interaction between the subject and his or her environment.

In several contributions in this volume, social construction forms the dominant scientific paradigm. In contemporary models about both leadership and religion in general, great emphasis is placed on the ongoing processes of social identity construction, presupposing that these processes allow for leadership. Leadership is much more than the qualities and skills of the leader. The relationship between leader and followers within the structure of the organization or society is much more important. It is not so much about the personality of the leader; the social perception and reception of the leader by the followers are central factors. Following the paradigm of social construction, leadership is created in those perception processes. The decision about effective or failed leadership also lies in the perception of the subject. This formulation already shows that the predictability of effective, successful leadership within this paradigm of social construction is much lower than in the paradigm of the effective leader. More variables than only the personality traits are taken into account in this new paradigm: the perception process, contextual factors, characteristics of the observer, characteristics of the leader and uncertainty about the purpose of leadership. All these variables affect the effectiveness of leadership.

The paradigm of social construction thus offers opportunities for leadership besides the person of the leader, but leadership also becomes more complex and uncertain.

Various contributions in this volume with a central focus on social identity construction reveal this complexity. The context of social construction makes leadership possible, but at the same time, this context sometimes problematizes leadership.

4. Social Construction in Religious Leadership

The contribution of Udi Lebel fits into the paradigm of social construction. He calls the social perception and reception of the leader Leadership Capital: the leader is perceived as such on the basis of the social constructs that lead to the perception of leadership. Lebel refers to Gunter (2010), stressing the important role of framing and reception of the leader. According to him, this explains why a leader in one community may be perceived as successful whereas he or she will not be seen as a leader at all in another community. Image and reputation are crucial. Potential leaders construct Leadership Capital as a result of this socio-cognitive process of perception. This Leadership Capital puts them in the right position to fill influential positions, contributing in turn to the Leadership Capital. In short, Leadership Capital arises within perception and consequently functions as a self-reinforcing cognitive effect. Formally and informally, people prefer a leader who has sufficient social Leadership Capital. In other words, this Capital gives access to the knowledge and experience of leadership; as a result, the associated skills and attributes are quasi naturally developed and strengthened. The concept Leadership Capital does not deny the personality traits of the leader as a predictor for success, but it claims that personality traits per se cannot explain the social reception of the leaders.

This concept of Leadership Capital shows that the paradigm of the social construction fits into the evolutionary perspective, in which leadership is conceived as an important factor for the survival and welfare of the group. Leadership Capital can grow because the group members perceive these leadership qualities and experiences as beneficial to the group.

Evolution is a very dominant concept in many contemporary social science theories. When it comes to leadership, I refer above all to the work of Mark van Vugt (Van Vugt & Ahuja, 2010; 2011). From an evolutionary point of view, Van Vugt and his research group connect leaders and followers. In this perspective, both leadership and followership can be conceived as adaptive forms of leadership and followership that emerge if they benefit the survival and development of the group. We choose the leaders whom we suspect will ensure the best survival of the group. Moreover, Van Vugt also convincingly shows that this assessment is often based on incorrect assumptions, which were previously in the evolution of interest, but not any more. Van Vugt calls this the "mismatch hypothesis": we mistakenly believe we have to make the same considerations as our ancestors on the savannah. As a result, we tend to choose strong male leaders from whom we expect protection and the greatest chance of survival.

So the paradigm of social construction is reinforced by the dominance of evolutionary ideas in the social sciences. In the field of leadership, this means that the focus is increasingly being placed on the social context within which the leadership process emerges, rather than on the personality traits and skills of the leader.

Indeed, if social construction is taken seriously, leadership itself is a form of sense-making. Leadership does not exist outside our perception or construction, it is a form of perception and interpretation. John Eliastam sums up this process of sense-making from theories as "discursive leadership." These theories stress the social, linguistic, and cultural aspects of leadership. Eliastam refers to Fairhurst, who describes discursive leadership theories as ways to explore the actual interactional processes and linguistic patterns that constitute leadership. From this theoretical perspective, Eliastam investigates the role of narratives in leadership. He shows that the leadership discourse provides for narratives supporting people to connect different experiences. These narratives help people to make sense of their conditions and lives. Leadership occurs when people recognize themselves in the values and ideas that are put forward to solve problems or to achieve goals. In this perspective, leadership becomes a social activity of reality construction and meaningfulness. From this paradigm, Eliastam reveals opportunities for religious leadership that provide new narratives to replace existing dominant stories. In his conclusion Eliastam connects this opportunity to the evolutionary principle of survival: A multiplicity of connected narratives creates a need for new sense-making processes in order to assimilate the various stories. This need is rooted in the human need to survive or adapt to the environment that gives rise to rationality.

From this point of view, leadership becomes more and more a form of adaptation and construction. Leadership is not fixed nor determined by the person of the leader, but the context in which leadership occurs is crucial for the effectiveness of leadership. That is why various authors in this volume advocate for an adapted language, tailored to a new context: complex, international, difficult to steer and digital.

Ian Nell takes up this last element. He shows that leadership is not limited to real face-to-face situations. Virtual Leadership exists in the form of online religion, which can be categorized to some extent by analogy with real-life religious leadership. In other words, Virtual Leadership is not a fundamentally different kind of leadership, it is a variant in which the same categories (social constructivist) show up that are applicable to real forms of leadership.

So this volume shows that the paradigm of the social construction has become very dominant in theories about religious leadership, as it is in secular theories about leadership and in social sciences in general. In this paradigm, leadership is a process of reciprocal influence wherein the meaning arises in the relationship between the leader and follower; a relationship that includes perception, structure and meaning. At the same time, we have not completely left the previous paradigm of leadership that focuses on the person of the leader and his or her characteristics and abilities.

In fact, if leadership fails, fingers point to the leader again, ignoring the construction process between leader and followers.

Rein Brouwer demonstrates this in his contribution to leadership in a deconstructed church. He refers to research by Marti & Ganiel showing that "emerging congregations resist institutionalization through flat leadership structures and an egalitarian form of government. (…) However, this does not exclude dependence on the leader. Although some communities (…) emphasize the viability of valid congregational life without a centralized leader, still it is recognized that the decentralization results in certain people having more influence in decision-making than others." In other words, a conception of leadership in which the relationship between leader and followers is more central than the characteristics of the leader may have an undesirable negative effect. The power is concentrated in a small elite group, without any accompanying constructive policy on that. The starting point lies in the relationship, and the result is a decisive role for the leader(s) in person.

5. The Paradox in Leadership Theories

The paradigm shift from personality traits to processes of social construction and relations can be found in the domain of leadership at large. However, within the domain of religion, this paradigm shift leads to several unexpected problems, related to specific religious factors, as shown, for example, by Brouwer in this volume.

I consider this the great paradox of modern ideas about leadership in a religious context. That leadership is under pressure, influenced by the fact that Western societies are individualized and secularized societies. Religion is no longer a matter of naturalness; the religious leader is no longer a priori an authority. Religious institutions and traditions seem to be crumbling. The individual believer becomes more and more the central focus, and it is accepted that the commitment is personal and sometimes temporary; large organizational structures are less weighty than they used to be.

Religious leadership has never been an easy task. Religious leaders always operate in a complex context in which their personal qualities and skills play an important role.

If we define leadership as a dynamic process in which the leader and group members interact in such a way that agreement arises about the group's targets and the way resources are used to accomplish these targets, both the leader and group members can influence this relationship. Problems with leadership can almost never be reduced to a failing leader or to a typical problematic congregation.

This description of leadership also reveals that leadership is not a static state, but a dynamic process. Both the leader and the religious group are constantly under the influence of various factors and experiences in the outside world and in the religious life. Attitudes and choices are constantly changing. These changes affect the process and the experience of leadership.

In my view, these changes are paradoxical. The paradox can be described as follows. Apparently, the role of the leader or preacher is decreasing, while individual believers are becoming more educated and empowered. For most church members, it is more and more a subjective decision of how to live or how to believe. Institutions and traditions are decreasing rapidly in influence. However, paradoxically, the role of the leader is not thereby reduced. Apparently that is the case: the role of leaders is decreasing, while the contributions of their group members are increasing. There is no longer an external criterion that determines how well one lives or believes. It cannot be imposed by something or someone; people think and decide for themselves. However, due to the uncertainty which characterizes our times, individual believers do need religion more than ever for their own identity. After all, that identity as a whole is undermined. We are constantly looking for what's important, and we are looking for those parts of ourselves that will help us determine who we are. Little or nothing is a foregone conclusion, we are constantly looking for what's important. What determines who I am, what is important for my identity? At that point, the congregation, the religious group, is important, as it is about values and perspective. The religious group meets the emotional need for closeness and security. The fundamental human fears of loneliness, uncertainty and mortality are enhanced by the social and religious context of today. At the same time, faith and a faith community provide salient clues to reduce these fears. And in this process of identification, the person of the predecessor, the religious leader, is very important. For the process of identity formation, the extent to which leadership skills are available does not count so much, but rather how the process of social identification or construction is supervised. For this process it is indeed important that the leader shows in person why it makes sense to be part of this community. The leader, the pastor, is a kind of prototype, from which the individual believers – at least partly – derive their identity. Not the classic leadership traits and skills prevail, but the way the leader presents himself or herself as a believer. The personal worldview and world orientation of the leader matter, the way he or she deals with the challenges posed by our time and society.

Bibliography

1. Book and Article References

Abu-Hilal, Maher M. and Kayed M. Salameh. "Validity and reliability of the Maslach burnout inventory for a sample of non-western teachers." *Educational and Psychological Measurement* 52 (1992): 161–169.

Adam, Barbara. "Memory of Futures." *KronoScope* 4, no. 2 (2004): 297–315.

Ahlbäck, Lennart. *Socialdemokratisk kyrkosyn: En studie i socialdemokraternas kyrkopolitiska riktlinjer 1979--1996*. [Social Democratic Ecclesiology: A study of the Social Democratic party's outlines of Church politics 1979–1996]. Lund: Arcus, 2003.

Ahrén, Per-Olov. "Den dubbla ansvarslinjen som kyrkorättsligt problem" [The double line of responsibility as a problem in Church law], in *Kyrka - universitet - skola: Teologi och pedagogik i funktion: Festskrift till Sven-Åke Selander*, eds. J.-O. Aggedal, C.-G. Andrén and A. J. Evertsson (Lund: Teologiska institutionen, 2000).

Alexander, Peter. "A Massive Rebellion of the Poor."] *Mail & Guardian*, April 13, 2012. http://www.mg.co.za/article/2012-04-13-a-massive-rebellion-of-the-poor.

Almog, O. *The Sabra: The Creation of the New Jew*. California: University of California Press, 2000.

Altbeker, Antony. *A country at war with itself: South Africa's crisis of crime*. Johannesburg: Jonathan Ball, 2007.

Alvesson, Mats, and Dan Kärreman. "Varieties of discourse: On the study of organizations through discourse analysis." *Human Relations* 53 (2000): 1125–1149.

Ammerman, Nancy T. *Sacred Stories, Spiritual Tribes. Finding Religion in Everyday Life*. Oxford: Oxford University Press, 2014.

Amrousi, E. "Pendulum." *Small World* 72 (2007): 11–12.

Aran, G. *Kookism*. Carmel Press: Jerusalem, 2013.

Anderson, Bernhard. *The Unfolding Drama of the Bible*. Fourth edition. Minneapolis: Fortress Press, 1988.

Andreasson, Stefan. "Orientalism and African Development Studies: The Reductive Repetition Motif in Theories of African Underdevelopment." *Third World Quarterly* 26, no. 6 (2005): 971–86.

Appiah, Kwame Anthony. *In My Father's House: Africa in the Philosophy of Culture*. New York: Oxford University Press, 1992.

Ashin, G. "A Change of Elite", *Sociological Research* 35, no. 1 (1996): 55–90.

Avery, Gayle C. *Understanding Leadership. Paradigms and Cases*. London: Sage Publications, 2004 (reprinted 2005).

Aviner, S. "Stop Crumbling the IDF." *Love and Belief* 500 (2005): 2–3.

Ayittey, George B.N. *Africa in Chaos*. New York: St. Martin's Press, 1998.

Baker, J. : "No Ivies, Oxbridge, or Grandes Écoles." *British Journal of Sociology of Education* 35, no. 6 (2014): 914–932.
Banaszak, A. *Why Movements Succeed to Fail*. NJ: Princeton University Press, 1996.
Banda, Felix, and Aquilina Mawadza. "'Foreigners are stealing our birth right': Moral panics and the discursive construction of Zimbabwean immigrants in South African media." *Discourse & Communication* 9, no. 1 (2015): 47–64.
Barak, O. and E. Tsur. "The Military Careers and Second Careers of Israel's Military Elite." *Middle East Journal* 66, no. 3 (2012): 473–492.
Barnard, Laura K. and John F. Curry. "The relationship of clergy burnout to self-compassion and other personality dimensions." *Pastoral Psychology* 61 (2012): 149–163.
Barratt, E. "C. Wright Mills, Power and the Power Elites – A Reappraisal." *Management and Organizational History* 9, no. 1 (2014): 92–106.
Baym, Nancy K. *Personal Connections in the Digital Age*. Cambridge: Polity Press, 2010.
Belcastro, Philip A., Robert S. Gold and Leon C. Hays. "Maslach Burnout Inventory: factor structures for samples of teachers." *Psychological Reports* 53 (1983): 364–366.
Bellah, R. N. "Biblical Religion and Civil Religion in America." *American Academy of Arts and Sciences* 96, no. 1 (1967): 1–21.
Berger, Peter. *The sacred canopy: elements of a sociological theory of religion*. New York: Anchor Books, 1967.
Berntson, M., B. Nilsson, and C. Wejryd. *Kyrka i Sverige: Introduktion till svensk kyrkohistoria* [Church in Sweden: Introduction to Swedish Church history]. Skellefteå: Artos, 2012.
Beuving, J., and G. de Vries. *Doing Qualitative Research. The Craft of Naturalistic Inquiry*. Amsterdam: Amsterdam University Press, 2015.
Bexell, O. "Präster och lekmän i kyrkomötet: Några linjer i allmänna kyrkomötets diskussion om sin egen sammansättning" [Clergy and Laity in the Church Assembly: Themes in the Church Assembly's discussion of its own composition] In *Med engagemang och medansvar: En bok om lekmannaskapet i Svenska kyrkan. Festskrift till Carl Henrik Martling*, edited by O. Bexell, S.-E. Brodd, G. Edqvist, S. Ekström and G. Weman, 126–165. Stockholm: Verbum, 1990.
Bhabha, Homi K. *The Location of Culture*. New York: Routledge, 1994.
Bick, E. "The Tal Law: A Missed Opportunity for 'Bridging Social Capital' in Israel." *Church and State* 52, no. 2 (2010): 298–322.
Billig, M., and U. Lebel. "Israeli public opinion on the settlement in Judea and Samaria." (index number 04) *Judea and Samaria Studies* 22 (2013): 11–22.
Biskopsvalkommitténs betänkande. D. 1, Biskopsval [Report by the Committee on the election of Bishops]. Stockholm, 1957.
Bob-Milliar, George. "Re: The Failure Of African Leadership, Cause Of Africa's Problems." Modern Ghana, 2005. https://www.ghanaweb.com/GhanaHomePage/diaspora/Re-The-Failure-Of-African-Leadership-Cause-Of-Africa-s-Problems-81437.

Bolden, Richard and Philip Kirk. "African Leadership: Surfacing New Understandings through Leadership Development." *International Journal of Cross Cultural Management* 9 (2009): 69–86. DOI: 10.1177/1470595808101156.

Booysen, Lize. "The duality in South African Leadership: Afrocentric or Eurocentric." *South African Journal of Labour Relations* 24, no. 3/4 (2001): 36–64.

Bourdieu, P. *Practical Reason: On the Theory of Action*. Stanford: Stanford University Press, 1998.

Bourdieu, P. "The Forms of Capital." In *Handbook of Theory and Research for the Sociology of Education*, edited by J. Richardson, 89–44. NY: Greenwood Press, 1986.

Bourdieu, P. *La Noblesse d'*État: Grandes écoles et esprit de corps. Paris: Minuit, 1989.

Bowers Du Toit, N. "Gangsterism on the Cape Flats: A challenge to 'engage the powers in 'Doing urban public theology in South Africa: Visions, approaches, themes and practices towards a new agenda.'" *HTS Teologiese Studies/ Theological Studies* 70, no. 3 (2014).

Bradburn, Norman M. *The structure of psychological well-being*. Chicago, IL: Aldine, 1969.

Braun, V. and V. Clark. "Using thematic analysis in psychology." *Qualitative Research in Psychology* 3 (2006): 77–101.

Brewster, Christine E. "The fate of the rural Anglican clergy: Caring for more churches and experiencing higher levels of stress." In *Religious identity and national heritage: Empirical – theological perspectives*, edited by Francis-Vincent Anthony and Hans-Georg Ziebertz, 149–169. Leiden: Brill, 2012.

Brewster, Christine E., Leslie J. Francis and Mandy Robbins. "Maintaining a public ministry in rural England: Work-related psychological health and psychological type among Anglican clergy serving in multi-church benefices." In *The public significance of religion*, edited by Hans-Georg Ziebertz and Leslie J. Francis, 241–265. Leiden: Brill, 2011.

Brodd, S.-E. "Kyrkan är det prästerskap som frambär andliga offer" [The Church is the Priesthood that offers spiritual sacrifices] In *Med engagemang och medansvar: En bok om lekmannaskapet i Svenska kyrkan. Festskrift till Carl Henrik Martling*, edited by O. Bexell, S.-E. Brodd, G. Edqvist, S. Ekström and G. Weman, 50–67. Stockholm: Verbum, 1990.

Brodd, S.-E. "Liturgy Crossing Frontiers: Interplay and Confrontation of Ecclesiological Patterns in Liturgical Change During the Twentieth Century" In *The meaning of Christian liturgy: Recent developments in the Church of Sweden*, edited by O. Bexell, 24–52. Grand Rapids, Mich.: W.B. Eerdmans Pub. Co., 2012.

Broodryk, J. *Understanding South Africa: The Ubuntu way of living*. 3rd ed. Waterkloof: Ubuntu school of philosophy, 2010.

Brouwer, R. "Theology, Perhaps. A Practical Theological Reflection on Kristien Hemmerechts' Novel The Woman Who Fed the Dogs." *International Journal of Public Theology* 9 (2015): 428–445.

Brouwer, R., K. de Groot, H. de Roest, E. Sengers and S. Stoppels, eds. *Levend lichaam. Dynamiek van christelijke geloofsgemeenschappen in Nederland*. Utrecht: Kok, 2007.
Brown, David. *God and Mystery in Words: Experience through Metaphor and Drama*. Oxford: Oxford University Press, 2008.
Brown, P. "Cultural Capital and Social Exclusion." *Work, Employment and Society* 9, no. 1 (1995): 29–51.
Brown, Sally A. "Hermeneutical Theory." In *The Wiley-Blackwell Companion to Practical Theology*, edited by Bonnie J. Miller-McLemore, 112–122. Oxford: Blackwell Publishing, 2012.
Bunge, M.J. (ed.). *The Child in the Bible*. Grand Rapids: Michigan, 2008.
Burr, Vivien. *An introduction to social constructionism*. London: Routledge, 1995.
Burton, Jean and Chris Burton. *Public people, private lives: Tackling stress in clergy families*. London: Continuum, 2009.
Burton, Lewis, Leslie J. Francis and Mandy Robbins. "Psychological type profile of Methodist circuit ministers in Britain: Similarities with and differences from Anglican clergy." *Journal of Empirical Theology* 23 (2010): 64–81.
Buys, Chenelle and Sebastian Rothman. "Burnout and engagement of reformed church ministers." *SA Journal of Industrial Psychology* 36, no. 1 (2010).
Byrne, Barbara M. "The Maslach Burnout Inventory: Validating factorial structure and invariance across intermediate, secondary, and university educators." *Multivariate Behavioral Research* 26 (1991): 583–605.
Byrne, Barbara M. "The Maslach Burnout Inventory: Testing for factorial validity and invariance across elementary, intermediate, and secondary teachers." *Journal of Occupational and Organizational Psychology* 66 (1993): 197–212.
Campbell, Heidi A. *When Religion meets New Media*. London: Routledge, 2011.
Campbell, Heidi A. "Community." In *Digital Religion: Understanding Religious Practice in New Media Worlds*, edited by Heidi A. Campbell, 3–67. Abingdon: Routledge, 2013.
Campbell, Heidi A. *Digital Religion: Understanding Religious Practice in New Media Worlds*. London: Routledge, 2013.
Campbell, Heidi A., and Steven S. Garner. *Networked Theology: Negotiating Faith in Digital Culture*. Grand Rapids: Baker Academic, 2016.
Campbell, Heidi A. "Understanding the relationship between religion online and offline in a networked society." *Journal of the American Academy of Religion* 80, no. 1 (2012): 64–93. Doi: https://doi.org/10.1093/jaarel/lfr074.
Canales, A.D. "Models of Christian Leadership in Youth Ministry." *Religious Education: The official journal of the Religious Education Association* 109, no. 1 (2014): 24–44, DOI: 10.1080/00344087.2014.868207.
Canales, A.D. "Integrating Christian discipleship IS Franciscanism." *Association of Franciscan Colleges and Universities Journal* 1, no. 1 (2004): 34–53.
Caputo, J.D. *Heidegger and Aquinas: An essay on overcoming metaphysics*. New York: Fordham University Press, 1982.
Caputo, J.D. *Demythologizing Heidegger*. Indianapolis: Indiana University Press, 1993.

Caputo, J.D. *The Prayers and Tears of Jacques Derrida. Religion without Religion*. Bloomington: Indiana University Press, 1997.
Caputo, J.D. *The Weakness of God. A Theology of the Event*. Bloomington: Indiana, 2006.
Caputo, J.D. *What Would Jesus Deconstruct? The Good News of Postmodernism for the Church*. Grand Rapids/Michigan: Baker Academic, 2007.
Caputo, J.D. *The Insistence of God. A Theology of Perhaps*. Bloomington: Indiana University Press, 2013.
Castells, Manuel. *End of Millennium: The Information Age: Economy, Society and Culture*. Oxford: Blackwell Publishing, 2006.
Cattell, Raymond, Alberta K. S. Cattell and Heather E. P. Cattell. *Sixteen Personality Factor Questionnaire*. Fifth edition. Windsor: NFER-Nelson, 1993.
Caulat, Ghislaine. "Virtual Leadership." *The Ashridge Journal* 3 (2006): 6–11.
Césaire, Aimé. *Discourse on Colonialism* (1955). Trans. Joan Pinkham. New York: Monthly Review Press, 1972.
Childers, Jana, and Clayton J. Schmit, eds. *Performance in Preaching: Bringing the Sermon to Life*. Grand Rapids: Baker Academic, 2008.
Church of England. *Mission and Pastoral Measure 2011: Code of recommended practice*. Volume 1. London: Church House Publishing, 2011.
Claiborne, S., and C. Haw. *Jesus for President. Politics for Ordinary Radicals*. Grand Rapids, Michigan: Zondervan, 2008.
Clayton, Philip. "Theology and the Church after Google." *The Princeton Theological Review* 15, no. 2 (2010): 7–20.
Cloete, Anita. "Living in a Digital Culture: The Need for Theological Reflection." *HTS Teologiese Studies / Theological Studies* 71, no. 2 (2015): 1–7. Doi: http://dx.doi.org/10.4102/hts.v71i2.2073.
Coate, Mary A. *Clergy stress: The hidden conflicts in ministry*. London: SPCK, 1989.
Cobb, Kelton. *The Blackwell Guide to Theology and Popular Culture*. Oxford: Blackwell Publishing, 2005.
Codone, S. "Megachurch Pastor Twitter Activity: An Analysis of Rick Warren and Andy Stanley, Two of America's Social Pasters Macon, GA." *Journal of Religion, Media and Digital Culture* 3, no. 2 (2014): 1–32. http://jrmdc.com/papers-archive/volume-3-issue-2-august-2014/.
Cohen, S. "From integration to segregation: the role of religion in the IDF." *Armed Forces and Society* 25, no. 3 (1999): 387–405.
Cohen, S. "The formation of military and war laws in Israel 1948–2004." *Iyunim Bitkumat Israel* [Studies in Israeli and modern Jewish society] 15 (2005): 239–274.
Cohen, S. "The Hesder Yeshivot in Israel: A church-state military arrangement." *Church and State* 35, no. 1 (1993): 113–130.
Cohen, S., *The Scroll or the Sword? Dilemmas of Religion and Military Service in Israel*. London: Harwood Academic Press, 1997.
Comaroff, John L., and Jean Comaroff. "Naturing the Nation: Aliens, Apocalypse and the Postcolonial State." *Journal of Southern African Studies* 27 (2001): 627–51.

Conforti, Y. "The New Jew in the Zionist movement: ideology and historiography." *Australian Journal of Jewish Studies* 25 (2011): 87–102.

Cooper, Adam. "'Let us eat airtime': youth identity and 'xenophobic' violence in a low-income neighbourhood in Cape Town." CSSR Working Paper No. 263 October 2009.

Coote, Belinda. "The trade trap." In *Introductory Reader on North-South Issues for the Autumn University "Play Fair Europe! Aachen, 25th of September – 8th of October 1995*, edited by S. Hernandez, 75–104. 1995.

Corcoran, Kevin J. "Measuring burnout: A reliability and convergent validity study." In *Journal of Social Behavior and Personality* 1 (1985): 107–112.

Costa, Paul T. and Robert R. McCrae. *The NEO Personality Inventory*. Odessa, FL: Psychological Assessment Resources, 1985.

Couldry, N. "Mediatization or Mediation? Alternative Understandings of the Emergent Space of Digital Storytelling." *New Media & Society* 10, no. 3 (2008): 373–391. Doi: https://doi.org/10.1177/1461444808089414.

Craig, Charlotte L., Bruce Duncan and Leslie J. Francis. "Safeguarding tradition: Psychological type preferences of male vergers in the Church of England." *Pastoral Psychology* 54 (2006): 457–463.

Crea, Giuseppe. *Stress e burnout negli operatori pastorali: Una ricerca tra i missionary*. Bologna: Editrice Missionaria Italiana, 1994.

Cronbach, Lee J. "Coefficient alpha and the internal structure of tests." *Psychometrika* 5 (1951): 297–334.

Cronje, Frans. *A time traveller's guide to our next ten years*. Cape Town: Tafelberg Press, 2014.

Croucher, Sheila. "South Africa's illegal aliens: constructing national boundaries in a post-apartheid state." *Ethnic and Racial Studies* 21, no. 4 (1998): 639–660.

Crush, Jonathan, and Sujata Ramachandran. "Xenophobia, International Migration and Human Development." United Nations Development Programme Human Development, Research Paper 2009/47. http://hdr.undp.org/sites/default/files/hdrp_2009_47.pdf.

Crush, Jonathan, and Vincent Williams. "Making up the Numbers: Measuring 'Illegal Immigration' to South Africa." *Migration Policy Brief*, 3. Southern African Migration Project, 2001.

Crush, Jonathan, ed., *The Perfect Storm: The Realities of Xenophobia in Contemporary South Africa*. Southern African Migration Programme. Cape Town: IDASA, 2008.

Crush, Jonathan, Sujata Ramachandran and Wade Pendleton. *Soft targets: Xenophobia, public violence, and changing attitudes to migrants after May 2008*. Southern African Migration Programme. Cape Town: Bronwen Dachs Muller, 2013.

Davey, John. *Burnout: Stress in ministry*. Leominster: Gracewing, 1995.

Davies, Bronwyn and Rom Harré. "Positioning: The discursive production of selves." *Journal for the Theory of Social Behaviour* 20, no. 1 (1990): 44–63.

Davis, Rebecca. "Lawmakers crunch xenophobia numbers." Eye Witness News, 29 April, 2015. http://ewn.co.za/2015/04/29/OPINION-Rebecca-Davis-Lawmakers-crunch-some-xenophobia-numbers.

Dawson, Lorne L. "Religion and the Quest for Virtual Community." In *Religion Online: Finding Faith on the Internet*, edited by Lorne L. Dawson and Douglas E. Cowan, 75–89. London: Routledge, 2004.
De Beer, S. & I. Swart. "Towards a fusion of horizons: Thematic contours for an urban public theological praxis-agenda in South Africa in 'Doing urban public theology in South Africa: Visions, approaches, themes and practices towards a new agenda." *HTS Teologiese Studies/Theological Studies* 70, no. 3 (2014).
De Vries, M. *Sustainable Youth Ministry: Why most youth ministry doesn't last and what you church can do about it.* USA: Inter Varsity Press, 2008.
De Wet, Chris L. "Entrepreneurial Leadership Training and Theological Education." In *Contested Issues in Training Ministers in South Africa*, edited by Marilyn Naidoo, 127–140. Stellenbosch: Sun Press, 2015.
Dean, K.C. *Almost Christian: What the faith of our teenagers is telling the American church.* New York: Oxford University Press, 2010.
DeMaria, Bill. "Neo-colonialism Through Measurement: A Critique of the Corruption Perception Index." *Critical Perspectives on International Business* 4, no 2/3 (2008): 184–202.
Derrida, Jacques. *Positions.* Transl. A. Bass. London: Athlone Press, 1981.
Derrida, Jacques. *Rogues: Two essays on reason.* Transl. P-A. Brault and M. Naas. Stanford: Stanford University Press, 2005.
Derrida, Jacques. *The beast and the Sovereign.* Volume 1. Transl. G. Bennington. Chicago: University of Chicago Press, 2009.
Derrida, Jacques. *The Beast and the Sovereign.* Volume II. Transl. G. Bennington. Chicago: University of Chicago Press, 2011.
Diocese of Southwark. *The Bridge.* 6, no. 1 (2001).
Diocese of Southwark. *Diocesan Year Book 2008.* London: Diocese of Southwark, 2009.
Diocese of Southwark. *Diocesan Year Book 2009.* London: Diocese of Southwark, 2010.
Diocese of Southwark. *Diocesan Year Book 2010.* London: Diocese of Southwark, 2011.
Don-Yehiya, E. "Messianism and Politics: The Ideological Transformation of Religious Zionism." *Israel Studies* 19, no. 2 (2014): 239–263.
Don-Yehiya, E. "Origins and Development of the Agudah and Mafdal Parties." *Jerusalem Quarterly* 20, no. 1 (1981): 49–64.
Don-Yehiya, E. "Religious Fundamentalism and Political Radicalism: The Nationalist Yeshivot in Israel." In *Atzmaut – 50 HaShanim HaRishononot* [Independence – the First 50 Years], edited by Anita Shapira, 431–470. Jerusalem: Zalman Shazar Center, 1998.
Doolittle, Benjamin R. "Burnout and coping among parish-based clergy." *Mental Health, Religion and Culture* 10 (2007): 31–38.
Doornenbal, R. *Crossroads. An Exploration of the Emerging-Missional Conversation with a special Focus on 'Missional leadership' and Its Challenges for Theological Education.* Delft: Eburon, 2012.

Duncan, Norman. "Reaping the whirlwind: Xenophobic violence in South Africa." *Global Journal of Community Psychology Practice* 3, no. 1 (2012): 104–112.
Dylan, T. "Godless Patriots: Towards a New American Civil Religion." *Polity* 45 no. 3 (2013): 372–392.
Eichler, M. "Leadership in Social Movements." *Sociological Inquiry* 47, no. 2 (1977): 99–107.
Einstein, M. *Brands of Faith: Marketing religion in a commercial age*. New York: Routledge, 2008.
Eliastam, John. "Re-storying xenophobia in South Africa: a postfoundational, narrative exploration of identity, competing interests, and ubuntu in the Eastern Cape." PhD Diss., University of Pretoria, 2015.
Elon, E. "The State's leadership will become increasingly religious." n *Eretz Acheret* 24 (2004): 71.
Esposito, R. *Terms of the Political: Community, Immunity, Biopolitics*. NY: Ferdham University Press, 2013.
Estes, Douglas. *SimChurch: Being Church in the Virtual World*. Grand Rapids: Zondervan, 2009.
Evenshpanger, N. "The contribution of the pre-military academies to the army and to the discourse between the religious and secular population." *Iyyunim BeBitakhon Leumi* 16, The Research Center, IDF National Security Academy (2011): 32–49.
Evers, Welko and Will Tomic. "Burnout among Dutch Reformed pastors." *Journal of Psychology and Theology* 31 (2003): 329–338.
Eysenck, Hans J. and Michael W. Eysenck. *Personality and individual differences: A natural science approach*. New York: Plenum Press, 1985.
Eysenck, Hans J. and Sybil B. G. Eysenck. *Manual of the Eysenck Personality Questionnaire (adult and junior)*. London: Hodder and Stoughton, 1975.
Eysenck, Hans J. and Sybil B. G. Eysenck. *Manual of the Eysenck Personality Scales*. London: Hodder and Stoughton, 1991.
Eysenck, Sybil B.G., Hans J. Eysenck and Paul Barrett. "A revised version of the psychoticism scale." *Personality and Individual Differences* 6 (1985): 21–29.
Ezzy, D. *Qualitative Analysis: Practice and Innovation*. Australia: Routledge, 2002.
Failing, Wolf-Eckart, and Hans-Günther Heimbrock. *Gelebte Religion wahrnehmen. Lebenswelt – Alltagskultur – Religionspraxis*. Stuttgart: Kohlhammer, 1998.
Fairhurst, Gail T. and David Grant. "The Social Construction of Leadership: A Sailing Guide." *Management Communication Quarterly* 24, no. 2 (2010): 171–210.
Fairhurst, Gail T. *Discursive leadership: In conversation with leadership psychology*. Thousand Oaks, CA: Sage, 2007.
Fanon, Frantz. "First Truths on the Colonial Problem." In *Toward the African Revolution*, edited by Frantz Fanon, 120–126. Translated by Haakon Chevalier. Harmondsworth: Penguin, 1967.

Fanon, Frantz. *On National Culture and the Pitfalls of National Consciousness in The Wretched of the Earth*. Translated by Constance Farrington. New York: Grove Press, 1968.
Fanon, Frantz. *The Wretched of the Earth*. Translated by Constance Farrington. Harmondsworth: Penguin, 1990.
Fletcher, Ben. *Clergy under stress: A study of homosexual and heterosexual clergy*. London: Mowbray, 1990.
Flew, Terry. *New Media. An Introduction*. Melbourne: Oxford University Press, 2008.
Församlingar i samverkan: Rapport från 1982 års kyrkokommitté [Congregations in cooperation: Report from the 1982 Church committee]. Stockholm, 1985.
Foucault, Michel. *The archaeology of knowledge and the discourse on language*. London: Tavistock, 1972.
Foucault, Michel. *The Foucault reader: An introduction to Foucault's thought*, edited by P Rabinow. Harmondsworth: Penguin, 1984.
Francis, Leslie J. and Douglas W. Turton. "Recognising and understanding burnout among the clergy: a perspective from empirical theology." In *Building Bridges over Troubled Waters: Enhancing pastoral care and guidance*, edited by David Herl and Mark L. Berman, 307–331. Lima, OH: Wyndham Hall Press, 2004b.
Francis, Leslie J. *Faith and psychology: Personality, religion and the individual*. London: Darton, Longman and Todd, 2005.
Francis, Leslie J. and Andrew Village. *Preaching with all our souls*. London: Continuum, 2008.
Francis, Leslie J. and Andrew Village. "The psychological temperament of Anglican clergy in ordained local ministry (OLM): The conserving, serving pastor?" *Journal of Empirical Theology* 25 (2012): 57–76.
Francis, Leslie J. and Christine E. Brewster. "Understanding stress from time-related over-extension in multi-parish benefices: The role of personal, environmental, psychological, and theological factors among rural Anglican clergy." *Rural Theology* 10 (2012): 161–178.
Francis, Leslie J. and Christopher J. F. Rutledge. "Are rural clergy in the Church of England under greater stress? A study in empirical theology." *Research in the Social Scientific Study of Religion* 11 (2000): 173–191.
Francis, Leslie J. and Douglas W. Turton. "Reflective ministry and empirical theology: Antidote to clergy stress?" In *Hermeneutics and empirical research in practical theology: The contribution of empirical theology by Johannes A van der Ven*, edited by Chris A. M. Hermans and Mary E. Moore, 245–265. Leiden: Brill, 2004a.
Francis, Leslie J. and Greg Smith. "Separating sheep from goats: Using psychological type theory in a preaching workshop on Matthew 25:31–46." *Journal of Adult Theological Education* 9, (2012): 175–191.
Francis, Leslie J. and Greg Smith. "Reading and proclaiming the Birth Narratives from Luke and Matthew: A study in empirical theology among curates and their training incumbents employing the SIFT method." *HTS Theological Studies* 69, no. 1 (2013): 1–13.

Francis, Leslie J. and Greg Smith. "Exploring organised and visionary approaches to designing an Advent Fun Day in an educational setting." *International Journal of Christianity and Education* 19 (2015): 57–72.

Francis, Leslie J. and Greg Smith. "Introverts and extraverts reflecting on the experience of parish ministry: Conversation between training incumbents and curates." *Journal of Research in Christian Education* 25 (2016): 76–85.

Francis, Leslie J. and Pat Holmes. "Ordained Local Ministers: The same Anglican orders, but of different psychological temperaments?" *Rural Theology* 9 (2011): 151–160.

Francis, Leslie J., Andrew Village, Mandy Robbins and Keith Wulff. "Work-related psychological health among clergy serving in The Presbyterian Church (USA): Testing the idea of balanced affect." *Review of Religious Research* 53 (2011): 9–22.

Francis, Leslie J., Charlotte L. Craig, Michael Whinney, David Tilley and Paul Slater. "Psychological profiling of Anglican clergy in England: Employing Jungian typology to interpret diversity, strengths, and potential weaknesses in ministry." *International Journal of Practical Theology* 11 (2007): 266–284.

Francis, Leslie J., Douglas W. Turton and Stephen Louden. "Dogs, cats and Catholic parochial clergy in England and Wales: Exploring the relationship between companion animals and work-related psychological health." *Mental Health, Religion and Culture* 10 (2007): 47–60.

Francis, Leslie J., Keith Littler and Mandy Robbins. "Psychological type and Offa's Dyke: Exploring differences in the psychological type profile of Anglican clergy serving in England and Wales." *Contemporary Wales* 23 (2010): 240–251.

Francis, Leslie J., Keith Wulff and Mandy Robbins. "The relationship between work-related psychological health and psychological type among clergy serving in The Presbyterian Church (USA)." *Journal of Empirical Theology* 21 (2008): 166–182.

Francis, Leslie J., Mandy Robbins and Keith Wulff. "Assessing the effectiveness of support strategies in reducing professional burnout among clergy serving in The Presbyterian Church (USA)." *Practical Theology* 6 (2013a): 319–331.

Francis, Leslie J., Mandy Robbins and Keith Wulff. "Are clergy serving yoked congregations under greater stress? A study among clergy serving in The Presbyterian Church (USA)." *Stress and Health* 29 (2013b): 113–116.

Francis, Leslie J., Mandy Robbins and Susan H. Jones. "The psychological type profile of clergywomen in ordained local ministry in the Church of England: Pioneers or custodians?" *Mental Health, Religion and Culture* 15 (2012): 945–953.

Francis, Leslie J., Mandy Robbins, Bruce Duncan and Michael Whinney. "Confirming the psychological type profile of Anglican clergymen in England: A ministry for intuitives." In *Psychology of intuition,* edited by Bartoli Ruelas and Vanessa Briseno, 211–219. New York: Nova Science Publishers, 2010.

Francis, Leslie J., Mandy Robbins, Peter Kaldor and Keith Castle. "Psychological type and work-related psychological health among clergy in Australia, England and New Zealand." *Journal of Psychology and Christianity* 28 (2009): 200–212.

Francis, Leslie J., Michael Whinney, Lewis Burton and Mandy Robbins. "Psychological type preferences of male and female Free Church Ministers in England." *Research in the Social Scientific Study of Religion* 22 (2011): 251–263.

Francis, Leslie J., Patrick Laycock and Christine E. Brewster. "The burdens of rural ministry: Identifying and exploring the correlates of five causes of stress among rural Anglican clergy serving in multi-parish benefices." *Research in the Social Scientific Study of Religion* 26 (2015): 218–236.

Francis, Leslie J., Peter Hills and Christopher J. F. Rutledge. "Clergy work-related satisfactions in parochial ministry: The influence of personality and churchmanship." *Mental Health, Religion and Culture* 11 (2008): 327–339.

Francis, Leslie J., Peter Kaldor, Mandy Robbins and Keith Castle. "Happy but exhausted? Work-related psychological health among clergy." *Pastoral Sciences* 24 (2005): 101–120.

Francis, Leslie J., Sean Gubb and Mandy Robbins. "Psychological type profile of Lead Elders within the Newfrontiers network of churches in the United Kingdom." *Journal of Belief and Values* 30 (2009): 61–69.

Francis, Leslie J., Sean Gubb and Mandy Robbins. "Work-related psychological health and psychological type among Lead Elders within the Newfrontiers network of churches in the United Kingdom." *Journal of Prevention and Intervention in the Community* 40 (2012): 233–245.

Francis, Leslie J., Stephen Louden and Christopher J. F. Rutledge. "Burnout among Roman Catholic parochial clergy in England and Wales: Myth or reality?" *Review of Religious Research* 46 (2004): 5–19.

Francis, Leslie J., V. John Payne and Mandy Robbins. "Psychological type and susceptibility to burnout: A study among Anglican clergymen in Wales." In *Psychology of burnout: New research*, edited by Benjamin R. Doolittle, 179–192, New York: Nova Science, 2013.

Francis, Leslie J., V. John Payne and Susan H. Jones. "Psychological types of male Anglican clergy in Wales." *Journal of Psychological Type* 56 (2001): 19–23.

Francis, Leslie. J., Mandy Robbins and Michael Whinney. "Women priests in the Church of England: Psychological type profile." *Religions* 2 (2011): 389–397.

Frank, T.E. "Leadership and Administration: An Emerging Field in Practical Theology. Research Report." *International Journal of Practical Theology* 10 (2006):113–152.

Friesen, Dwight J. *Thy Kingdom Connected: What the Church can Learn from Facebook, the Internet, and Other Networks*. ēmersion: Emergent Village Resources for Communities of Faith Series. Grand Rapids: Baker Books, 2009.

Fuchs, Christian. *Social Media – A Critical Introduction*. London: Sage Publications, 2014.

Furedi, F. *Authority: a sociological history*. Cambridge: Cambridge University Press, 2013.
Gallagher, Eugene V. "Religion." In *Encyclopedia of Leadership*, edited by George R. Goethals, Georgia J. Sorenson and James MacGregor Burns, 1308–1315. Thousand Oaks: Sage Publications, 2014. http://dx.doi.org.vu-nl.idm.oclc.org/10.4135/9781412952392.n299
Ganzevoort, R. Ruard, and Johan H. Roeland. "Lived religion. The praxis of practical theology." *International Journal of Practical Theology* 1 (2014): 91–101.
Ganzevoort, Ruard R. "Teaching that Matters. A Course on Trauma and Theology." *Journal of Adult Theological Education* 5, no. 1 (2008): 8–19. http://dx.doi.org/10.1558/jate2008v5i1.8.
Ganzevoort, Ruard R. "Forks in the Road when Tracing the Sacred: Practical Theology as Hermeneutics of Lived Religion." Last modified April 24, 2009. http://www.ruardganzevoort.nl/pdf/2009_Presidential.pdf.
Ganzevoort, Ruard R. "Hoe leiden we anno 2014 goede theologen op?" *Handelingen* 41, no. 3 (2014): 20–30
Ganzevoort, Ruard R., and Johan Roeland. "Lived Religion: The Praxis of Practical Theology." *International Journal of Practical Theology* 18, no. 1 (2014): 91–101.
Gaum, Fritz. *Die Kerkbode*. December 8, 2014.
Geertz, Clifford. "Religion as a cultural system." In *The interpretation of cultures: selected essays*, edited by Clifford Geertz, 87–125. London: Fontana Press, 1993.
Gelb, Stephen. "Behind Xenophobia in South Africa – Poverty or Inequality?" In *Go Home or Die Here: Violence, Xenophobia and the Reinvention of Difference in South Africa*, edited by Shireen Hassim, Eric Worby and Tawana Kupe, 79–92. Johannesburg: Wits University Press, 2008.
Giddens, A. *Modernity and Self-Identity.* Stanford: Standford University Press, 1991.
Girmalm, Thomas and M. Rosenius, "From state church to faith community: An analysis of worldly and spiritual power in the Church of Sweden" *International journal for the Study of the Christian Church* 13. No. 1. (2013): 48–58.
Gish, S.D. *Desmond Tutu: A Biography*. Greenwood Biographies. Westport, CT: Greenwood, 2014.
Gold, Yvonne. "The factoral validity of the Maslach Burnout Inventory in a sample of California elementary and junior high school classroom teachers." *Educational and Psychological Measurement* 44 (1984): 1009–1016.
Gold, Yvonne, Patricia Bachelor and William B. Michael. "The dimensionality of a modified form of the Maslach Burnout Inventory for university students in a teacher-training program." *Educational and Psychological Measurement* 49 (1989): 549–561.
Gold, Yvonne, Robert A. Roth, Claudia R. Wright, William B. Michael and Chin-Yi Chen. "The factorial validity of a teacher burnout measure (educators survey) administered to a sample of beginning teachers in elementary and secondary schools in California." *Educational and Psychological Measurement* 52 (1992): 761–768.

Golden, Jonathan, Ralph L. Piedmont, Joseph W. Ciarrocchi and Thomas Rodgerson. "Spirituality and Burnout: An incremental validity study." *Journal of Psychology and Theology* 32 (2004): 115–125.
Goldshlag, I. "Shapira, Ḥayyim Moshe." In *Encyclopaedia Judaica*, edited by M. Berenbaum and F. Skolnik, 400. Michigan: Macmillan, 2007.
Goldstone, J. "Towards a Fourth Generation of Revolutionary Theory." *Annual Review of Political Science* 4 (2001): 139–187.
Gore, Al. *The future*. London: W.H. Allen (Kindle Edition), 2013.
Gräb, Wilhelm. *Lebensgeschichten, Lebensentwürfe, Sinndeutungen. Eine Praktische Theologie gelebter Religion*. Gütersloh: Chr. Kaiser, Gütersloher Verlagshaus, 1998.
Graham, Elaine. "Being, Making and Imagining: Towards a Practical Theology of Technology." *Culture and Religion* 10, no. 2 (2009): 221–236. Doi: 10.1080/14755610903077588.
Green, Dianne E. and Frank H. Walkey. "A confirmation of the three-factor structure of the Maslach burnout inventory." *Educational and Psychological Measurement* 48 (1988): 579–585.
Green, Dianne E., Frank H. Walkey and Antony J. Taylor. "The three factor structure of the Maslach Burnout Inventory: a multicultural, multinational confirmatory study." *Journal of Social Behaviour and Personality* 6 (1991): 453–472.
Grint, Keith. *The arts of leadership*. Oxford: Oxford University Press, 2000.
Gritsch, Eric W. *A History of Lutheranism*. Second edition. Minneapolis: Fortress Press, 2010.
Grobbelaar, J. *Child Theology and the African Context*. United Kingdom: Child theology movement Ltd, 2012.
Gruber, Daniel A., Smerek, Ryan E., Thomas-Hunt, Melissa C., and Erika H. James. "The Real-time Power of Twitter: Crisis Management and Leadership in an Age of Social Media." *Business Horizons* 85 (2015): 163–172.
Gunter, H. "A Sociological Approach to Educational Leadership." *British Journal of Sociology of Education* 31, no. 4 (2010): 519–527.
Hadari-Ramage, Y. *Osim Choshvim*. Yad Tabenkin: Ramat Efal, 1994.
Harari, A. "The President: Ready for a religious Chief of Staff." *Channel 7*, December 17, 2014. http://www.inn.co.il/News/News.aspx/289432.
Harel A. *Every Jewish mother should know*. Tel Aviv: Kinneret Zmora-Bitan, 2013.
Harel I. "Tel-Aviv Menuteket uMishtametet." *Haaretz*, November 12, 2010. Accessed December 11, 2014. http://www.haaretz.co.il/opinions/1.1231717.
Harnoy, Meir. *The Settlers*. Tel Aviv: Maariv, 1994.
Harris, Philip R., Robert T. Moran and Sarah V. Moran. *Managing Cultural Differences: Global Leadership Strategies for the Twenty-first Century*. Sixth edition. Burlington, MA: Elsevier Butterworth-Heinemann, 2004.
Haslam, S.A., S.D. Reicher, and M.J. Platow. *The New Psychology of Leadership. Identity, Influence and Power*. Hove and New York: Psychology Press, 2011.
Hassan, Robert. *The Information Society: Digital Media and Society Series*. Cambridge: Polity Press, 2008.
Hayem, Judith. "From May 2008 to 2011: Xenophobic violence and national subjectivity in South Africa." *Journal of Southern African Studies* 39, no. 1 (2013): 77–97.

Healy, Nicholas. *Church, World and the Christian life: Practical-prophetic Ecclesiology*. Cambridge: Cambridge University Press, 2000.
Heelas, P., and L. Woodhead. *The Spiritual Revolution. Why Religion is giving way to Spirituality*. Oxford: Blackwell Publishing, 2005.
Heidegger, Martin. *Being and time: A translation of Sein und Zeit*. Translated by J. Stambaugh. New York: State University of New York Press, 1996.
Heidegger, Martin. *Die Grundbegriffe der Metaphysik: Welt – Endlichkeit – Einsamkeit*. Reissued by Friedrich-Wilhelm von Herrmann. Frankfurt am Main: Vittorio Klostermann, 1983.
Heidegger, Martin. *Identität und Differenz*. Pfullingen: Verlag Günther Neske, 1957.
Heidegger, Martin. *Poetry, language and thought*. Translated by A. Hofstadter. New York: Harper & Row, 1971.
Heidegger, Martin. *What is called thinking?* Translated by J. G. Gray. New York: Harper & Row, 1968.
Helland, Christopher, "Online Religion as Lived Religion. Methodological Issues in the Study of Religious Participation on the Internet." *Heidelberg Journal of Religions on the Internet* 1 (2005).
Heller, O. "Army enlistment to combat units: 61% in Judea and Samaria compared with 36% in Gush Dan." *NANA10*, November 17, 2011.
Helms, L. *Presidents, Prime Ministers and Chancellors*. Basingstoke: Palgrave, 2005.
Hendel, A. "Gated Community." Pages 493-535 in Gated Communities. Edited by A. Lahavy, Tel Aviv: Nevo Publish House, 2010.
Hermans, Chris A.M. "From Practical Theology to Practice-oriented Theology." *International Journal of Practical Theology* 18, no. 1 (2014): 113–126.
Hills, Peter, Leslie J. Francis and Christopher J.F. Rutledge. "The factor structure of a measure of burnout specific to clergy, and its trial application with respect to some individual personal differences." *Review of Religious Research* 46 (2004): 27–42.
Hinton, Sam, and Larissa Hjorth. *Understanding Social Media*. London: Sage Publications, 2013.
Hipps, Shane. *Flickering Pixels: How Technology Shapes your Faith*. Grand Rapids: Zondervan, 2009.
Hjarvard, S. "The Mediatization of Religion: A Theory of the Media as Agents of Religious Change." *Northern Lights* 6 (2008): 1–29.
HMSO. *Parochial Church Councils (Powers) Measure 1956*. London: HMSO, 1956.
HMSO. *Churchwardens Measure 2001*. London: HMSO, 2001.
HMSO. *Charities Act 2011, s177*. London: HMSO, 2011.
Hofstadter, Albert. "Introduction." In *Poetry, Language, Thought,* translated by Albert Hofstadter, ix–xxii. New York: Harper & Row, 1971.
Hofstede, Geert. "Cultural Constraints in Management Theories." *Academy of Management Executive* 7, no. 1 (1993): 81–94.
Hofstede, Geert. *Culture's Consequences: International Differences in Work-related Values*. Beverly-Hills, CA: Sage, 1980.

Holman, David, and Richard Thorpe. *Management and language: The manager as a practical author.* London: Sage, 2003.
Hoover, S. *Mass Media Religion: The Social Sources of the Electronic Church.* Beverley Hills: Sage, 1988.
Hoover, S., ed. *Religious Authority in the Media Age. In the Media and Religious Authority.* University Park, Pennsylvania: Penn State University Press, 2016.
Hope Cheong, P. "Tweet the Message? Religious Authority and Social Media Innovation." *Journal of Religion, Media & Digital Culture* 3, no. 3 (2014): 2–19.
Hope Cheong, P. "Religious Authority and Social Media Branding in a Culture of Religious Celebrification." In *The Media and Religious Authority*, edited by S. Hoover. University Park, Pennsylvania: Penn State University Press, 2016.
Horowitz, A. *The Culture War.* Hebron: Emek Hebron, 2007.
House, Robert, Paul Hanges, Marcus Dickson, S. Antonio Ruiz-Quintanilla and Globe CCI's. Culture and leadership scales. Unpublished manuscript, 1998.
House, Robert, J. A proposal to conduct a multination study of leadership and organizational practices. Unpublished manuscript. Pennsylvania, 1993.
House, Robert, J. Prospectus: an update on the GLOBE study. Unpublished manuscript. Pennsylvania, 1996.
House, Robert, J., N.S. Wright and Ram N. Aditya. "Cross-cultural research on organizational leadership. a critical analysis and a proposed theory." In *New perspectives on international industry/organizational psychology*, edited by P.C. Earley and M. Erez, 535–625. San Francisco, CA: New Lexington: 1997.
Huberman, H. "Knitted Beret." *Besheva*, July 8, 2004: 20–18.
Human Rights Watch. *Prohibited persons: abuse of undocumented migrants, asylum seekers, and refugees in South Africa.* New York: Human Rights Watch, 1998.
Inbari, A. "One Hundred Years of Solitude." *Maariv*, September 15, 2002. http://www.nrg.co.il/online/archive/ART/347/558.html.
Ingerson, Katharyn, and Jaclyn Bruce. "Leadership in the Twitterverse." *Journal of Leadership Studies* 7, no. 3 (2013): 74–83.
Iwancki, Edward F. and Richard L. Schwab. "A cross validation study of the Maslach Burnout Inventory." *Educational and Psychological Measurement* 41 (1981): 1167–1174.
Jackson, J. *Pastorpreneurs.* Friendswood: Baxter, 2003.
Jinkins, Michael. "Religious Leadership." In *The Wiley-Blackwell Companion to Practical Theology*, edited by Bonnie J. Miller-McLemore, 307–317. Aldershot: Ashgate, 2012.
Johnson, G. "Strategic Leadership Development Program." *Strategic HR Review* 9, no. 4 (2010): 5–12.
Jorgenson, Allen G. "Contours of the Common Priesthood" In *The Global Luther: Theologian for Modern times*, edited by C. Helmer, 249–265. Minneapolis: Fortress Press, 2009.
Joseph, Eugene N., Jozef Corveleyn, Patrick Luyten and Hans de Witte. "Does commitment to celibacy lead to burnout or enhanced engagement." *European Journal of Mental Health* 5 (2010): 187–204.

Joseph, Eugene N., Patrick Luyten, Jozef Corveleyn and Hans de Witte. "The relationship between personality, burnout, and engagement among the Indian clergy." *International Journal for the Psychology of Religion* 21 (2011): 276–288.
Joubert, Stephan J. "Annus Virualis: Enkele Uitdagings wat die Virtuele Era van Web 2.0 aan Relevante Kerklike Bedieninge Stel." *Nederduitse Gereformeerde Teologiese Tydskrif* 51, no. 3/4 (2010): 48–60.
Jung, Carl G. *Psychological types: The collected works*. Volume 6. London: Routledge and Kegan Paul, 1971.
Kaldor, Peter and Rod Bullpitt. *Burnout in church leaders*. Adelaide, South Austrialia: Openbook Publishers, 2001.
Kalmijn, M. "Status Homogamy in the United States." *American Journal of Sociology* 97, no. 2 (1991): 496–523.
Kane, J. *The Politics of Moral Capital*. Cambridge: Cambridge University Press, 2001.
Kaputa, C. *You are a brand! In persona and online, how smart people brand themselves for business success*. Boston (MA): Nicholas Brealey Publishing, 2012.
Kay, William K., Leslie J. Francis and Mandy Robbins. "A distinctive leadership for a distinctive network of churches? Psychological type theory and the Apostolic Networks." *Journal of Pentecostal Theology* 20 (2011): 306–322.
Kay, William K. *Pentecostals in Britain*. Carlisle: Paternoster, 2000.
Keirsey, David and Marilyn Bates. *Please understand me*. Del Mar, CA: Prometheus Nemesis, 1978.
Kelly, Simon. "Leadership: a categorical mistake?" *Human Relations* 61 (2008): 763–782.
Kelly, Simon. "Towards a negative ontology of leadership." *Human Relations* 67, no. 8 (2014): 905–922.
Kenway, J. and Koh, A. "The Elite School as 'Cognitive Mechane' and 'Social Paradise.'" Journal of Sociology 49, no. 3 (2013): 272–290.
Kerfoot, Karlene M. "Listening to See: The Key to Virtual Leadership." *Nursing Economics* 28, no. 2 (2010): 114–119.
Kerr, Philippa, and Kevin Durrheim. "The Dilemma of Anti-Xenophobia Discourse in the Aftermath of Violence in De Doorns." *Journal of Southern African Studies* 39, no. 3 (2013): 577-596.
Kerr, R., and Robinson, S. "Leadership as an Elite Field." *Leadership* 7, no. 2 (2011): 151–173.
Khoza, R. "The need for an Afrocentric management approach. A South African based management approach." In *African management. Philosophies, concepts and applications*, edited by P. Christie, R. Lessem and L. Mbigi, 117–124. Pretoria: Sigma, 1994.
Kimmerling, B., "Patterns of Militarism in Israel." *European Journal of Sociology* 34, no. 2 (1993): 196–223.
Kirk, Mary and Tom Leary. *Holy matrimony? An exploration of marriage and ministry*. Oxford: Lynx, 1994.
Klaver, M. "Pentecostal Pastorpreneurs and the Global Circulation of Authoritative Aesthetic Styles." *Culture and Religion* 16, no. 2 (2015): 146–159. https://doi.org/10.1080/14755610.2015.1058527.

Kotze, J. *Understanding Black South Africans through their experiences of life.* Cape Town: Juta, 1993.
Küçüksüleymanoğlu, Rüyam. "Occupational burnout levels of Turkish imams," *Review of Religious Research* 55 (2013): 27–42.
Kungörelse om beslutad ny regeringsform. Svensk författningssamling [Proclamation about decided new Constitution. Swedish Code of Statues]. Stockholm, 1974.
Kyrkoordning 2016: Med angränsande lagstiftning för Svenska kyrkan [Church Ordinance 2016: With corresponding legislation for the Church of Sweden]. Stockholm: Verbum, 2016.
Laclau, Ernesto, and Chantal Mouffe. *Hegemony and Socialist Strategy: Towards a Radical Democratic Politics.* London: Verso, 1985.
Laclau, Ernesto. "Paul de Man and the Politics of Rhetoric." *Pretexts* 7, no. 2 (1998): 153–70.
Laclau, Ernesto. *New Reflections on the Revolution of Our Time.* London: Verso, 1990.
Lag om Svenska kyrkan. Svensk författningssamling [Law of the Church of Sweden. Swedish code of statutes]. Stockholm, 1998.
Landau, Loren B. ed., *Exorcising the Demons Within: xenophobia, violence and statecraft in contemporary South Africa.* Johannesburg: Wits University Press, 2012.
Lankshear D.W. and Francis, L.J. *Signs of Growth – Listening to the churches in the Woolwich Episcopal Area.* London: Diocese of Southwark, 2009.
Laruelle, François. "Etho-techno-logy: Of Ethics in an Intense Technological Milieu." Translated by Alyosha Edlebi. *Qui Parle: Critical Humanities and Social Sciences* 21, no. 2 (2013b): 157–167.
Laruelle, François. *Principles of Non-Philosophy.* Translated by N. Rubczak and A.-P. Smith. London: Bloomsbury, 2013a. Kindle edition: www.bloomsbury.com.
Leadbeater, Charles. *We-think: Mass Innovation, not Mass Production.* Second edition. London: Profile, 2009.
Lebel, U. "'Casualty Panic': Military Recruitment Models, Civil-Military Gap and their Implications for the Legitimacy of Military Loss." *Democracy and Security* 6, no. 2 (2010): 183–206.
Lebel, U. "Postmodern or Conservative? Competing Security Communities over Military Doctrine – Israeli National-Religious Soldiers as Counter [Strategic] Culture Agents." *Political and Military Sociology: An Annual Review* 40 (2013): 23–57.
Lebel, U. and H. Dahan-Kaleb. "Marshalling a Second Career: Generals in the Israeli School System." *Journal of Educational Administration and History* 36, no. 2 (2004): 145–157.
Lebel, U. "Casualties." in: Joseph, P. (ed.), *SAGE Encyclopedia of War: Social Science Perspectives*, Sage: London, 275–276, 2016.
Lebel, U. and G. Hatuka. "Israeli Labor Party and the security elite 1977–2015: De-Militarization as Political Self-Marginalization." *Israel Affairs* 22, no. 3/4 (2016): 641–663.

Lebel, U. and S. Lubish-Omer. "The return to who we were." In *Between the Yarmulke and the Beret*, edited by R. Gal and T. Libel, 151–203. Tel Aviv: Modan, 2012.
Lebel, U., and E. Orkibi. Settlers and Settlement in Israeli Academic Research. Ariel University, in preparation.
Lebovitz, A. "Regional framing: Judea, Samaria and the Gaza Strip in the eyes of the security elite." *Israel Affairs* 21, no. 3 (2015): 422–442.
Lee, S. and P. Sinitiere. *Holy Mavericks: Evangelical innovators and the spiritual marketplace*. New York: New York University Press, 2009.
Leithwood, K. and B. Mascall. "Collective Leadership Effects on Student Achievement." *Educational Administration Quarterly* 44, no. 4 (2008): 529–561.
Leon, N. "Self-segregation of the vanguard." *Israel Affairs* 21, no. 3 (2015): 348–360.
Leon, N. "The 1977 sub-revolutions and their place in the development of the Shas political movement." *Israel Affairs* 15 (2009): 1–32.
Less, A. and G. Weiz. "We have a problem." *Yediot Aharonot*, July 4, 2003.
Letender, K., R. Gonzales and N. Takako. "Feeding the Elite." *Higher Education Policy* 19, no. 1 (2006): 7–30.
Levinstein-Malz, R. *Proclaim Liberty – The Story of Colonel Dror Weinberg*. Tel Aviv: Yediot Aharonot, 2010.
Levy, Y. "Is There a Motivation Crisis in Military Recruitment in Israel?" *Israel Affairs* 15, no. 2 (2009): 135–158.
Levy, Y. "The Theocratization of the Israeli Military." *Armed Forces and Society* 40, no. 2 (2014): 269–294.
Liu, Helena. "When leaders fail: A typology of failures and framing strategies." *Management Communication Quarterly* 24, no. 2 (2010): 323–259.
Luhrmann, T.M. *When God Talks Back. Understanding the American Evangelical Relationship with God*. New York: Vintage Books, 2012.
Lundby, K. "Media logic: Looking for social interaction changes." In *Mediatization: Concept, changes, consequences*, edited by K. Lundby, 101–121. New York: Peter Lang, 2009.
Lundstedt, Göran. *Biskopsämbetet och demokratin: Biskopsrollens förändring i Svenska kyrkan under 1900-talets senare del: En kyrkorättslig undersökning* [The Office of Bishop and the Democracy: Changes in the Role of Bishops in the Church of Sweden in the Latter Part of the 20th Century. An investigation into Canon Law]. Skellefteå: Artos, 2006.
Luther, Martin. "An den christlichen Adel deutscher Nation von des christlichen Standes Besserung." In *D. Martin Luther Werke: Kritische Gesamtausgabe*, 6. Weimar: Hermann Böhlau, 1888.
Luther, Martin. "Der 82. Psalm Ausgelegt." In *D. Martin Luther Werke: Kritische Gesamtausgabe*, 31 I. Weimar: Hermann Böhlaus Nachfolger, 1913.
Luther, Martin. *On the Councils and the Church*. In *Luther's Works* 41. Philadelphia: Fortress, 1966.
Luther, Martin. *Psalm 82*. In *Luther's Works*, 13. Saint Louis: Concordia, 1956.
Luther, Martin. *To the Christian Nobility of the German Nation Concerning the Reform of the Christian Estate*. In *Luther's Works*, 44. Philadelphia: Fortress, 1968.

Luther, Martin. *Von den Konziliis und Kirchen*. In *D. Martin Luthers Werke: Kritische Gesamtausgabe*, 50. Weimar: Hermann Böhlaus Nachfolger, 1914.
Lutz, Barend, and Pierre du Toit. *Defining Democracy in a Digital Age: Political Support on Social Media*. London: Palgrave MacMillan (Kindle Edition), 2014.
MacGuire, Meredith B. *Lived Religion. Faith and Practice in Everyday Life*. Oxford: Oxford University Press, 2008.
Maiko, S.M. *Youth, Faith and Culture: Contemporary theories and practices of youth ministry*. USA: Author House, 2007.
Malherbe, J. *Saved by the Lion? Stories of African Children encountering outsiders*. London: ChildNet, 2011.
Malhota, N. and Y. Margalit. "Expectation Setting and Retrospective Voting." *Journal of Politics* 76, no. 4 (2014): 1000–1016.
Mamdani, Mahmood. *Citizen and Subject: Contemporary Africa and the Legacy of Late Colonialism*. Princeton, NJ: Princeton University Press, 1996.
Managa, A. "Unfulfilled promises and their consequences: A reflection on local government performance and the critical issue of poor service delivery in South Africa." *Policy Brief*, number 76 May 2012. Africa Institute of South Africa.
Mandela, N.R and The Nelson Mandela Foundation. *Nelson Mandela: Conversations with Myself*. London: Macmillan, 2010.
Mangaliso, Mzamo P. "Building Competitive Advantage from Ubuntu: Management Lessons from South Africa." *Academy of Management Executive* 15, no. 3 (2001): 23–32.
Mangcu, X. *The Arrogance of Power: South Africa's Leadership Meltdown*. Cape Town: NB Publishers, 2014.
Marti, G., and G. Ganiel. *The Deconstructed Church. Understanding Emerging Christianity*. New York: Oxford University Press, 2014.
Martin, William G. "Africa's Futures: from North–South to East–South?" *Third World Quarterly* 29, no. 2 (2008): 339–56.
Martinsson, Johan. *Värdet av valdeltagande* [The value of participation in the electoral process]. Stockholm: Grundlagsutredningen, 2007.
Maslach, Christina. *Burnout: The cost of caring*. Cambridge, MA: Malor Books, 2003.
Maslach, Christina and Susan E. Jackson. *Maslach Burnout Inventory manual*. Second edition. Palo Alto, CA: Consulting Psychologists Press, 1986.
Matsengarwodzi, Derick. "Leadership Crisis in Africa: Words have turned into bullets that maim the innocent." *Nehanda Radio*, September 8, 2013. http://nehandaradio.com/2013/09/30/words-have-turned-into-bullets-that-maim-the-innocent/.
Matsinhe, D. Mario. "Africa's Fear of Itself: the ideology of Makwerekwere in South Africa." *Third World Quarterly* 32, no. 2 (2011): 295–313.
Maxwell, J.C. *Developing the leader within you*. Nashville: Thomas Nelson Publishers, Meyers, 1993.
Mbembe, Achille. "African Modes of Self-Writing." Translated by S. Rendall. *Public Culture* 14, no. 1 (2002a): 239–73.

Mbembe, Achille. "On the Power of the False." Translated by Judith Inggs. *Public Culture* 14, no. 3 (2002b): 629–41.

Mbembe, Achille. "Provisional Notes on the Postcolony." *Africa* 62, no. 1 (1992): 3–37.

Mbembe, Achille. *On the Postcolony*. Berkeley, CA: University of California Press, 2001.

McCarthy, J., and Mayer, Z. "The Enduring Vitality of the Resource Mobilization Theory of Social Movements." In *Handbook of Sociological Theory*, edited by J. Turner, 533–565. NY: Plenum Publishers, 2002.

Meindl, James R. "The romance of leadership as a follower-centric theory: A social constructionist approach." *Leadership Quarterly* 6 (1995): 329–341.

Meyers, C. "The Family in Early Israel." In *Families in Ancient Israel*, edited by Leo G. Perdue, Jospeh Blenkinsopp, John J. Collins and Carol Meyers, 1–47. Louisville KY: Westminster John Knox Press, 1997.

Miller, Vincent. *Understanding Digital Culture*. Thousand Oaks: Sage, 2011.

Miner, Maureen H. "Changes in burnout over the first 12 months in ministry: Links with stress and orientation to ministry." *Mental Health, Religion and Culture* 10 (2007a): 9–16.

Miner, Maureen H. "Burnout in the first year of ministry: Personality and belief style as important predictors." *Mental Health, Religion and Culture* 10 (2007b): 17–29.

Misago, Jean Pierre, Loren B. Landau and Tamlyn Monson. *Towards Tolerance, Law, and Dignity: Addressing Violence against Foreign Nationals in South Africa*. Report for the International Organisation of Migration. Pretoria: International Organisation of Migration, 2009.

Misago, Jean Pierre, Tamlyn Monson, Tara Polzer and Loren B. Landau. *May 2008 violence against foreign nationals in South Africa: Understanding causes and evaluating responses*. Report for the Forced Migration Studies Programme (FMSP), University of the Witwatersrand and Consortium for Refugees and Migrants in South Africa (CoRMSA). Johannesburg: FMSP, 2010.

Misago, Jean Pierre. "Disorder in a changing society: authority and the micropolitics of violence." In *Exorcising the Demons Within: xenophobia, violence and statecraft in contemporary South Africa*, edited by Loren B. Landau, 90–108. Johannesburg: Wits University Press, 2012.

Mngxitama, Andile. "We are not all like that: race, class and nation after apartheid." in *Go Home or Die Here: violence, xenophobia and the reinvention of difference in South Africa*, edited by S. Hassim, T. Kupe and E. Worby. Johannesburg: Wits University Press, 2008.

Monson, Tamlyn, and Jean Pierre Misago. "Why History Has Repeated Itself: The Security Risks of Structural Xenophobia." *SA Crime Quarterly* 29 (2009): 25–34.

Monson, Tamlyn. "Everyday politics and collective mobilisation against foreigners in a South African shack settlement." *Africa: The Journal of the International African Institute* 85, no. 1 (2015): 131–152.

Moore, D. and S. Aweiss. "Hatred of "Others" Among Jewish, Arab, and Palestinian Students in Israel." *Analyses of Social Issues and Public Policy* 2, no. 1 (2002): 151–172

Moore, D. and S. Aweiss. *Bridges over Troubled Water: A Comparative Study of Jews, Arabs, and Palestinians.* London: Prager, 2004.
Moore, L.R. *Selling God. American Religion in the Marketplace of Culture.* Oxford: Oxford University Press, 1995.
Morris, A. *The Origin of the Civil Rights Movement.* NY: Free Press, 1984.
Mosselson, Aidan. "'There is no difference between citizens and non-citizens anymore': Violent Xenophobia, Citizenship and the Politics of Belonging in Post-Apartheid South Africa." *Journal of Southern African Studies* 36, no. 3 (2010): 641–655.
Mothoagae, Ithumeleng. "Identity as a social construct of empire: then and now." *Studia Historiae Ecclesiasticae* 37 (2011): 115–130.
Moynagh, M., with Ph. Harrold 2012. *Church for Every Context. An Introduction to Theology and Practice.* London: SCM Press.
Mozes, H. "From religious Zionism to Post-modern religious: trends and developments in Religious-Zionism since the Rabin Assassination." PhD diss., Bar Ilan University, 2009.
Mudimbe, Valentin-Yves. *The Invention of Africa: Gnosis, Philosophy, and the Order of Knowledge.* Bloomington, IN: Indiana University Press, 1988.
Mueller, W. *Engaging the soul of youth culture: Bridging teen worldviews and Christian truth.* USA: InterVarsity Press, 2006.
Müller, Julian C. "Transversal rationality as a practical way of doing Interdisciplinary Work." *Practical Theology in South Africa* 24, no. 2 (2009): 199–228.
Murthy, Dhiraj. *Twitter, Social Communication in the Twitter Age.* Cambridge: Polity Press (Kindle Edition), 2013.
Myers, Isabel B. and Mary H. McCaulley. *Manual: A guide to the development and use of the Myers-Briggs Type Indicator.* Palo Alto, CA: Consulting Psychologists Press, 1985.
Myers, Isabel B., Mary H. McCaulley, Naomi L. Quenk and Allen L. Hammer. *MBTI Manual: A guide to the development and use of the Myers-Briggs Type Indicator.* Palo Alto, CA: Consulting Psychologists Press, 1998.
Nauss, A. "Assessing ministerial effectiveness. A review of measures and their use." *Research in the Social Scientific Study of Religion* 7 (1996): 221–251.
Nash, S. and J. Whitehead, ed. *Christian Youth Work in Theory and Practice.* Lomdon: SCM Press, 2014.
Ndou, Clive. "Foreigners must go home – King Zwelithini." *The Citizen*, 23 March, 2015. http://citizen.co.za/349347/foreigners-must-go-home-king-zwelithini/.
Nel, R.W. "Discerning the role of faith communities in responding to urban youth marginalisation." *HTS Teologiese Studies/Theological Studies* 70, no. 3 (2014). http://dx.doi.org/10.4102/hts.v70i3.2743.
Nell, I. and E. Nell. "Practical Theology and Missiology." *Stellenbosch University, South Africa – Rural theology* 12, no. 1 (2014): 29–41.
Nell, I. "The end of leadership?: The shift of power in local congregations." *HTS Teologiese Studies/ Theological Studies* 71, no. 3 (2015). http:// dx.doi.org/10.4102/hts. v71i3.2934.

Nell, I. "Teaching leadership and administration at a Faculty of Theology: Practical Theological Reflections." *Scriptura* 113 (2014): 1–18.
Neocosmos, Michael. "The Politics of Fear and the Fear of Politics: Reflections on Xenophobic Violence in South Africa." *Journal of Asian and African Studies* 43 (2008): 586.
Ngomane, R.M. and E. Mahlangu. "Leadership mentoring and succession in the Charismatic churches in Bushbuckridge." *HTS Teologiese Studies/ Theological Studies* 70, no. 1 (2014). http:// dx.doi.org/10.4102/hts. v70i1.2065.
Nickels, H.C., L. Thomas, M.J. Hickman, and S. Silvestri. "De-Constructing 'Suspect' Communities: A Critical Discourse Analysis of British Newspaper Coverage of Irish and Muslim Communities." *Journalism Studies* 13, no. 2 (2012): 340–355.
Nieftagodien, Noor. "Xenophobia in Alexandra." in *Go Home or Die Here: Violence, Xenophobia and the Reinvention of Difference in South Africa*, edited by Shireen Hassim, Eric Worby and Tawana Kupe, 65–78. Johannesburg: Wits University Press, 2008.
Nietzsche, Friedrich Wilhelm. *Also sprach Zarathustra. Ein Buch für Alle und Keinen*. Köln: Anaconda Verlag, 2005. Project Gutenberg, 2005. www.gutenberg2000.de/nietzsche/zara.also.htm.
Nietzsche, Friedrich Wilhelm. *The Gay Science*. Translated and edited by W. Kaufmann. New York: W. Vintage, 1974.
Nkomo, Stella. "A Post-colonial and anti-colonial reading of 'African' leadership and management in organization studies: tensions, contradictions and possibilities." *Organization* 18 (2011): 365–386. DOI: 10.1177/1350508411398731.
Ntsebeza, Lungisile and Ruth Hall, eds. *The Land Question in South Africa: the challenge of transformation and redistribution*. Cape Town: HSRC Press, 2007.
Nyembezi, Babalwa. "Min. Lindiwe Zulu to foreigners: 'Share your ideas with local business owners.'" 702 News, 28 January, 2015. http://www.702.co.za/articles/1505/zulu-foreign-business-owners-must-share.
Obiakor, Festus E. "Building Patriotic African Leadership through African-centred education." *Journal of Black Studies* 34 (2004): 402–420.
Öppna kyrkan: Kyrkopolitiskt program för Socialdemokraterna i Svenska kyrkan. Antaget av den socialdemokratiska partistyrelsen den 21 juni 2000 [Open the Church: Church Political Platform for the Social Democrats in the Church of Sweden. Approved by the Social Democratic Party's executive committee on 21 of June 2000]. Stockholm: Socialdemokraterna, 2000.
Orobator, A.E. *Theology brewed in an African pot*. New York: Orbis books, 2009.
Orsi, Robert. "Everyday Miracles: The Study of Lived Religion." In *Lived Religion in America. Toward a History of Practice*, ed. David D. Hall, 3–21. Princeton: Princeton University Press, 1997.
Osmer, Richard R. *Practical Theology: An Introduction*. Grand Rapids: Wm. B. Eerdmans, 2008.
Osmer, Richard R. *The Teaching Ministry of Congregations*. Louisville: Westminster, 2005.

Parker, Philip D. and Andrew J. Martin. "Clergy motivation and occupational well-being: Exploring a quadripolar model and its role in predicting burn-out and engagement." *Journal of Religion and Health* 50 (2011): 656–674.

Paulus, Trena M., Jessica N. Lester and Paul G. Dempster. *Digital Tools for Qualitative Research.* London: Sage Publications, 2014.

Pearson, Clive. "Twittering the Gospel." *International Journal of Public Theology* 9 (2015): 176–192.

Pedahzur, A. *The Triumph of Israel's Radical Right.* NY: Oxford University Press, 2012.

Perdue, L.G., ed. The household, Old Testament Theology and Contemporary Hermeneutics in Families in Ancient Israel. Louisville: Westminster John Knox Press, 1997.

Peyton, Nigel and Caroline Gatrell. *Managing clergy lives: Obedience, sacrifice, intimacy.* London: Bloomsbury, 2013.

Phillips, Simon. *The Complete Guide to Professional Networking. The Secrets of Online and Offline Success.* London: Kogan Page, 2014.

Pierce, C. Mark B. and Geoffrey N. Molloy. "The construct validity of the Maslach Burnout Inventory: some data from Down Under." *Psychological Reports* 65 (1989): 1340–1342.

Pillay, D. "Relative Deprivation, Social Instability and Cultures of Entitlement." In *Go Home or Die Here: Violence, Xenophobia and the Reinvention of Difference in South Africa*, edited by Shireen Hassim, Eric Worby and Tawana Kupe, 93–103. Johannesburg: Wits University Press, 2008.

Posel, Deborah. "Races to consume: revisiting South Africa's history of race, consumption and the struggle for freedom." *Ethnic and Racial Studies* 33, no. 2 (2010): 157–175.

Powers, Stephen and Kenneth F. Gose. "Reliability and construct validity of the Maslach Burnout Inventory in a sample of university students." *Educational and Psychological Measurement* 46 (1986): 251–255.

Quash, Ben. *Theology and the Drama of History: Cambridge Studies in Christian Doctrine.* Cambridge: Cambridge University Press, 2005.

Rabin, Y. *Service Book.* Tel Aviv: Maariv, 1979.

Raj, Anthony and Karol E. Dean. "Burnout and depression among Catholic priests in India." *Pastoral Psychology* 54 (2005): 157–171.

Rakow, K. "Religious Branding and the Quest to Meet Consumer Needs: Joel Osteen's 'Message of Hope.'" In *Religion and the Marketplace in the United States,* edited by J. Stievermann, P. Goff and D. Junker. New York: Oxford University Press, 2015.

Randall, Kelvin. "Burnout as a predictor of leaving Anglican parish ministry." *Review of Religious Research* 46 (2004): 20–26.

Randall, Kelvin. "Examining the relationship between burnout and age among Anglican clergy in England and Wales." *Mental Health, Religion and Culture* 10 (2007): 39–46.

Randall, Kelvin. "Clergy burnout: Two different measures." *Pastoral Psychology* 62 (2013): 333–341.

Reader, John. *Reconstructing Practical Theology. The Impact of Globalization.* Aldershot: Ashgate, 2008.

Reid, Jean. "The relationships among personality type, coping strategies, and burnout in elementary teachers." *Journal of Psychological Type* 51 (1999): 22–33.

Religionsfrihetslag. Svensk författningssamling [Law of Religious Freedom. Swedish code of statutes]. Stockholm, 1951.

Renner, Judith. "The Local Roots of the Global Politics of Reconciliation: The Articulation of 'Reconciliation' as an Empty Universal in the South African Transition to Democracy." *Millennium: Journal of International Studies* 42, no. 2 (2014): 263–285.

Rice, Jesse. *The Church of Facebook: How the Hyperconnected are Redefining Community.* London: Routledge, 2009.

Ricoeur, Paul. *Time and Narrative.* Volume 1. Translated by Kathleen McLaughlin and David Pellauer. Chicago: University of Chicago Press, 1984.

Riesebrodt, M. "Charisma in Max Weber's Sociology of Religion." *Religion* 29, no. 1 (1999): 1–14.

Robbins, Mandy and Leslie J. Francis. "Work-related psychological health among Church of England clergywomen: Individual differences and psychological type." *Review of Religious Research* 52 (2010): 57–71.

Robbins, Mandy, Leslie J. Francis and Ruth Powell. "Work-related psychological health among clergywomen in Australia." *Mental Health, Religion and Culture* 15 (2012): 933–944.

Rodgerson, Thomas E. and Ralph L. Piedmont. "Assessing the incremental validity of the Religious Problem-Solving Scale in the prediction of clergy burnout." *Journal for the Scientific Study of Religion* 37 (1998): 517–527.

Roebben, B. *Seeking sense in the city: European Perspectives on Religious Education.* Germany: Lit Verlag, 2009.

Rogers, R. *Digital Methods.* Cambridge (MA): MIT Press, 2013.

Rollins, P. *Insurrection. To Believe is Human; to Doubt, Divine.* London: Hodder & Stoughton (2012 paperback edition), 2011.

Rollins, P. *The Idolatry of God. Breaking the Addiction to Certainty and Satisfaction.* London: Hodder & Stoughton, 2012.

Rollins, P. *How (Not) to Speak of God.* London: SPCK, 2006.

Roof, W.C. *Spiritual Marketplace: Baby Boomers and the Remaking of American Religion.* New Jersey: Princeton University Press, 1999.

Root, A. *Revisting Relational youth ministry: From strategy of influence to a theology of incarnation.* Westmont, Illinois: Intervarsity Press, 2007.

Rosenius, Marie. "Lex orandi, lex credendi eller lex credendi, lex orandi: Om liturgi och ecklesiologi i Teologiska grundprinciper för arbetet i 2006 års kyrkohandboksgrupp och Mässans grundordning," In *Svensk Teologisk Kvartalskrift* 88, no. 2 (2012): 78–88.

Rossetti, Stephen J. *Why priests are happy: A study of the psychological and spiritual health of priests.* Notre Dame: Ave Maria Press, 2011.

Rossman-Stollman, E. "Religion and the Military as Greedy Frameworks." PhD diss., Bar-Ilan University, 2006.

Roth, A. "Something New Begins – Religious Zionism in the 2013 Elections: From Decline to Political Recovery." In *Israel Affairs* 21, no. 2 (2015): 209–229.

Rowling, C. and P. Gooder. *Reader Ministry Explored*. London: SPCK, 2011.

Russell, I. *The Churchwarden's Handbook – A Practical Guide*. Bury St Edmunds: Kevin Mayhew, 2000.

Rutledge, Christopher J.F. "Burnout and the practice of ministry among rural clergy: Looking for the hidden signs." *Rural Theology* 4, no. 1 (2006): 57–65.

Rutledge, Christopher J.F. and Leslie J. Francis. "Burnout among male Anglican parochial clergy in England: Testing a modified form of the Maslach Burnout Inventory." *Research in the Social Scientific Study of Religion* 15 (2004): 71–93.

Sadan, E. *A Call for Direction for the Religious Zionism*, no name or place of print, 2007.

Sagawa, S., and J. Schramm. *High Schools as Launch Pads*. Washington DC: College Summit, 2008.

Sahar, E. "The home that produced our finest boys." *Israel Today*, June 12, 2014.

Said, Edward. *Culture and Imperialism*. London: Chatto and Windus, 1993.

Said, Edward. *Orientalism*. New York, NY: Vintage, 1979.

Sanford, John A. *Ministry burnout*. London: Arthur James, 1982.

Sarid, Y. "Dance of the Parasites." *Haaretz*, December 26, 1991.

Schaufeli, Wilmar B. and Dirk van Dierendonck. "The construct-validity of 2 burnout measures." *Journal of Organizational Behavior* 14 (1993): 631–647.

Schrag, Calvin O. *Convergence amidst difference: Philosophical conversations across national boundaries*. Albany: State University of New York Press, 2004.

Schrag, Calvin O. *The resources of rationality: A Response to the postmodern challenge*. Bloomington: Indiana University Press, 1992.

Schulz, W. "Reconsidering Mediatization as an Analytical Concept." *European Journal of Communication* 19, no. 1 (2004): 87–101.

Schwartz, D. *Religious Zionism: History and Ideology*. Tel Aviv: Ministry of Defense, 2003.

Senghor, Leopold Sedar. "Negritude: A Humanism of the Twentieth Century." In *Colonial Discourse and Postcolonial Theory*, edited by P. Williams and L. Chrisman, 27–35. New York, NY: Columbia University Press, 1994.

Senghor, Leopold Sedar. *On African Socialism*. Translation by Mercer Cook. London: Pall Mall, 1964.

Sharon, R. "The father of the pre-military academies in a rare interview." NANA10, October 20, 2014. http://news.nana10.co.il/Article/?ArticleID=1087411.

Shotter, John and Ann L. Cunliffe. "Managers as practical authors: Everyday conversations for action." In *Management and Language*, edited by David Holman and Richard Thorpe, 15–37. London: Sage, 2003.

Shotter, John. *Conversational realities: Constructing life through language*. London: Sage, 1993.

Siegel, Lee. *Against the Machine: Being Human in the Age of the Electronic Mob. Spiegel Sociology of Knowledge*. New York: Anchor, 2008.

Silverstone, R. "Complicity and Collusion in the Mediation of Everyday Life." *New Literary History* 33, no. 5 (2002): 754–764.
Sloterdijk, Peter. *Bubbles: Spheres 1.* Translation by W. Hoban. Los Angeles: Semiotext(e), 2011.
Smircich, Linda, and Caret Morgan. "Leadership: the management of meaning." *Journal of Applied Behavioural Science* 18 (1982): 257–273.
Smith, C. and M. Lundquist Denton. *Soul Searching: The Religious and Spiritual Lives of American Teenagers.* New York: Oxford University Press, 2005.
Smith, Greg and Leslie J. Francis. "Experiencing and reflecting on thinking and feeling in pastoral care: Deploying psychological type theory in continuing ministerial formation." *Journal of Adult Theological Education* 12 (2015): 69–78.
Spener, Philipp. J. *Pia Desideria*, 3. durchgesehene. Aufl. Berlin: Walter de Gruyter & Co., 1964a.
Spener, Philip. J. *Pia Desideria*. Minneapolis: Augsburg Fortress Publishers, 1964b.
Spivak, Gayatri Chakravorty. "Can the Subaltern Speak?" In *Marxism and the Interpretation of Culture*, edited by C. Nelson and L. Grossberg, 271–313. London: Macmillan, 1988.
Stanton-Rich, Howard M. and Seppo E. Iso-Ahola. "Burnout and leisure." *Journal of Applied Social Psychology* 28 (1998): 1931–1950.
Stern, A. "Towards a Jewish Leadership." *Tzohar* 10 (2002): 59–61.
Stevenson, J. *Sensational devotion: Evangelical performance in twenty-first century America.* Ann Arbor: Michigan University Press, 2013.
Stiver, Dan. R. "Theological Method." In *The Cambridge Companion to Postmodern Theology*, edited by Kevin J. Vanhoozer, 170–185. Cambridge: Cambridge University Press, 2003.
Stogdill, R.M. *Handbook of Leadership: A suvery of literature.* New York: Free Press, 1974.
Streib, Heinz, Astrid Dinter, and Kerstin Söderblom. *Lived Religion. Conceptual, Empirical and Practical-Theological Approaches. Essays in Honor of Hans-Günter Heimbrock.* Leiden: Brill, 2008.
Strümpfer, D. J. W. and J. Bands. "Stress among clergy: An exploratory study on South African Anglican priests." *South African Journal of Psychology* 26, no. 2 (1996): 67–75.
Swart, I. and S. de Beer. "Doing urban public theology in South Africa: Introducing a new agenda." *HTS Teologiese Studies/Theological Studies* 70, no. 3 (2014). http://dx.doi.org/10.4102/hts.v70i3.2811.
Sweet, Len. *Viral: How Social Networking is Poised to Ignite Revival.* Colorado Springs: Waterbrook Press (Kindle edition), 2012.
Sweet, Len. "Twitter Theology: 5 Ways Twitter has Changed my Life and Helped me be a Better Disciple of Jesus." Last modified April 28, 2014. http://www.leonardsweet.com/article_details.php?id=55.
Taylor, C. *A Secular Age.* Cambridge (MA): Harvard University Press, 2007.
Tappert, Theodore G. *Philip Jacob Spener, Pia Desideria.* Minneapolis: Augsburg Fortress Publishers, 1964.

Thomas, Christopher G. "Why the Homeless Rebel: Housing Struggles in post-Apartheid South Africa." *African Historical Review* 42, no. 2 (2010): 27–47.
Thompson, Geoffrey. "Religious Diversity, Christian Doctrine and Karl Barth." *International Journal of Systematic Theology* 8, no. 1 (2006): 3–24.
Thurau-Gray, L. "The trend towards turning public education into a gated community." *Cornell Journal of Law and Public Policy* 11, no. 3 (2002): 665–690.
Tomlinson, M., D. Oreilly and M. Wallace. "Developing Leaders as Symbolic Violence." *Management Learning* 44, no. 1 (2013): 81–97.
Triandis, Harry C. "A theoretical framework for the study of diversity." In *Diversity in Organizations: New Perspectives for a Changing Workplace*, ed. Martin M. Chemers, Stuart Oskamp and Mark A. Costanzo (California: Sage Publications, 1995). http://dx.doi.org/10.4135/9781452243405.n2.
Turkle, Sherry. *Alone Together. Why we Expect more from Technology and Less from Each Other*. New York: Basic Books (Kindle Edition), 2011.
Turton, Douglas W. and Leslie J. Francis. "The relationship between attitude toward prayer and professional burnout among Anglican parochial clergy in England: Are praying clergy healthier clergy?" *Mental Health, Religion and Culture* 10 (2007): 61–74.
Twitchell, J. *Shopping for God: How Christianity went from in your heart to in your face*. New York: Simon Schuster, 2007.
UNHCR, *UNHCR Global Trends 2012 – displacement: the new 20th century challenge*. Geneva: United Nations High Commissioner for Refugees, 2012.
Van den Berg, Jan-Albert. "The story of the hashtag(#): A practical theological tracing of the hashtag(#) symbol on Twitter." *HTS Teologiese Studies/Theological Studies* 70, no. 1 (2014). http://dx.doi.org/10.4102/hts.v70i1.2706
Van den Berg, Jan-Albert, and Ruard R. Ganzevoort. "The Art of Creating Futures – Practical Theology and a Strategic Research Sensitivity for the Future." *Acta Theologica* 34, no. 2 (2014): 166–185.
Van den Berg, Jan-Albert. "Theoretical Signposts for Tracing Spirituality within the Fluid Decision-making of a Mobile Virtual Reality." *HTS Teologiese Studies / Theological Studies* 68, no. 2 (2012): 1–6. Doi: 10.4102/hts.v68i2.1290.
Van der Ven, Johannes A. "An Empirical or a Normative Approach to Practical-theological Research? A false Dilemma." In *Normativity and Empirical Practical Theology*, ed. Johannes A. van der Ven and Michael Scherer-Rath, 101–135. Leiden: Brill, 2005.
Van Dijk, José. "Tracing Twitter: The Rise of a Micro Blogging Platform." *International Journal of Media and Cultural Politics* 7, no. 3 (2012): 333–348.
Van Huyssteen, J. Wentzel. *Essays in postfoundationalist theology*. Grand Rapids: Eerdmans, 1997.
Van Huyssteen, J. Wentzel. *The shaping of rationality: Toward interdisciplinarity in theology and science*. Grand Rapids: Eerdmans, 1999.
Van Huyssteen, J. Wentzel. *Alone in the World? Science and Technology on Human Uniqueness*. Grand Rapids: Eerdmans, 2006.
Van Huyssteen, J. Wentzel. *Theology and the justification of faith: Constructing theories in systematic theology*. Grand Rapids: Eerdmans, 1989.

Van Saane, Joke W. *Geloofwaardig Leiderschap*. Zoetermeer: Uitgeverij Meinema, 2012.
Van Velsor, E., C.D. McCauley and M.N. Ruderman, eds. *The Center for Creative Leadership handbook of leadership development*. San Fransisco: Jossey-Bass, 2010.
Van Vugt, M. and A. Ahuja. *Naturally selected. The evolutionary science of leadership*. New York: Harper Business, 2010.
Van Vugt, M. and A. Ahuja. *De natuurlijke leider*. Utrecht: Bruna Levboeken, 2011.
Vanhoozer, Kevin J. "What is Everyday Theology? How and Why Christians should Read Culture." In *Everyday Theology: How to Read Cultural Texts and Interpret Cultural Trends*, edited by Kevin J. Vanhoozer, Charles A. Anderson, and Michael J. Sleasman, 15–60. Grand Rapids: Baker Academic, 2007.
Vanhoozer, Kevin J.. *The Drama of Doctrine: A Canonical-linguistic Approach to Christian Theology*. Louisville: Westminster John Knox, 2005.
Vigneswaran, Darshan. "Undocumented Migration: Risk and Myths (1998–2005)." In *Migration in Post-Apartheid South Africa: Challenges and Questions to Policy-Makers*, edited by Aurelia Wa-Kabwe Segatti and Loren Landau, 135–158. Paris: Agence Française de Development, 2007.
Vigneswaran, Darshan. "Taking out the trash? A 'garbage can' model of immigration policing." In *Exorcising the Demons Within: xenophobia, violence and statecraft in contemporary South Africa*, edited by Loren B. Landau, 150–171. Johannesburg: Wits University Press, 2012.
Village, Andrew. "Gifts differing? Psychological type among stipendiary and non-stipendiary clergy." *Research in the Social Scientific Study of Religion* 22 (2011): 230–250.
Village, Andrew. "Traditions within the Church of England and psychological type: A study among the clergy." *Journal of Empirical Theology* 26 (2013): 22–44.
Virginia, Stephen G. "Burnout and depression among Roman Catholic secular, religious, and monastic clergy." *Pastoral Psychology* 47 (1998): 49–67.
Vogt, William P. and Malcolm Williams. "Introduction: Sampling, Inference and Measurement." In *The SAGE Handbook of Innovation in Social Research Methods*, edited by Malcolm Williams and William P. Vogt, 467–472. London: Sage Publications, 2011.
Von Balthasar, Hans U. *Theo-drama: Theological Dramatic Theory*. Vol. 1: Prologomena. Transl. by Graham Harrison. (San Francisco: Ignatius Press, 1988).
Von Holdt, Karl. "South Africa: the transition to violent democracy." *Review of African Political Economy* 40, no. 138 (2013): 589–604. Doi: http://dx.doi.org/10.1080/03056244.2013.854040.
Voorberg, R. *De dominee leert vloeken. Over woede, onmacht en daadkracht*. [The Reverend learns to curse] Amsterdam: Uitgeverij De Arbeiderspers, 2016.
Wagner, Rachel. *Godwired, Religion, Ritual and Virtual Reality*. Hoboken: Routledge, 2012.

Walker, Cherryl. "The limits to land reform: rethinking 'the land question.'" *Journal of Southern African Studies* 31 (2005): 805–824.
Walkey, Frank H. and Dianne E. Green. "An exhaustive examination of the replicable factor structure of the Maslach burnout inventory." *Educational and Psychological Measurement* 52 (1992): 309–323.
Walton, Sara, and Bronwyn Boon. "Engaging with a Laclau & Mouffe Informed Discourse Analysis: A Proposed Framework." *Qualitative Research in Organizations and Management: An International Journal*, 9 no. 4 (2014): 351–370.
Ward, P. *Liquid Church*. Peabody, MA: Hendrickson Publishers, 2002.
Warner, Janelle and John D. Carter. "Loneliness, marital adjustment and burnout in pastoral and lay persons." *Journal of Psychology and Theology* 12 (1984): 125–131.
Warren, Yvonne. *The cracked pot: The state of today's Anglican parish clergy*. Stowmarket: Kevin Mayhew Ltd, 2002.
Wasserman, A. "To Settle in the Centers of Power." *Besheva*, 30 July, 2015.
Weber, S.M. "Faith formation of young people in an evangelical context: An empirical and theoretical investigation." PhD diss., University of Stellenbosch, 2014.
Weedon, Chris. *Feminist practice and poststructuralist theory*. Malden, MA: Blackwell, 1987.
Weick, Karl E. *The Social Psychology of Organising*. New York: Random House, 1979.
Weick, Karl E., Kathleen M. Sutcliffe and David Obstfeld. "Organising and the process of sensemaking." *Organization Science* 16 (2005): 409–421.
Wengert, Timothy J. *Priesthood, pastors, bishops: Public ministry for the Reformation and Today*. Philadelphia: Fortress, 2008.
Wesley, W.J. "Sociolinguistic Challenges to Minority Collegiate Success: Entering the Discourse Community of the College." *College Student Retention* 6, no. 4 (2005): 369–393.
Wiggins, Sally and Jonathan Potter. "Discursive Psychology." In *The SAGE Handbook of Qualitative Research in Psychology*, edited by Carla Willig and Wendy Stainton-Rogers, 73–90. London: SAGE Publications, 2008.
Wilhoit, J.C. *Spiritual Formation as if the Church Mattered: Growing in Christ through Community*. Grand Rapids: Baker Academic, 2008.
Wilson, Len and Jason Moore. *The Wired Church 2.0*. Nashville: Abingdon Press, 2008.
Woolard, Ingrid, Murray Leibbrandt and Hayley McEwen. "The persistence of high income inequality in South Africa: Some recent evidence." In *Transformation audit: Recession and recovery*, edited by Jan Hofmeyr, 98–105. Cape Town: Institute for Justice and Reconciliation, 2009.
Wright, Tom. *The New Testament and the People of God*. Minneapolis: Fortress Press, 1992.
Ya'alon, Moshe. "Speech in Honour of 25th Anniversary of Bnei David Academy." [In Hebrew], 2003. Accessed 11 December, 2014. https://www.youtube.com/watch?v¼dE3Z2rFtbjU.

Yukl, Gary A. *Leadership in Organizations,* seventh global edition. Upper Saddle River: Pearson, 2010.
Zald, M.N., and J.D. McCarthy. *Social Movements in an Organizational Society.* New Brunswick, NJ: Transaction Books, 1987.
Zappavigna, Michele. *Discourse of Twitter and Social Media: How we Use Language to Create Affiliation on the Web.* Sydney: Continuum International Publishing, 2012.

2. Webcontent References

#Fullywelcome, Twitter, https://twitter.com/hashtag/fullywelcome.
"About Joel Osteen Ministries," Joel Osteen Ministries, Facebook, https://www.facebook.com/JoelOsteen/info/?tab=page_info.
"About Joel Osteen," Joel Osteen Ministries, http://www.joelosteen.com/Pages/AboutJoel.aspx.
"Africa: The Lost Continent?" The Socialist Party of Great Britain, http://www.worldsocialism.org/spgb/education/depth-articles/politics-and-conflict/africa-lost-continent.
"Investigation crash MH17, 17 July 2014 Donetsk," Dutch Safety Board, October 13, 2015, http://www.onderzoeksraad.nl/en/onderzoek/2049/investigation-crash-mh17-17-july-2014.
"Let's Fully Welcome Refugees," Facebook, https://www.facebook.com/fully-welcome/timeline.
"Obama and the power of social media and technology." The European Business Review, last modified July 16, 2013. http://www.europeanbusinessreview.com/?p=1627.
"Rikko Voorberg doodgewenst om Benno L.," *EO Visie,* https://visie.eo.nl/2014/02/rikko-voorberg-doodgewenst-om-benno-l/.
"Rikko Voorberg," Lazarus.nl, http://www.7keer7.nl/portfolio/rikko-voorberg.
"South African Fellows Fight on in the Name of Mandela," The Aspen Institute, December 10, 2013, http://www.aspeninstitute.org/leadership-programs/africa-leadership-initiative/south-africa.
"Tsvangirai: Puppet on a string," *The Herald,* August 9, 2013, http://www.herald.co.zw/tsvangirai-puppet-on-a-string/.
"We Are Here," Facebook, https://www.facebook.com/WijZijnHier.
"Your Complete Media Monitoring Solution." Fuseware.net. Last modified April 17, 2015. http://www.fuseware.net.
"Zwelethini likens immigrants to lice, ants." *The Herald,* 17 April, 2015. http://www.herald.co.zw/zwelithini-likens-immigrants-to-lice-ants/.
African Leadership Academy, www.africanleadershipacademy.org/.
Benno L. welkom in onze straat [Benno L., welcome in our street], Facebook, February, 2014, https://nl-nl.facebook.com/BennoLwelkom.
Bob-Milliar, George. "Re: The Failure Of African Leadership, Cause of Africa's Problems," Modern Ghana, 2005. https://www.ghanaweb.com/GhanaHomePage/diaspora/Re-The-Failure-Of-African-Leadership-Cause-Of-Africa-s-Problems-81437.

Branson, Richard (@richardbranson), Twitter, https://twitter.com/richard-branson/status/536920967348772864?lang=en.
Branson, Richard (@richardbranson). "My top 10 quotes on leadership." Twitter, November 24, 2014a. https://twitter.com/richardbranson.
Branson, Richard (@richardbranson). "Tie-loathing adventurer, philanthropist & troublemaker, who believes in turning ideas into reality. Otherwise known as Dr Yes at
Branson, Richard. "My top 10 quotes on leadership." Richard Branson's Blog. November 25, 2014b. https://www.virgin.com/richard-branson/my-top-10-quotes-leadership.
Bullas, J. "33 Social Media Facts and Statistics You Should Know in 2015," Jeffbullas.com, http://www.jeffbullas.com/2015/04/08/33-social-media-facts-and-statistics-you-should-know-in-2015/.
Christensen, Christian (@chrchristensen). "Prof. of Journalism at Stockholm University. American. Tweets are my own opinion, not my employer's." Twitter, November 9, 2015. https://twitter.com/ChrChristensen.
Church of England, https://www.churchofengland.org/
De Wever, Robin "Dominee wil meer 'God verdomme' horen," *Trouw*, September 4, 2014, http://www.trouw.nl/tr/nl/4716/Christendom/article/detail/3737316/2014/ 09/04/Dominee-wil-meer-God-verdomme-horen.dhtml.
Devika, "10 weken, 10 kerken – week 1 de Pop-up Kerk," [10 weeks, 10 churches – week 1 the Pop-up Church] Something Righteous, January 31, 2015, http://somethingrighteous.nl/2015/01/10-kerken-in-10-weken-de-popup-kerk.
Ekklesia Amsterdam, prekenarchief, http://ekklesia-amsterdam.nl/prekenarchief/.
Emiroglu, Sema. "The Role of Social Media in Arab Spring." Academia.edu. Last modified July 16, 2013. http://www.academia.edu/8590902/The_Role_of_Social_Media_in_Arab_Spring.
Forbes Media, www.forbes.com/leadership/.
Gillissen, Daniël. "Vloekende Rikko Voorberg vraagt om kwaad weg te werpen," *Nederlands Dagblad*, September 5, 2014, https://www.nd.nl/nieuws/geloof/vloekende-rikko-voorberg-vraagt-om-kwaad-weg-te.433511.lynkx.
Hoover, S. "Faith Online. A report of the Pew Internet & American Life Project." Pew Research Center, 2004. http://www.pewinternet.org/Reports/2004/Faith-Online.aspx.
Incubators for immigrants, http://incubatorsforimmigrants.com.
Joel Osteen (@joelosteen), Instagram, https://instagram.com/joelosteen/.
Joel Osteen Ministries (@JoelOsteen), Twitter, https://twitter.com/JoelOsteen.
Joel Osteen Ministries, Facebook, https://www.facebook.com/JoelOsteen/.
Joel Osteen Ministries, YouTube, https://www.youtube.com/joelosteen.
Joubert, Stephan. "God is Altyd Tuis." E-kerk. http://www.ekerk.org/#!God-is-altyd-tuis/ckfj/56d01dae0cf24bcda475f710.
Leadership Magazine, www.leadershiponline.co.za.
Let's Fully Welcome Refugees, http://www.fullywelcome.eu.

Mbembe, Achille. "South Africa's Second Coming: The Nongqawuse Syndrome." Open Democracy, 2006. https://www.opendemocracy.net/democracy-Africa_democracy/southafrica_succession_3649.jsp.

Nicolson, Greg. "#FeesMustFall: Wits splits – the beginning, not the end, of a chapter," Daily Maverick, October 27, 2015, http://www.dailymaverick.co.za/article/2015-10-27-feesmustfall-wits-splits-the-beginning-not-the-end-of-a-chapter/#.VsLXzYTWXU0.

Orme, Brian. "Top 100 Christian Leaders to Follow on Twitter," ChurchLeaders, Febraury 5, 2013, http://www.churchleaders.com/pastors/pastor-articles/165262-brian-orme-top-100-christian-leaders-to-follow-on-twitter.html.

Palmary, Ingrid. "Refugees, Safety and Xenophobia in South African Cities: The Role of Local Government." Research report written for the Centre for the Study of Violence and Reconciliation, 2002. http://www.csvr.org.za/docs/foreigners/refugeessafteyand.pdf.

Patreon, Peter Rollins, https://www.patreon.com/peterrollins.

Peters, Tom. "The Brand Called You," FastCompany, August 31, 1997. http://www.fastcompany.com/28905/brand-called-you.

Regterschot, Albert-Jan. "Spreker EO-Jongerendag wil 'voor verwarring zorgen,'" *Reformatorisch Dagblad,* May 30, 2013, http://www.refdag.nl/kerkplein/kerknieuws/spreker_eo_jongerendag_wil_voor_verwarring_zorgen_1_742281.

Rollins, Peter. "'You're Looking For Nothing': John Caputo Responds to My Work," Goodreads, https://www.goodreads.com/author_blog_posts/8653298-you-re-looking-for-nothing-john-caputo-responds-to-my-work.

Smith, Craig. "4000 Interesting Twitter Facts, Demographics and Statistics (November 2017)," DMR Business Statistics, last updated November 14, 2017, http://expandedramblings.com/index.php/march-2013-by-the-numbers-a-few-amazing-twitter-stats/#.UvRWovmSzHQ.

South African Press Association. "Minister's Facebook post unrelated to Soweto unrest – dept." News 24, 29 January, 2015. http://www.news24.com/SouthAfrica/News/Mokonyanes-status-unrelated-to-Soweto-unrest-dept-20150129.

Spaull, Nicholas. "South Africa's Education Crisis: The quality of education in South Africa 1994-2011." Centre for Development and Enterprise, 2013. http://www.cde.org.za/images/pdf/South%20Africas%20Education%20Crisis%20N%20Spaull%202013.pdf.

Stroomwest, http://www.stroomwest.nl.

Svenska kyrkan, "Slutgiltigt resultat för val till kyrkomöte 2013" [Final result for the election to the Church Assembly 2013] http://kyrkoval.svenskakyrkan.se/Valresultat2013/slutg/valresultat/Resultat/Kyrkomote.aspx, accessed February 1, 2016.

Sveriges Radio, "Kyrkovalet kostar 145 miljoner" [The Church election costs 145 million] http://sverigesradio.se/sida/artikel.aspx?programid=86&artikel=5644418, accessed February 1, 2016.

The echurch, http://www.ekerk.org/.
The Malphurs Group (@amalphurs), "Envision Tomorrow Today, Husband, Father, Consultant
Voorberg, Rikko, and Tjarko van de Pol, "Op de koffie bij Benno L.," *NRC*, May 14, 2015, http://www.nrc.nl/next/2014/05/03/op-de-koffie-bij-benno-l-1372666.
Voorberg, Rikko. "Rollende godverdommes," *NRC*, September 4, 2014, http://www.nrc.nl/next/2014/09/04/rollende-godverdommes-1416050.

Index of Authors

Abu-Hilal, M.M. 118, 217
Adam, B. 92, 217
Aditya, R.N. 231
Aggedal, J.-O. 217
Ahlbäck, L. 180, 217
Ahrén, P.-O. 169, 217
Ahuja, A. 213, 244
Alexander, P. 29, 217
Allen, D. 5
Almog, O. 191, 217
Altbeker, A. 29, 217
Alvesson, M. 27, 42, 217
Amarusi 207
Ammerman, N.T. 5, 217
Amrousi, E. 217
Anderson, B. 74, 217
Anderson, C.A. 244
Andreasson, S. 11, 217
Andrén, C.-G. 217
Anthony, F.-V. 219
Appiah, K.A. 12, 217
Aran, G. 202, 217
Ashin, G. 187
Avery, G.C. 2, 217
Aviner, S. 205, 217
Aweiss, S. 194, 237
Ayittey, G.B.N. 11, 217
Bachelor, P. 118, 228
Baker, J. 189, 218
Bakke, R. 164
Banaszak, A. 188, 218
Banda, F. 36, 218
Bands, J. 118, 242
Barak, O. 192, 218
Barna, G. 80
Barnard, L.K. 122, 218
Barnes, A.C. 5
Barratt, E. 204, 218
Barrett, P. 123, 224
Barth, K. 74

Bass, B.M. 5
Bates, M. 126, 232
Baym, N.K. 68, 69, 77, 78, 218
Belcastro, Ph.A. 118, 218
Bellah, R.N. 190, 218
Bennington, G. 17
Berenbaum, M. 229
Berger, P. 18, 218
Berman, M.L. 225
Berntson, M. 170, 218
Beuving, J. 51, 218
Bexell, O. 170, 171, 218, 219
Bhabha, H.K. 12, 20, 218
Bick, E. 199, 218
Bijsterveld, E. van 7
Billig, M. 195, 207, 218
Blenkinsopp, J. 236
Bob-Milliar, G. 10, 11, 218, 246
Bolden, R. 11, 18, 219
Boon, B. 39
Booysen, L. 16, 219
Botha, N. 72
Botha, P. 72
Bourdieu, P. 187–189, 219
Bowers Du Toit, N. 219
Bradburn, N.M. 121, 219
Branson, R. 83, 247
Braun, V. 155, 219
Brewster, C.E. 122, 128, 131, 132, 219, 225, 227
Briseno, V. 226
Brodd, S.-E. 169, 177, 178, 180, 218, 219
Broodryk, J. 219
Brouwer, R. 1, 3, 4, 6, 48, 63, 211, 214, 215, 219, 220
Brown, A. 5
Brown, D. 74, 220
Brown, P. 190, 220
Brown, S.A. 93, 220

Bruce, J. 91, 92, 94, 96, 97, 231
Bullas, J. 100, 247
Bullpitt, R. 116, 232
Bunge, M.J. 168
Burr, V. 27, 220
Burton, C. 116, 132, 220
Burton, J. 116, 132, 220
Burton, L. 127, 128, 220, 227
Busisiwe 32
Buthelezi 35
Buys, C. 118, 220
Byrne, B.M. 118, 220
Calvin, J. 74
Campbell, H.A. 77, 78, 90, 91, 100, 106, 220
Canales, A.D. 151, 152, 220
Caputo, J.D. 15, 24, 63, 64, 220, 221
Carter, J.D. 245
Carter, W. 118
Castells, M. 51, 90, 221
Castle, K. 121, 122, 128, 227
Cattell, A.K.S. 123, 221
Cattell, H.E.P. 123, 221
Cattell, R. 123, 221
Caulat, G. 70, 221
Césaire, A. 12, 221
Chemers, M.M. 243
Chen, C.-Y. 118, 228
Chevalier, H. 224
Childers, J. 74, 221
Chrisman, L. 241
Christensen, C. 247
Christie, P. 10, 232
Ciarrocchi, J.W. 118, 229
Claiborne, S. 64, 221
Clark, V. 155, 219
Clayton, Ph. 97, 98, 221
Cloete, A. 68, 69, 221
Coate, M.A. 132, 221
Cobb, K. 93, 221
Codone, S. 100, 106, 107, 112, 221
Cohen, S. 199, 201, 204, 221
Collins, J.J. 236
Comaroff, J. (Jean) 221
Comaroff, J.L. 32, 221
Conforti, Y. 192, 222

Cooper, A. 33, 222
Coote, B. 10, 222
Corcoran, K.J. 118, 222
Corveleyn, J. 118, 231, 232
Costanzo, M.A. 243
Costa, P.T. 123, 222
Couldry, N. 104–106, 222
Craig, C.L. 127, 128, 222, 226
Crea, G. 118, 222
Cronbach, L.J. 119, 222
Cronje, F. 29, 222
Croucher, S. 35, 222
Crush, J. 30, 31, 33–35, 222
Cunliffe, A.L. 42, 241
Curry, J.F. 122, 218
Dahan-Kaleb, A. 191
Davey, J. 132, 222
Davies, B. 44, 222
Davis, R. 29, 222
Dawson, L.L. 75, 223
Dean, K.C. 118, 155, 160, 166, 223, 239
De Beer, S. 153, 164, 223, 242
DeMaria, B. 11, 223
Dempster, P.G. 88, 239
Denton, M.L. 242
De Roest, H. 220
Derrida, J. 8, 14, 16, 17, 20–23, 63, 223
Devika 51, 247
De Vries, G. 218
De Vries, M. 51, 151, 152, 158, 161, 163, 223
De Wet, C.L. 79–81, 223
De Wever, R. 61, 247
De Witte, H. 118, 231, 232
Diamond, D.M. 5
Dickson, M. 231
Dinter, A. 5, 242
Don-Yehiya, E. 192–194, 223
Doolittle, B.R. 118, 223, 227
Doornenbal, R. 52, 223
Dugan, J.P. 5
Duncan, B. 222, 226
Duncan, N. 33, 127, 128, 224
Durrheim, K. 27, 232
Du Toit, P. 88, 235
Dylan, T. 224

Earley, P.C. 231
Edlebi, A. 233
Edqvist, G. 218, 219
Eichler, M. 188, 224
Einstein, M. 99–103, 106, 111, 224
Ekström, S. 218, 219
Eliastam, J. 3, 4, 6, 7, 26, 29, 40, 43, 213, 214, 224
Eloff, Th. 72
Elon, E. 224
Emiroglu, S. 85, 247
Erez, M. 231
Esposito, R. 224
Estes, D. 78, 224
Evenshpanger, N. 201, 224
Evers, W. 118, 224
Evertsson, A.J. 217
Eysenck, H.J. 123, 124, 224
Eysenck, M.W. 224
Eysenck, S.B.G. 123, 124, 224
Ezzy, D. 155, 224
Failing, W.-E. 5, 224
Fairhurst, G.T. 2, 26, 41–44, 213, 224
Fanon, F. 12, 224, 225
Farrell, F. 5
Farrington, C. 225
Fisher, R. 5
Fletcher, B. 132, 225
Flew, T. 90, 225
Foucault, M. 30, 225
Francis, L.J. 3, 4, 6, 116, 117, 119, 120, 122, 125–132, 134, 138, 139, 210, 219, 220, 222, 225–227, 230, 232, 233, 240–243
Frank, T.E. 163, 227
Friesen, D.J. 75, 227
Fuchs, C. 85, 227
Furedi, F. 113, 228
Gallagher, E.V. 1, 228
Gal, R. 234
Ganiel, G. 48, 49, 52, 53, 59, 60, 62–64, 214, 235
Ganzevoort, R.R. 5, 84, 93, 97, 228
Garner, S.S. 90, 91
Garrow, D. 5
Gatrell, C. 116, 239

Gaum, F. 65, 228
Geertz, C. 18, 228
Gelb, S. 33, 228
Giddens, A. 104, 228
Gillissen, D. 61, 247
Girmalm, T. 3, 4, 7, 169, 171, 172, 228
Gish, S.D. 39
Goethals G.R. 228
Goff, P. 239
Gold, R.S. 218
Gold, Y. 118, 228
Golden, J. 118, 229
Goldshlag, I. 192, 229
Goldstone, J. 189, 229
Gonzales, R. 234
Gooder, P. 136, 241
Gore, A. 97, 229
Gose, K.F. 118, 239
Gräb, W. 5, 229
Graham, E. 68, 229
Grant, D. 2, 41, 224
Gray, J.G. 230
Green, D.E. 118, 229, 245
Grint, K. 41, 229
Gritsch, E.W. 178, 229
Grobbelaar, J. 229
Groome 167, 168
Groot, K. de 220
Grossberg, L. 242
Gruber, D.A. 90, 95, 229
Gubb, S. 122, 128, 227
Gunter, H. 187, 212, 229
Hadari-Ramage, Y. 194, 229
Hall, R. 31, 238
Hammer, A.L. 128, 237
Hanges, P. 231
Harari, A. 229
Harel, A. 202, 203, 229
Harel, I. 229
Harnoy, M. 193, 195, 229
Harré, R. 44, 222
Harrison, G. 73
Harris, Ph.R. 11, 229
Harrold, Ph. 237
Haslam, S.A. 50, 54, 59, 60, 229
Hassan, R. 90, 229

Hassim, S. 228, 236, 238
Hatuka, G. 191, 192, 234
Haw, C. 64, 221
Hayem, J. 34, 229
Hays, L.C. 118, 218
Healy, N. 74, 230
Heelas, P. 48, 230
Heidegger, M. 14, 15, 17, 18, 21, 23, 230
Heimbrock, H.-G. 5, 224
Helland, C. 106, 230
Heller, O. 202, 230
Helmer, C. 231
Helms, L. 188–190, 230
Hendel, A. 203
Herl, D. 225
Hermans, C.A.M. 84, 225, 230
Hernandez, S. 10
Hickman, M.J. 238
Hills, P. 119, 125, 227, 230
Hinton, S. 87, 230
Hipps, S. 75, 76, 230
Hirsch, A. 71
Hjarvard, S. 104, 105, 230
Hjorth, L. 87, 230
Hofmeyr, J. 245
Hofstadter, A. 15, 230
Hofstede, G. 16, 230
Holman, D. 42, 231, 241
Holmes, P. 127, 226
Hoover, S. 99, 100, 231, 247
Hope Cheong, P. 100, 103, 231
Horowitz, A. 197, 198, 201, 231
House, R. 16, 231
Huberman, H. 199, 200, 231
Hybels, B. 80, 87
Inbari, A. 203, 231
Ingerson, K. 91, 92, 94, 96, 97, 231
Iso-Ahola, S.E. 118, 242
Iwancki, E.F. 118, 231
Jackson, J. 103, 117, 118, 231
Jackson, S.E. 235
Jakes, T.D. 80
James, E.H. 90, 95, 229
Jinkins, M. 67, 91, 231
Jobs, S. 83

Johnson, G. 190, 231
Jones, S.H. 127, 226, 227
Jorgenson, A.G. 231
Joseph, E.N. 118, 231, 232
Joseph, J. 233
Joubert, S.J. 65, 66, 70–73, 75–79, 81, 82, 232, 247
Jung, C.G. 125, 127, 232
Junker, D. 239
Kaldor, P. 116, 121, 122, 128, 227, 232
Kalmijn, M. 189, 232
Kane, J. 190, 232
Kant, I. 22
Kaputa, C. 102, 103, 232
Kärreman, D. 27, 42, 217
Kay, W.K. 119, 128, 232
Keirsey, D. 126, 232
Kelly, S. 41, 42, 232
Kenway, J. 189, 232
Kerfoot, K.M. 69, 70, 232
Kerr, Ph. 27, 232
Kerr, R. 189, 232
Khoza, R. 36, 232
Kimmerling, B. 232
King, L. 109
Kirk, M. 11, 18, 132, 232
Kirk, Ph. 219
Klaver, M. 103, 114, 232
Koh, A. 189, 232
Kotze, J. 233
Küçüksüleymanoğlu, R. 118, 233
Kupe, T. 228, 236, 238
Kurana, R. 5
Laclau, E. 39, 40, 41, 45, 46, 233
Landau, L.B. 27, 30, 31, 35, 233, 236, 244
Lankshear, D.W. 3, 4, 6, 135, 138, 139, 233
Laruelle, F. 15, 22, 233
Laycock, P. 132, 227
Leadbeater, C. 76, 233
Leary, T. 132, 232
Lebel, U. 3, 4, 6, 186, 191, 195, 196, 198, 206, 207, 212, 218, 233, 234
Lebovitz, A. 234
Lee, S. 100, 103, 234

Leibbrandt, M. 245
Leithwood, K. 190, 234
Leon, N. 192, 193, 195, 234
Less, A. 234
Lessem, R. 10, 232
Lester, J.N. 88, 239
Letender, K. 188, 234
Levinstein-Malz, R. 234
Levy, Y. 198, 234
Libel, T. 234
Littler, K. 127, 226
Liu, H. 42, 234
Louden, S. 119, 125, 129, 226, 227
Lubish-Omer, S. 196, 206, 234
Lucado, M. 87
Luhrmann, T.M. 49, 234
Lumumba, P. 10
Lundby, K. 105, 234
Lundquist, M. 155
Lundstedt, G. 169, 174, 181, 182, 234
Luther, M. 175–179, 181, 184, 185, 234, 235
Lutz, B. 88, 235
Luyten, P. 118, 231, 232
MacGregor Burns, J. 228
MacGuire, M.B. 5, 235
Mahlangu, E. 162, 238
Maiko, S.M. 159, 167, 168, 235
Malherbe, J. 235
Malhota, N. 189, 235
Mamdani, M. 32, 235
Managa, A. 29, 32, 235
Mandela, N.R. 235
Mangaliso, M.P. 20, 235
Mangcu, X. 151, 160–163, 165, 235
Margalit, Y. 189, 235
Marti, G. 48, 49, 52, 53, 59, 60, 62–64, 214, 235
Martin, A.J. 239
Martinsson, J. 183, 235
Martin, W.G. 11, 118, 235
Mascall, B. 190, 234
Masetlha 35
Maslach, C. 117, 118, 235
Matsengarwodzi, D. 9, 10, 13, 235
Matsinhe, D.M. 30, 235

Mawadza, A. 36, 218
Maxwell, J.C. 80, 160, 235
Mayer, Z. 236
Mbembe, A. 12, 32, 235, 236, 248
Mbigi, L. 10, 232
McCarthy, J. 188, 236
McCauley, C.D. 244
McCaulley, M.H. 126, 128, 237
McCrae, R.R. 123, 222
McEwen, H. 245
McLaren, B. 80
McLaughlin, K. 240
Meindl, J.R. 41, 42, 236
Meyer, J. 80, 99, 100, 102
Meyers, C. 236
Meylahn, J.-A. 3, 4, 6, 8
Michael, W.B. 118, 228
Miller-McLemore, B.J. 220
Miller, V. 68, 69, 77, 78, 236
Mills, C.W. 204
Miner, M.H. 118, 236
Misago, J.P. 27, 30, 31, 33, 35, 37, 236
Mngxitama, A. 30, 236
Molloy, G.N. 118, 239
Monson, T. 29, 30, 32, 236
Moore, D. 194, 236, 237
Moore, J. 245
Moore, L.R. 100, 103, 237
Moore, M.E. 225
Moore, S. 237
Moran, R.T. 229
Moran, S.V. 229
Morgan, C. 42, 43, 242
Morris, A. 188, 237
Mosselson, A. 34, 237
Mothoagae, I. 237
Mouffe, C. 39, 41, 45, 46, 233
Moynagh, M. 51, 52, 237
Mozes, H. 194, 237
Mudimbe, V.-Y. 12, 237
Mueller, W. 155, 165, 237
Müller, J.C. 26, 27, 237
Murthy, D. 85, 94, 96, 237
Myers, I.B. 126, 128, 237
Naidoom M. 223
Nash, S. 161, 163, 237

Nauss, A. 209, 237
Ndou, C. 36, 237
Nell, E. 154, 159, 160
Nell, I. 83, 154, 159, 160, 214, 237, 238
Nel, R.W. 237
Nelson, C. 242
Neocosmos, M. 32, 34, 238
Ngomane, R.M. 162, 238
Nicholson 85
Nickels, H.C. 187, 238
Nicolson, G. 248
Nieftagodien, N. 32, 238
Nietzsche, F.W. 24, 238
Nilsson, B. 218
Nkomo, S. 10, 12, 19, 20, 238
Nkrumah, K. 10
Nohria, D. 5
Northouse, P. 5
Ntsebeza, L. 31, 238
Nyembezi, B. 36, 238
Obiakor, F.E. 13, 238
Obstfeld, D. 245
Ogilvy, D. 102
Oreilly, D. 243
Orkibi, E. 195, 234
Orme, B. 87, 248
Orobator, A.E. 238
Orsi, R. 5, 238
Oskamp, S. 243
Osmer, R.R. 74, 86, 87, 89, 92, 93, 95, 238
Osteen, Joel 80, 99–114, 247
Osteen, John 101
Osteen, Victoria 108, 109
Palmary, I. 35, 248
Parker, Ph.D. 118, 239
Patton, B. 5
Paulus, T.M. 88, 239
Payne, V.J. 122, 127, 128, 227
Pearson, C. 96, 239
Pedahzur, A. 194, 239
Pellauer, D. 240
Pendleton, W. 222
Perdue, L.G. 236, 239
Peters, T. 102, 248
Peyton, N. 116, 239

Phillips, S. 86, 239
Piedmont, R.L. 118, 229
Pierce, C.M.B. 118, 239
Pillay, D. 33, 239
Pinkham, J. 221
Platow, M.J. 229
Polzer, T. 236
Posel, D. 33, 239
Potter, J. 245
Powell, R. 122, 128, 159, 240
Powers, S. 118, 239
Pretorius, B. 72
Quash, B. 74, 239
Quenk, N.L. 128, 237
Rabin, Y. 194, 239
Raj, A. 118, 239
Rakow, K. 99, 100, 102, 103, 106, 111, 113, 239
Ramachandran, S. 31, 222
Randall, K. 119, 122, 239
Reader, J. 92, 240
Regterschot, A.-J. 61, 248
Reicher, S.D. 229
Reid, J. 128, 240
Renner, J. 39, 40, 240
Rice, J. 75, 240
Ricoeur, P. 13, 240
Riesebrodt, M. 187, 240
Rivlin, R. 207
Robbins, M. 121, 122, 127, 128, 131, 132, 219, 220, 226, 227, 232, 240
Robinson, S. 189, 232
Rodgerson, T.E. 118, 229, 240
Roebben, B. 153, 166, 167, 240
Roeland, J.H. 5, 84, 97, 228
Rogers, R. 106, 240
Rollins, P. 53, 62, 63, 240, 248
Roof, W.C. 105, 240
Root, A. 160, 164, 240
Rosenius, M. 171, 172, 182, 228, 240
Rossetti, S.J. 118, 240
Rossman-Stollman, E. 201, 240
Roth, A. 118, 203, 204, 241
Rothman, S. 118, 220
Roth, R.A. 228
Rowling, C. 136, 241

Index of Authors

Rubczak, N. 233
Ruderman, M.N. 244
Ruelas, B. 226
Ruiz-Quintanilla, S.A. 231
Russell, I. 137, 241
Ruster, Th. 166
Rutledge, C.J.F. 119, 120, 125, 130, 225, 227, 230, 241
Sadan, E. 196, 197, 204, 241
Sagawa, S. 188, 241
Sahar, E. 241
Said, E. 12, 241
Salameh, K.M. 118, 217
Sanford, J.A. 132, 241
Sarid, Y. 194, 241
Schaufeli, W.B. 118, 241
Schmit, C.J. 74, 221
Schmitt, C. 21
Schrag, C.O. 28, 43, 45, 241
Schramm, J. 188, 241
Schuller, R. 80
Schulz, W. 104, 105, 241
Schwab, R.L. 118, 231
Schwartz, D. 241
Segatti, A.W. 244
Sengers, E. 220
Senghor, L.S. 12, 241
Sharon, R. 204, 241
Shotter, J. 42, 241
Siegel, L. 76, 241
Silverstone, R. 105, 242
Silvestri, S. 238
Sinitiere, P. 100, 103, 234
Sipho 33
Skolnik, F. 229
Slater, P. 127, 226
Sleasman, M.J. 244
Sloterdijk, P. 22, 242
Smerek, R.E. 90, 95, 229
Smircich, L. 42, 43, 242
Smith, A.-P. 233
Smith, C. 242, 248
Smith, G. 85, 134, 155, 225, 226, 242
Söderblom, K. 5, 242
Sorenson, G.J. 228
Spaull, N. 29, 248

Spener, Ph.J. 178, 179, 181, 184, 242
Spivak, G.C. 12, 19, 242
Stainton-Rogers, W. 245
Stambaugh, J. 230
Stanley, A. 106, 112
Stanton-Rich, H.M. 118, 242
Stern, A. 205, 242
Stevenson, J. 103, 106, 242
Stievermann, J. 239
Stiver, D.R. 92, 242
Stogdill, R.M. 208, 242
Stoppels, S. 220
Streib, H. 5, 242
Strümpfer, D.J.W. 118, 242
Sutcliffe, K.M. 245
Swart, I. 153, 164, 223, 242
Swartz 155
Sweet, L. 71, 73, 80, 81, 86, 87, 93, 98, 242
Takako, N. 234
Tappert, T.G. 184, 242
Taubman, W. 5
Taylor, A.J. 229
Taylor, C. 51, 103, 118, 242
Thomas, C.G. 32, 243
Thomas-Hunt, M.C. 90, 95, 229
Thomas, L. 238
Thompson, G. 74, 243
Thorpe, R. 42, 231, 241
Thurau-Gray, L. 199, 243
Tilley, D. 127, 226
Tomic, W. 118, 224
Tomlinson, M. 189, 243
Triandis, H.C. 16, 243
Tsur, E. 192, 218
Turkle, S. 83, 84, 90, 243
Turman, N.T. 5
Turner, J. 236
Turton, D.W. 119, 125, 129, 130, 225, 226, 243
Twitchell, J. 243
Van den Berg, J.-A. 3, 4, 6, 68, 74, 83–85, 99, 243
Van de Pol, T. 58, 249
Van der Ven, J.A. 6, 243
Van Dierendonck, D. 118, 241

Van Dijk, J. 85, 243
Vanhoozer, K.J. 74, 93, 242, 244
Van Huyssteen, J.W. 28, 243
Van Saane, J.W. 5, 6, 66, 67, 113, 208, 244
Van Velsor, E. 209, 244
Van Vugt, M. 213, 244
Vigneswaran, D. 31, 35, 244
Village, A. 122, 125, 127, 225, 226, 244
Virginia, S.G. 118, 244
Vogt, W.P. 88, 244
Von Balthasar, H.U. 73, 244
Von Herrmann, F.-W. 17, 230
Von Holdt, K. 29, 244
Voorberg, R. 48, 49–51, 55–64, 244, 249
Wagner, R. 85, 90, 244
Walker, C. 31, 245
Walkey, F.H. 118, 229, 245
Wallace, M. 243
Walton, S. 39
Ward, P. 49, 152, 245
Warner, J. 118, 245
Warren, R. 80
Warren, Y. 87, 99, 100, 106, 112, 116, 132, 245
Wasserman, A. 205, 245
Weber, S.M. 3, 4, 6, 151, 152, 155, 156, 158, 161, 167, 245
Weedon, C. 45, 245

Weick, K.E. 44, 245
Weiz, G. 234
Wejryd, C. 218
Weman, G. 218, 219
Wengert, T.J. 175–177, 179, 184, 245
Wesley, W.J. 187, 245
Whinney, M. 127, 128, 226, 227
Whitefield, G. 100
Whitehead, J. 161, 163, 237
Wiggins, S. 245
Wilhoit, J.C. 167
Williams, M. 88, 244
Williams, P. 241
Williams, V. 35
Willig, C. 245
Wilson, L. 76, 245
Woodhead, L. 48, 230
Woolard, I. 29, 245
Worby, E. 228, 236, 238
Wright, C.R. 228
Wright, N.S. 231
Wright, N.T. (Tom) 62, 74, 118, 245
Wulff, K. 122, 128, 132, 226
Ya'alon, M. 186, 245
Yukl, G.A. 66, 67, 210, 246
Zald, M.N. 188
Zappavigna, M. 87, 94, 246
Ziebertz, H.-G. 219
Zijderveld, T. 3, 4, 6, 68, 83, 99
Zulu, L. 35, 36